05/09

SALMON
doubts

Adam Sacks

Salmon Doubts
First printing Spring 2004
ISBN: 1-891867-71-7
Printed in Canada

Talk to Adam
Adam@AdamSacks.com
www.AdamSacks.com

Published by Alternative Comics
503 NW 37th Ave.
Gainesville, FL 32609-2204
352 373 6336
jmason@indyworld.com
www.indyworld.com/altcomics

For Mom and Dad

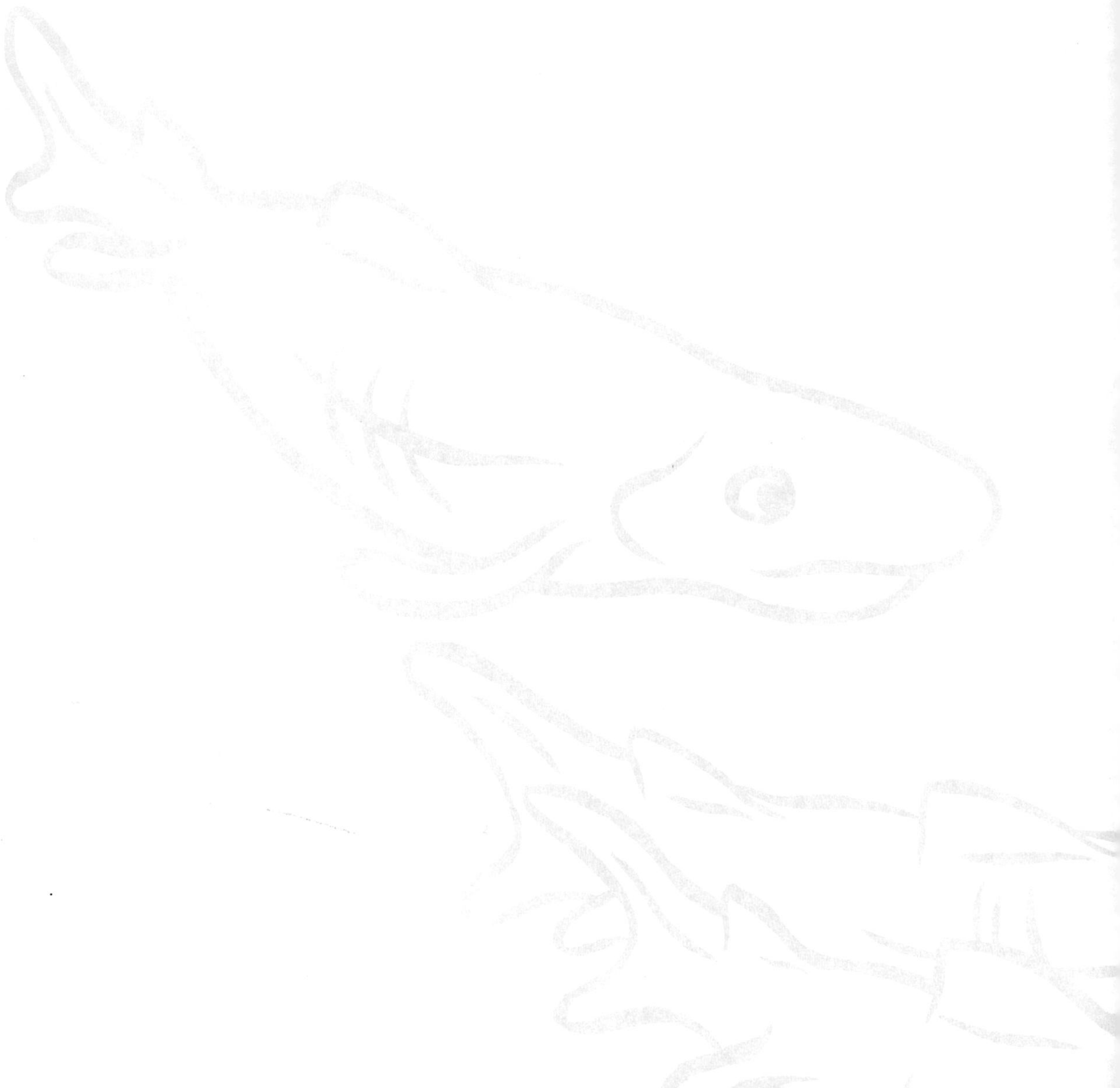

The first man to discover
Chinook salmon in Columbia
caught 264 in a day and
carried them across the
river by walking on the
backs of other fish. His
greatest feat, however, was
learning the Chinook jargon
in 15 minutes from listening
to Salmon talk.

Oregon: End of the trail
(The WPA Guide to Oregon) 1940

Salmon hatch in rivers, travel
to the sea, fatten on rich
ocean fare, return at maturity
to spawn in their natural
rivers and die shortly
after spawning.

National Geographic
July 1990

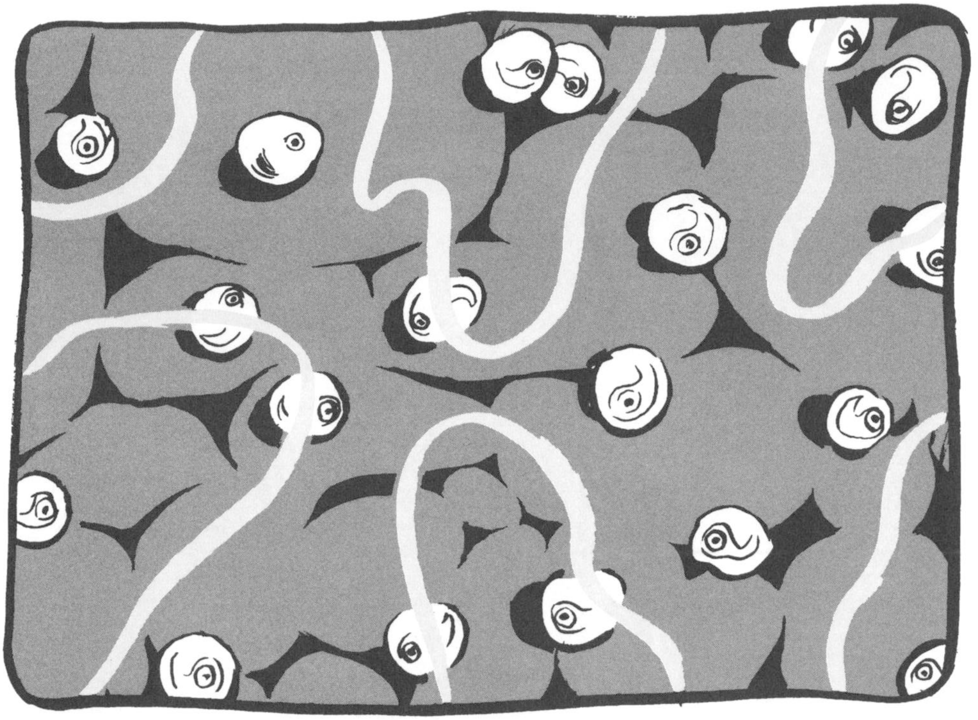
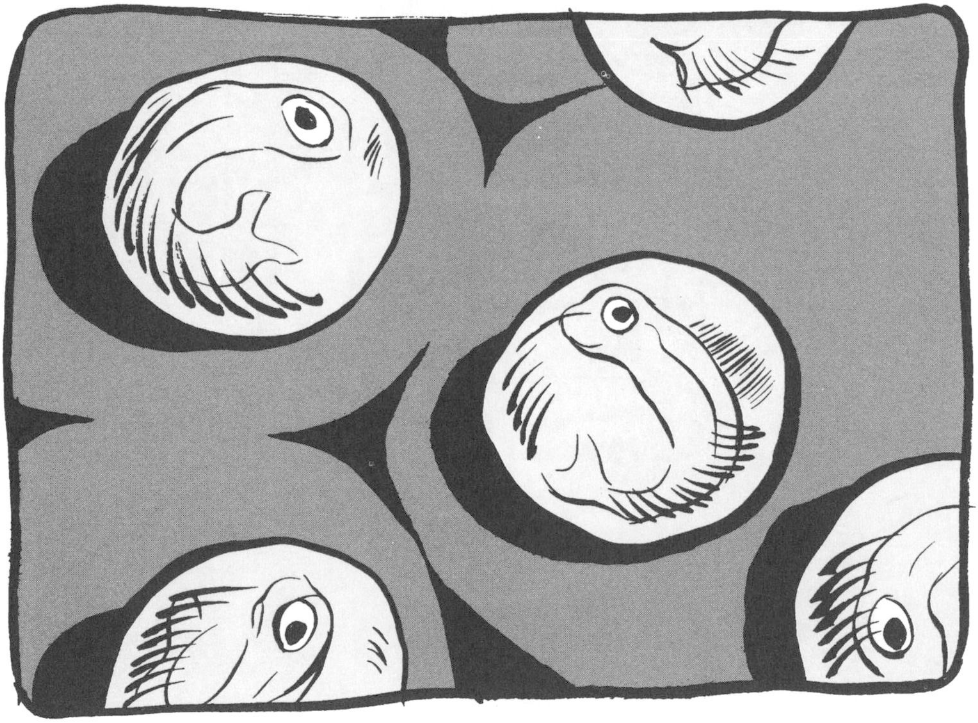

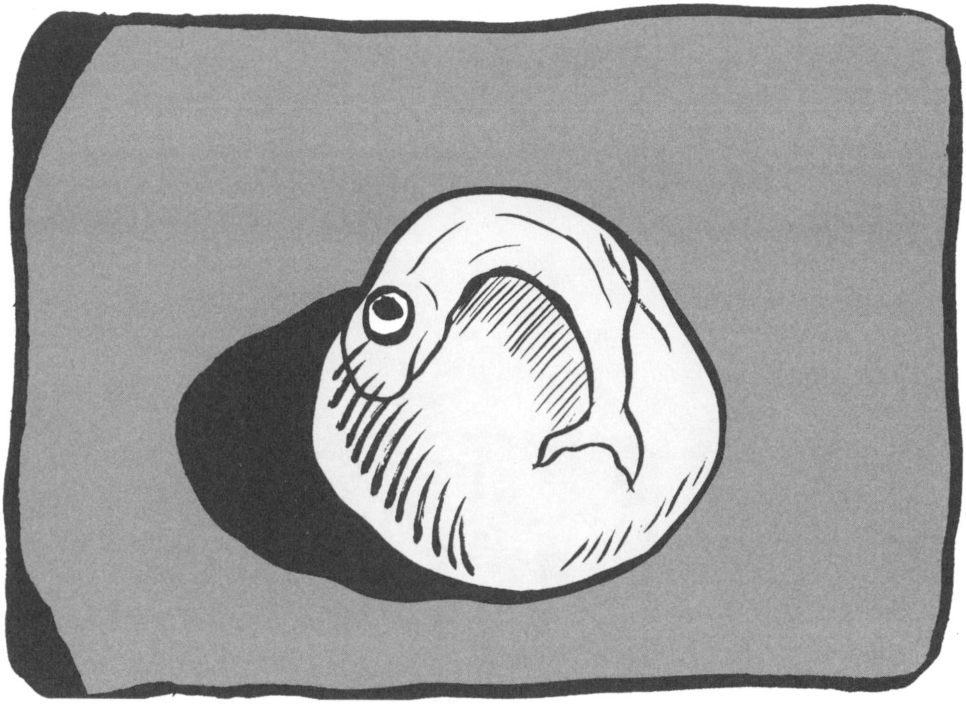

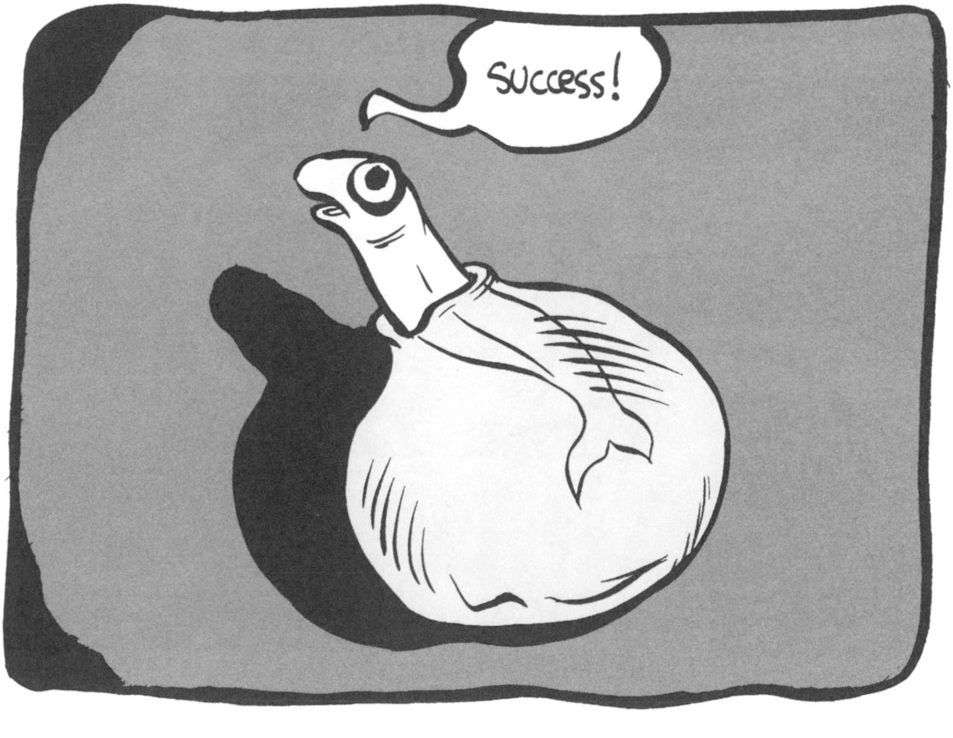
SUCCESS!

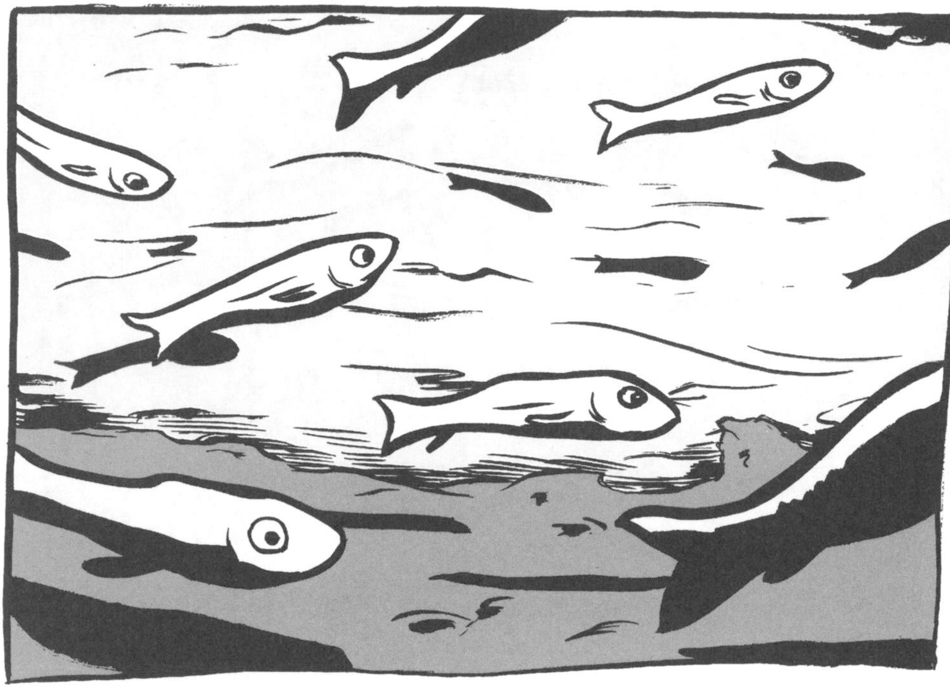
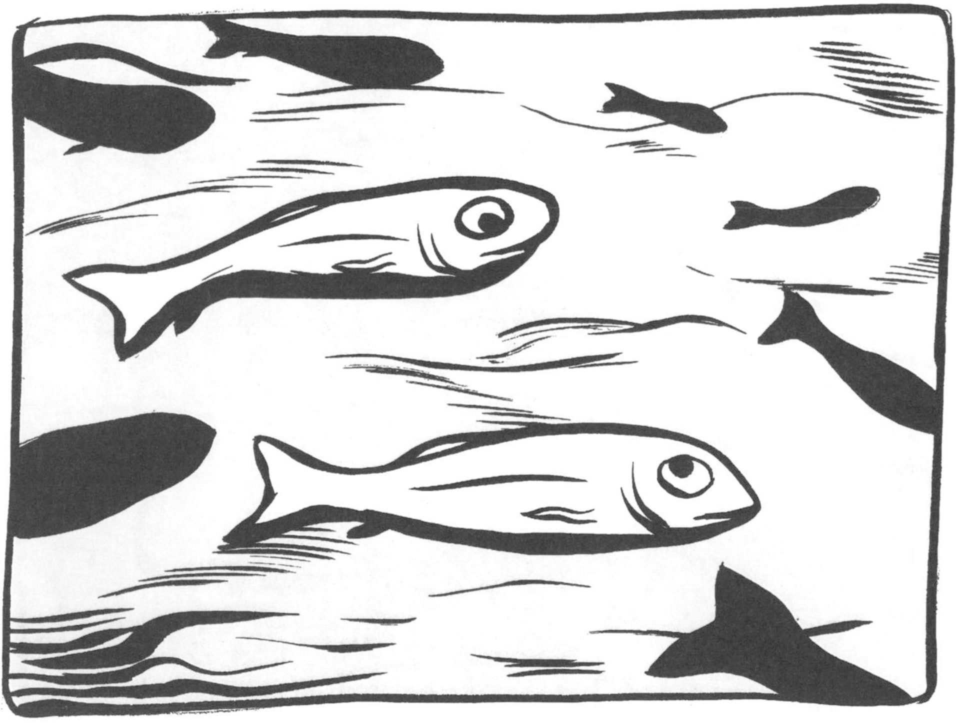

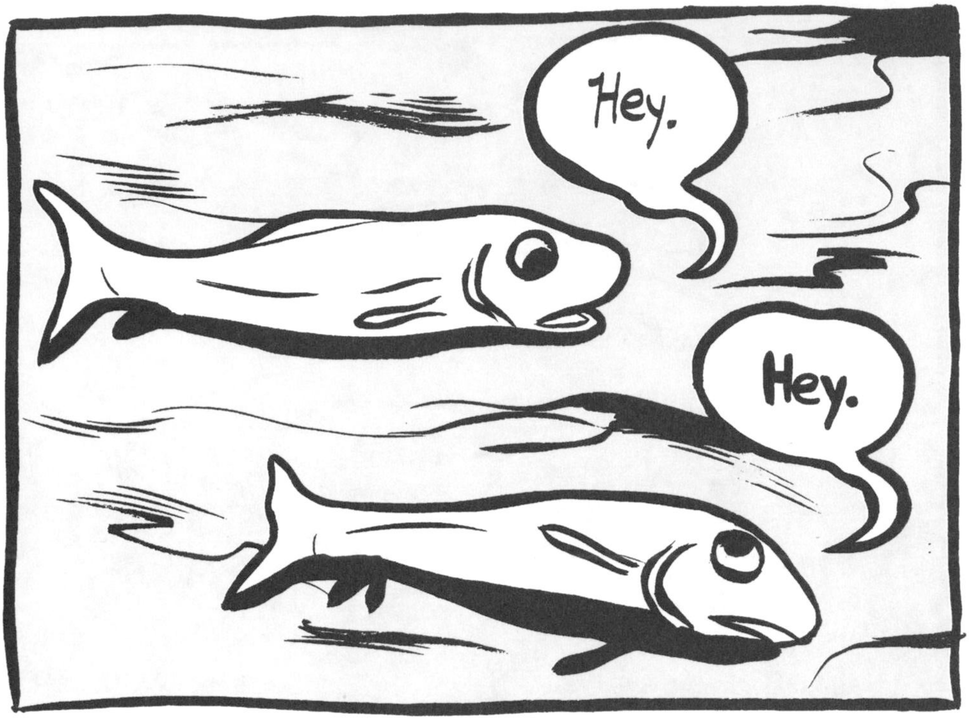
Hey.
Hey.

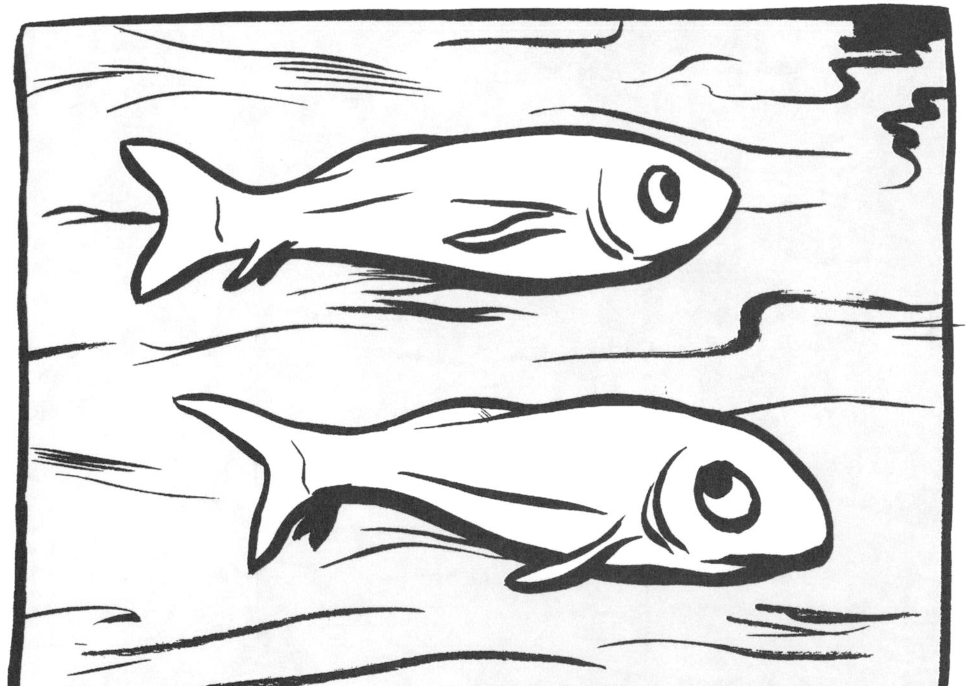

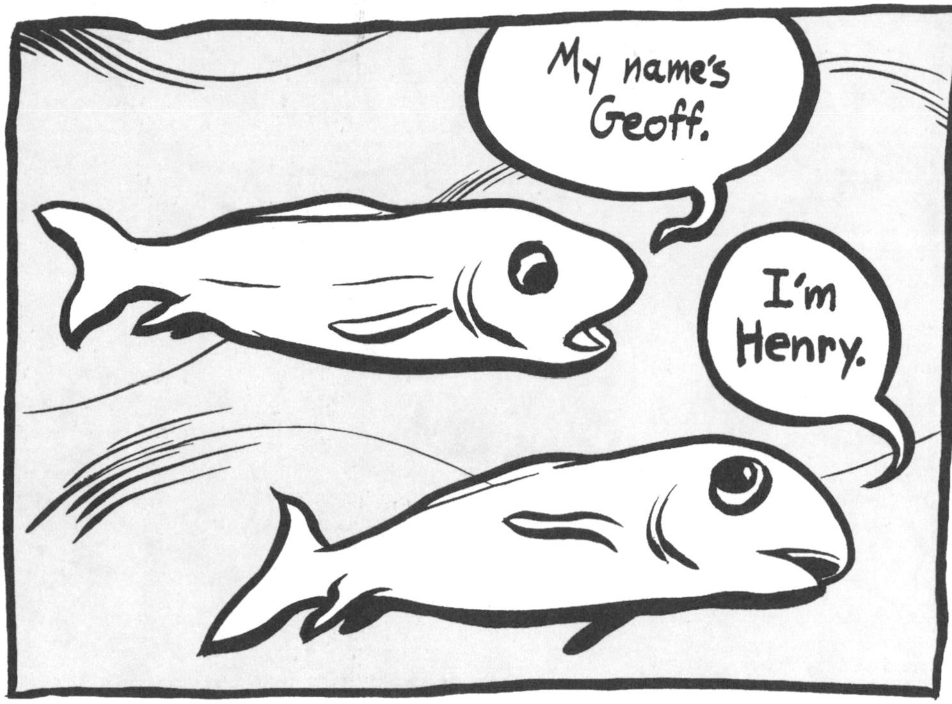
My name's Geoff.
I'm Henry.

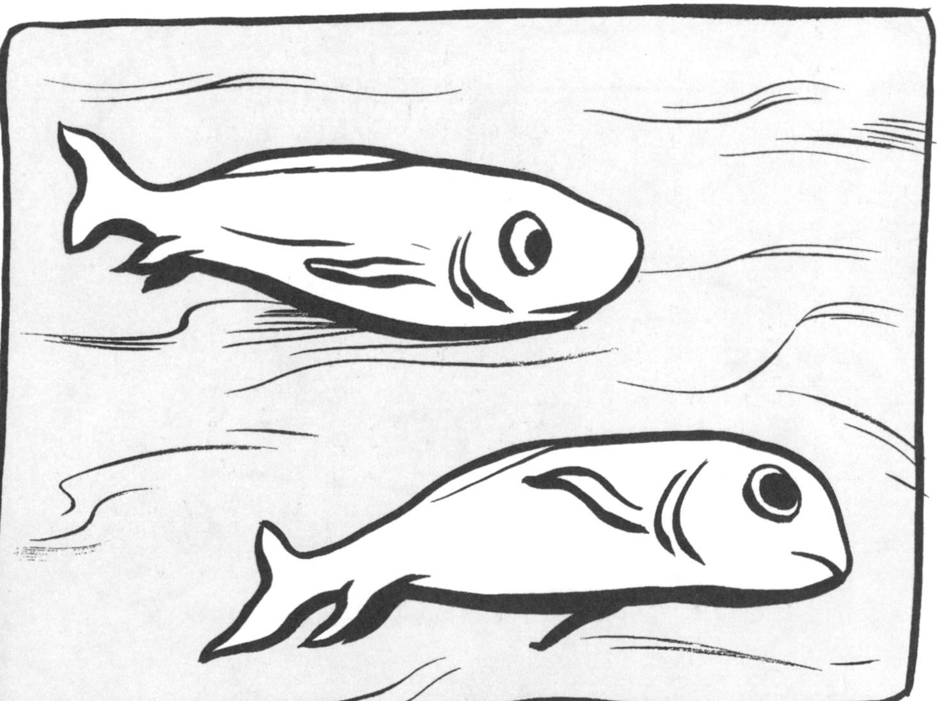

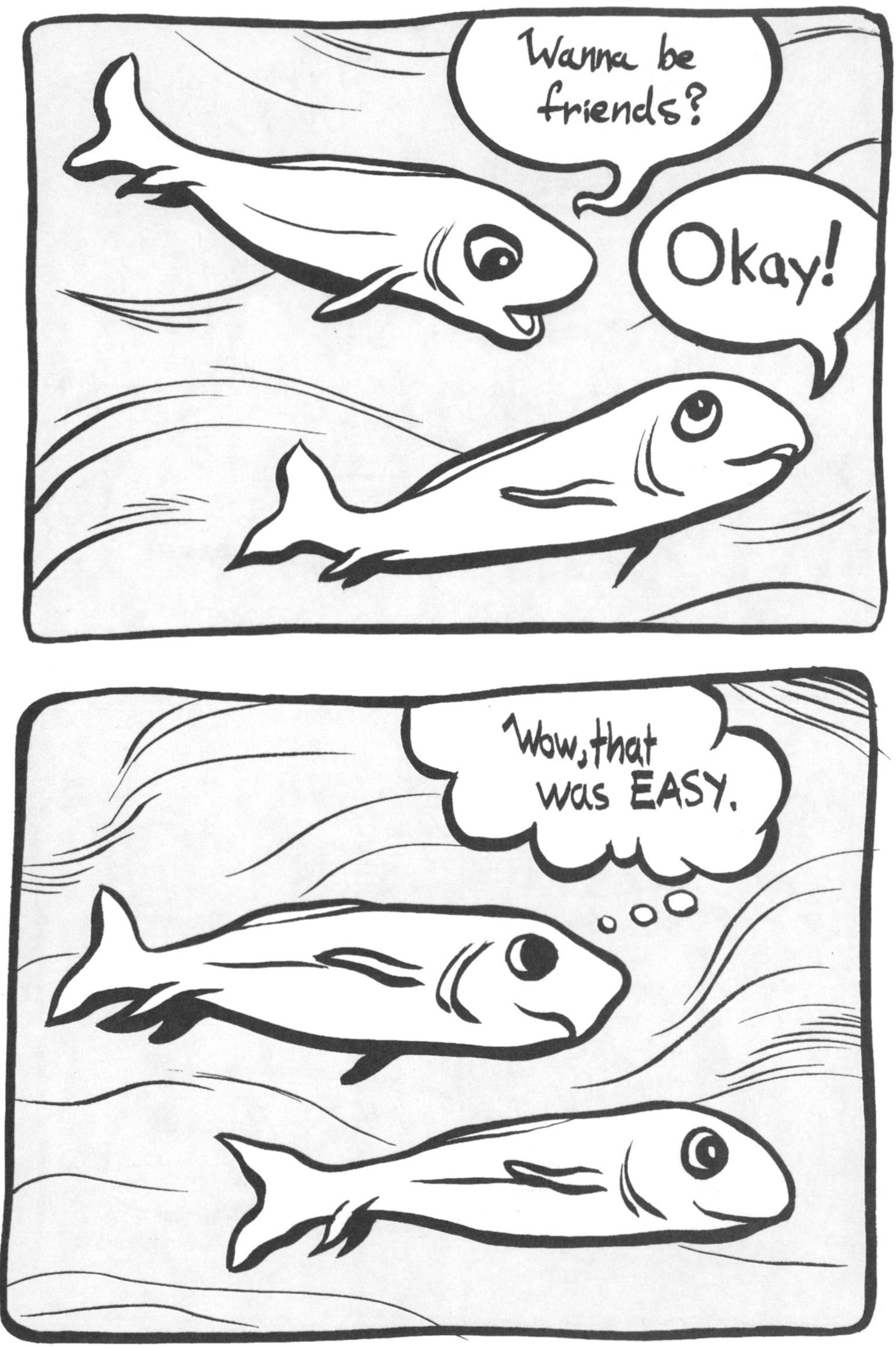
Wanna be friends?
Okay!
Wow, that was EASY.

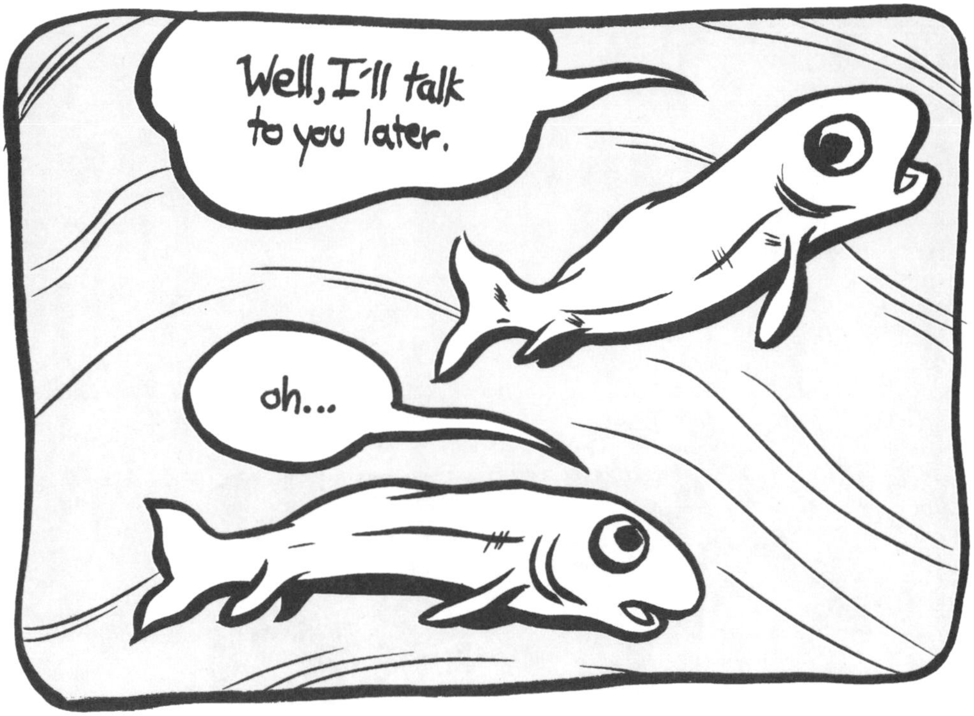
Well, I'll talk to you later.
oh...

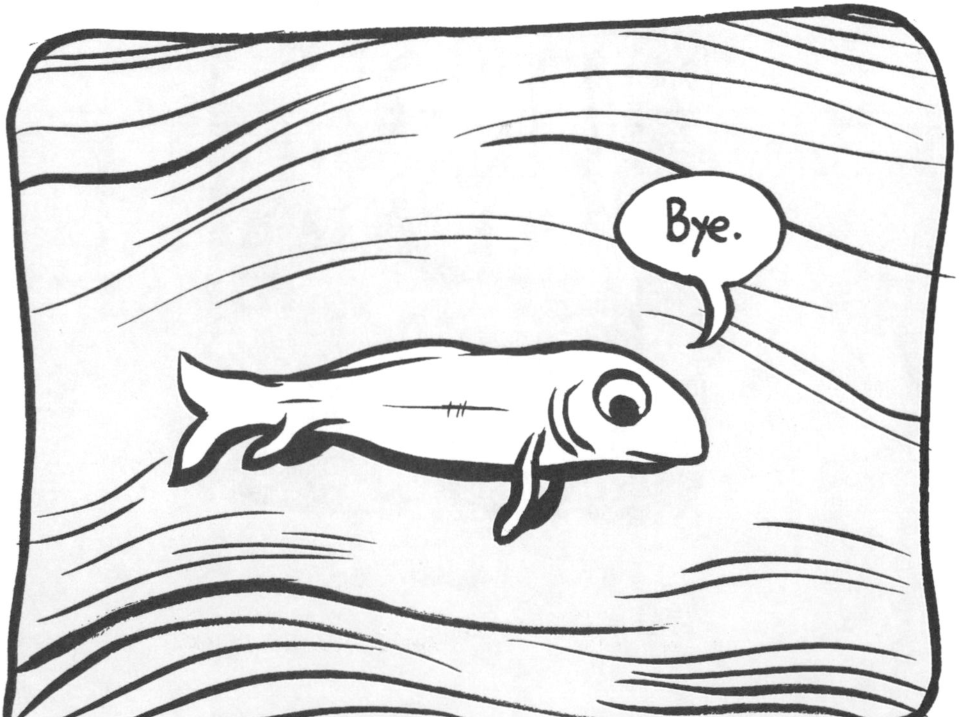
Bye.

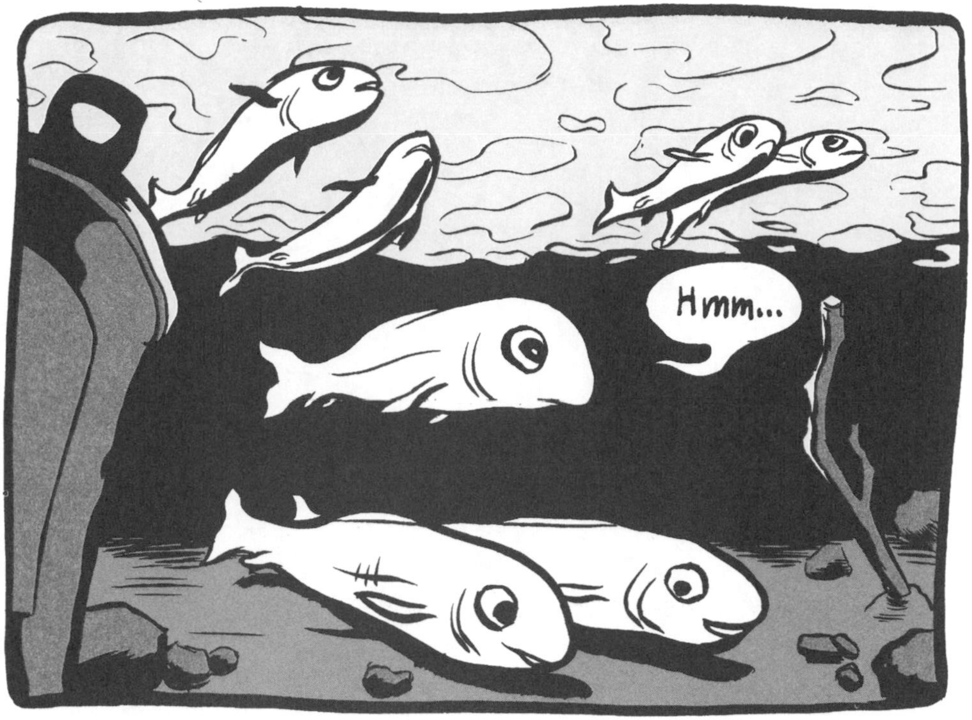
Hmm...

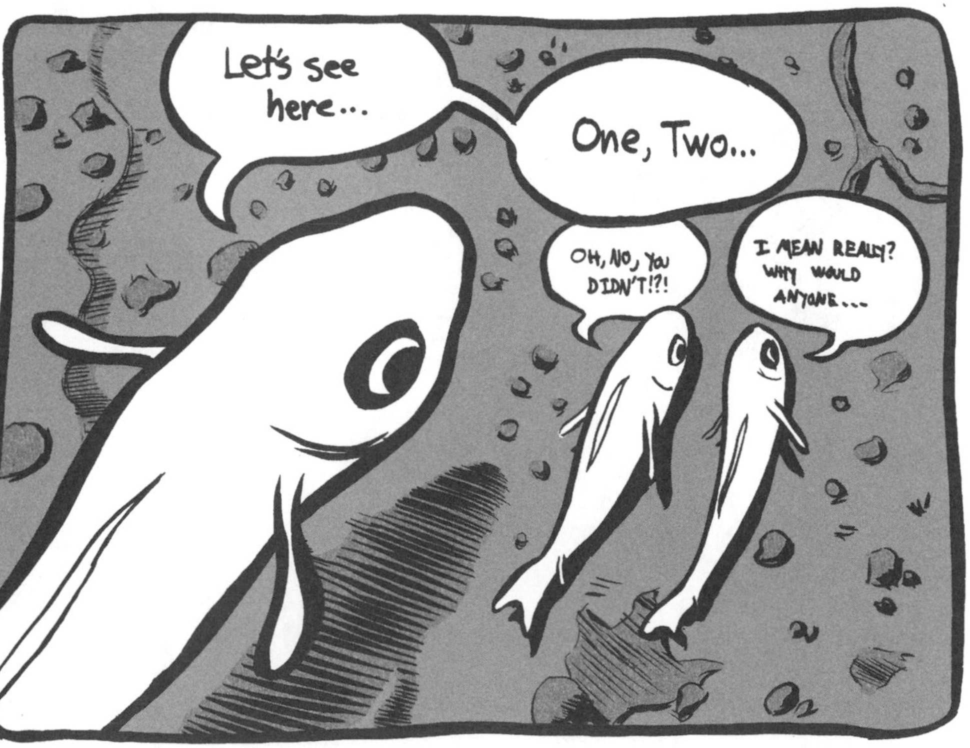
Let's see here...
One, Two...
OH, NO, YOU DIDN'T!?!
I MEAN REALLY? WHY WOULD ANYONE...

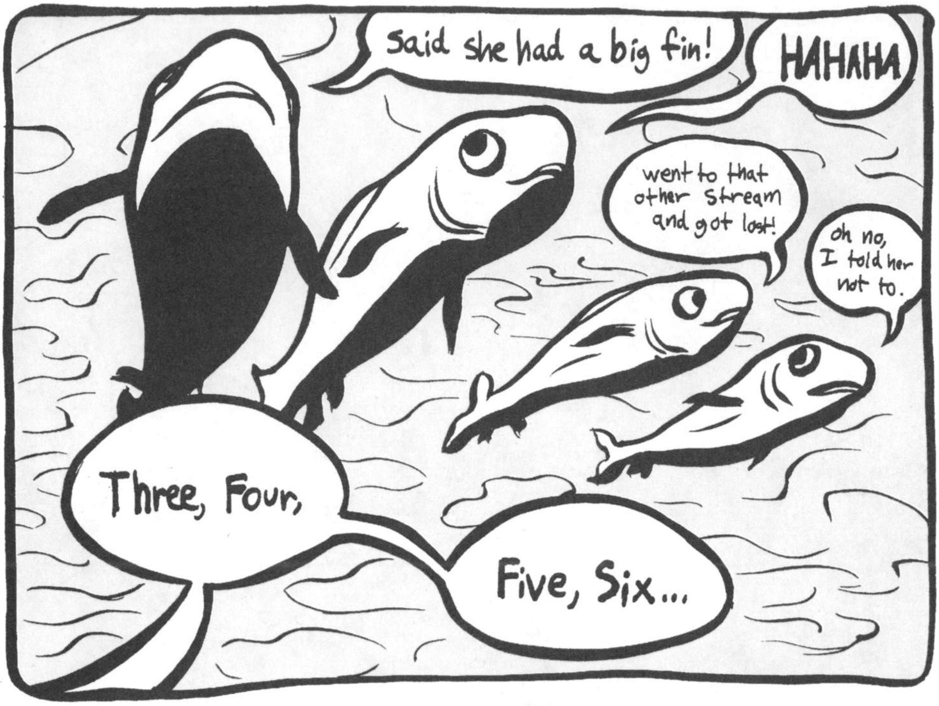
Said she had a big fin!
HAHAHA
went to that other stream and got lost!
oh no, I told her not to.
Three, Four,
Five, Six...

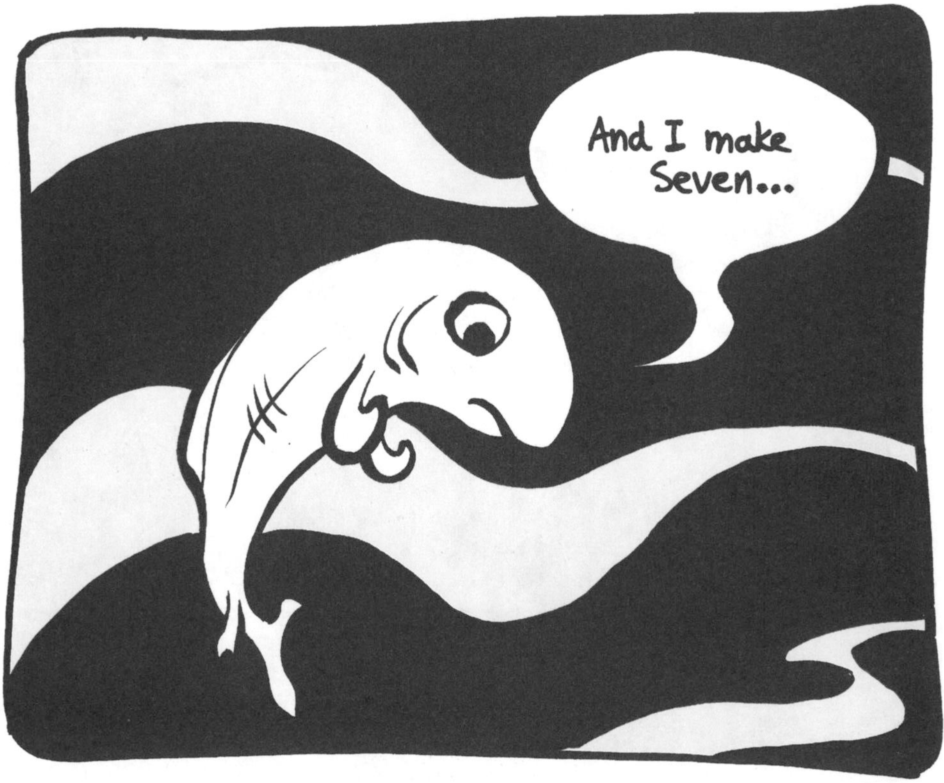
And I make Seven...

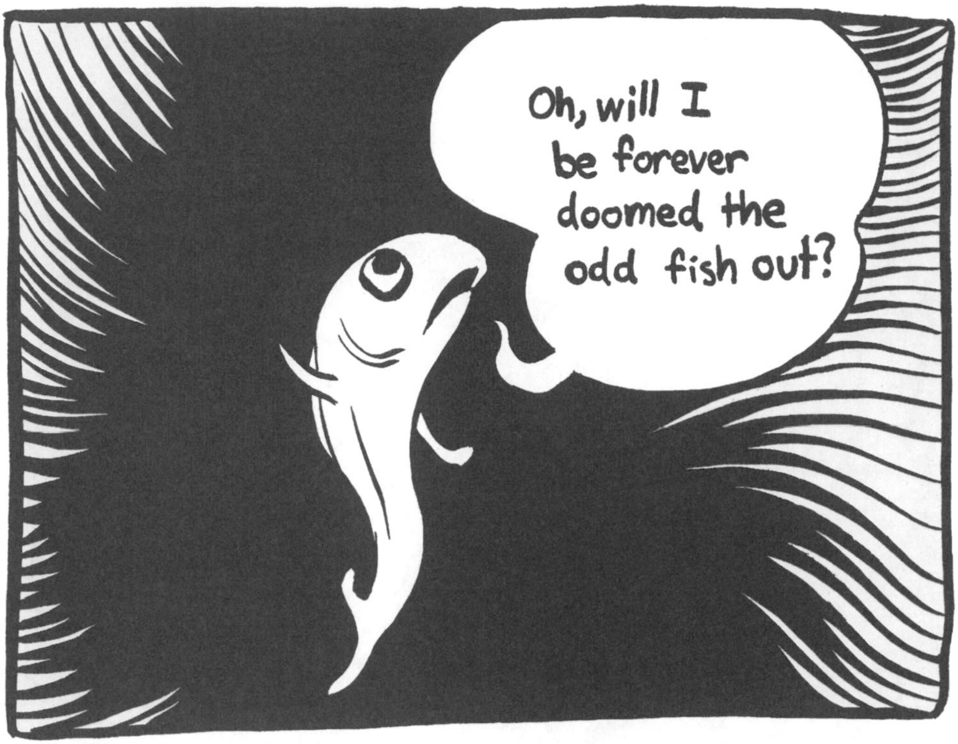
Oh, will I be forever doomed the odd fish out?

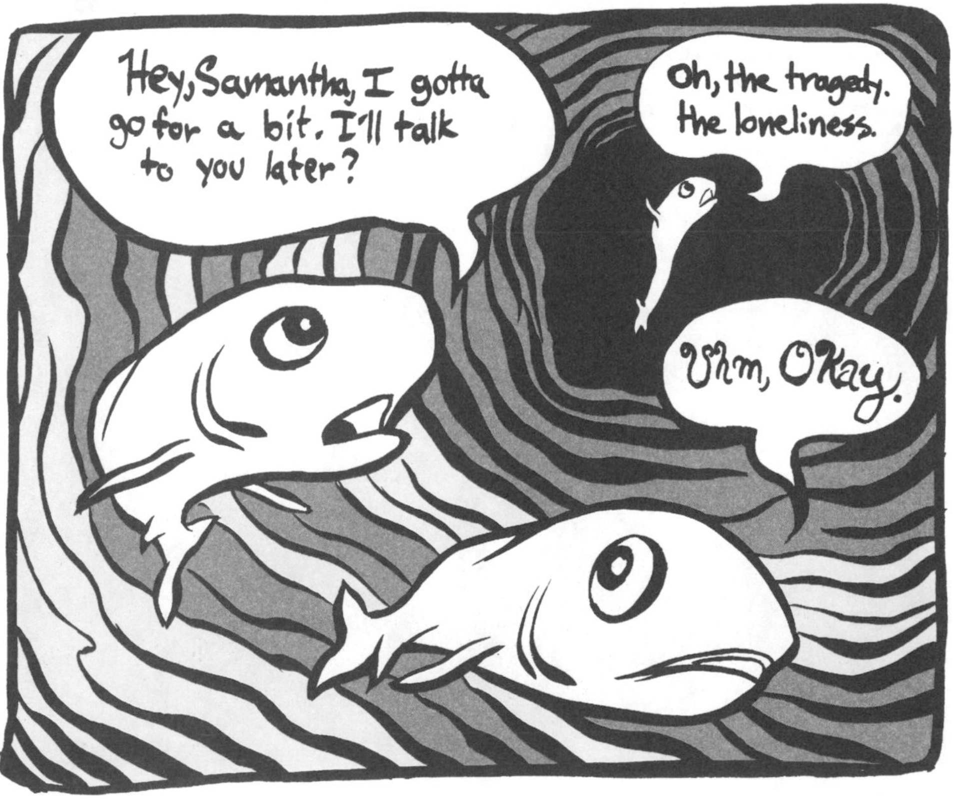
Hey, Samantha, I gotta go for a bit. I'll talk to you later?
Oh, the tragedy. the loneliness.
Uhm, Okay.

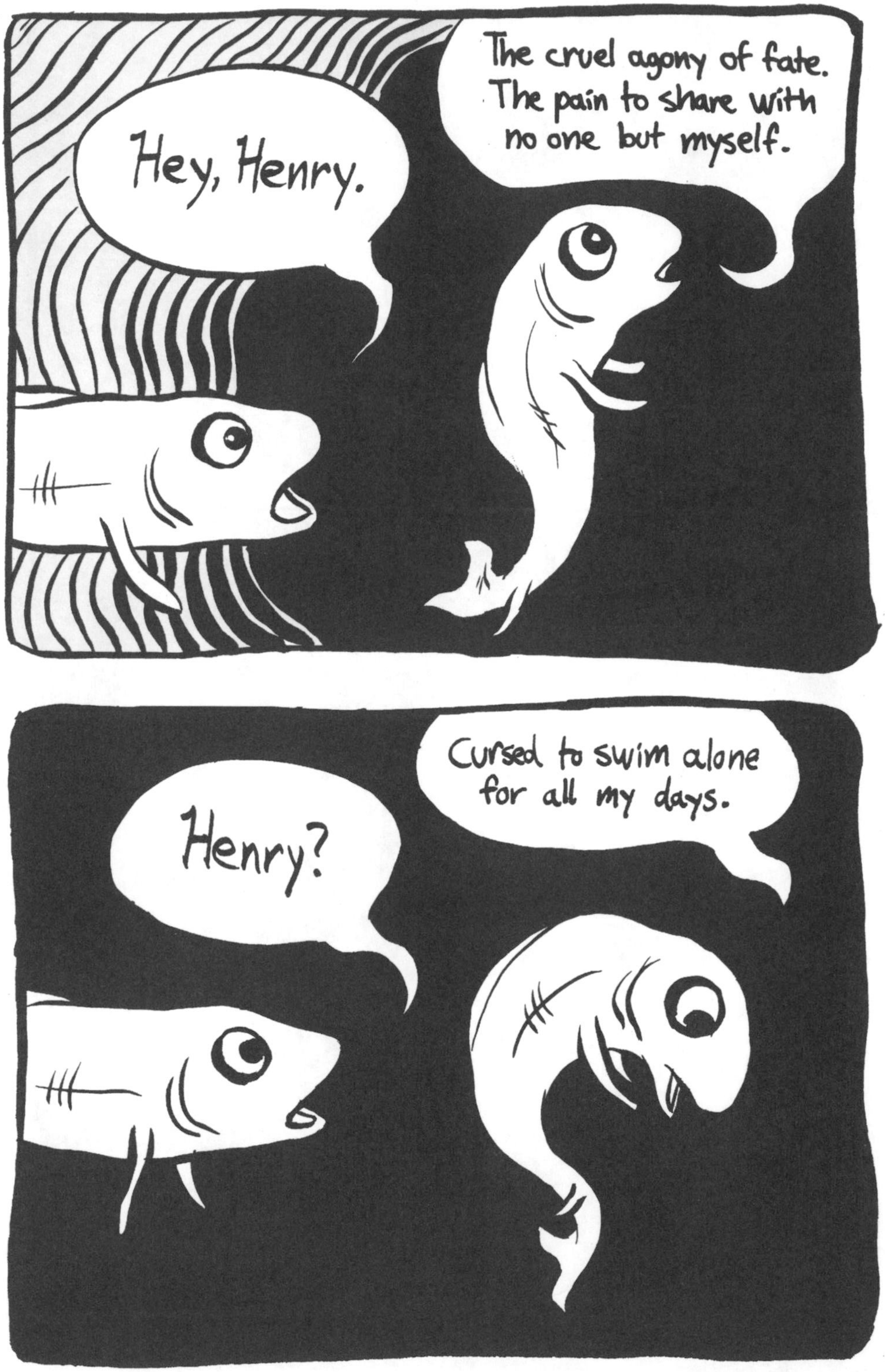
Hey, Henry.
The cruel agony of fate. The pain to share with no one but myself.
Henry?
Cursed to swim alone for all my days.

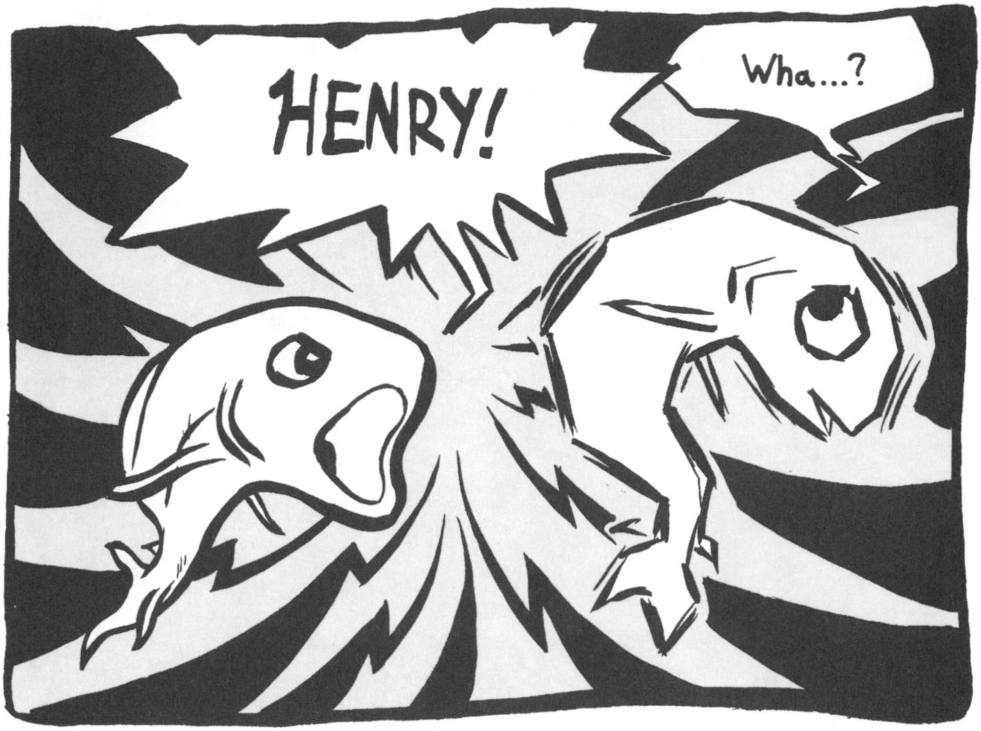
HENRY!
Wha...?

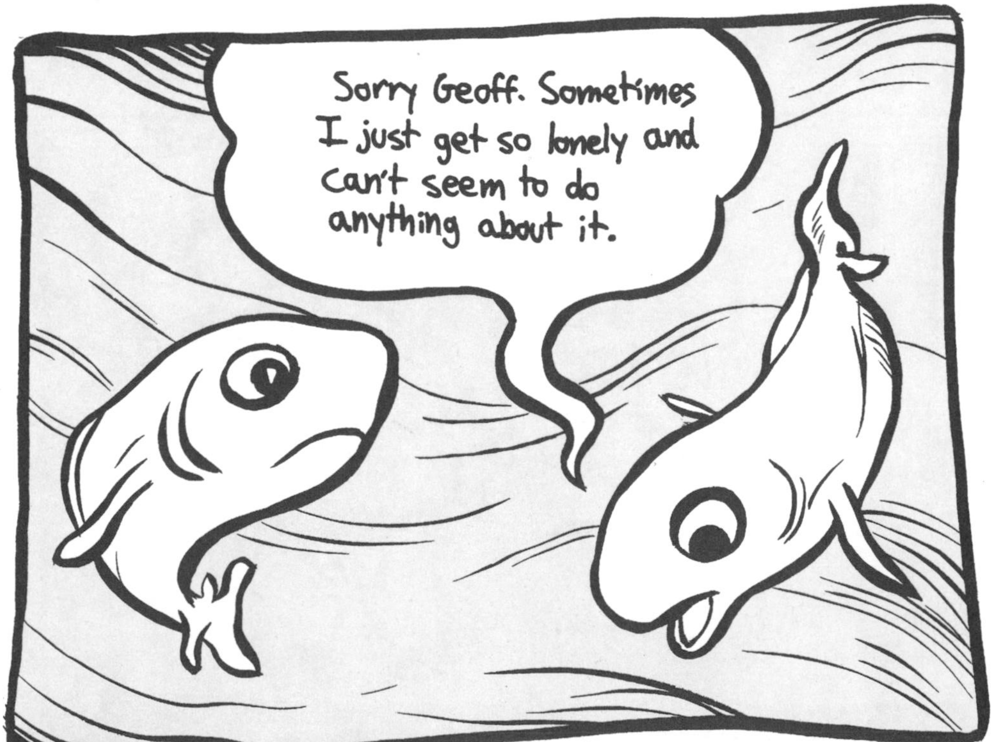
Sorry Geoff. Sometimes I just get so lonely and can't seem to do anything about it.

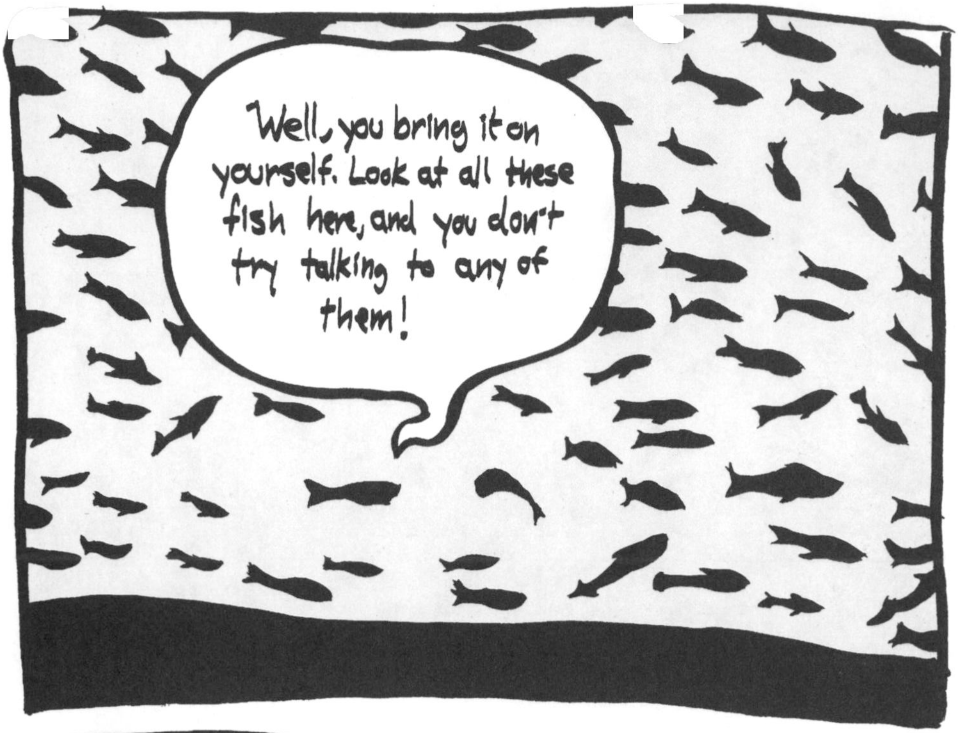
Well, you bring it on yourself. Look at all these fish here, and you don't try talking to any of them!

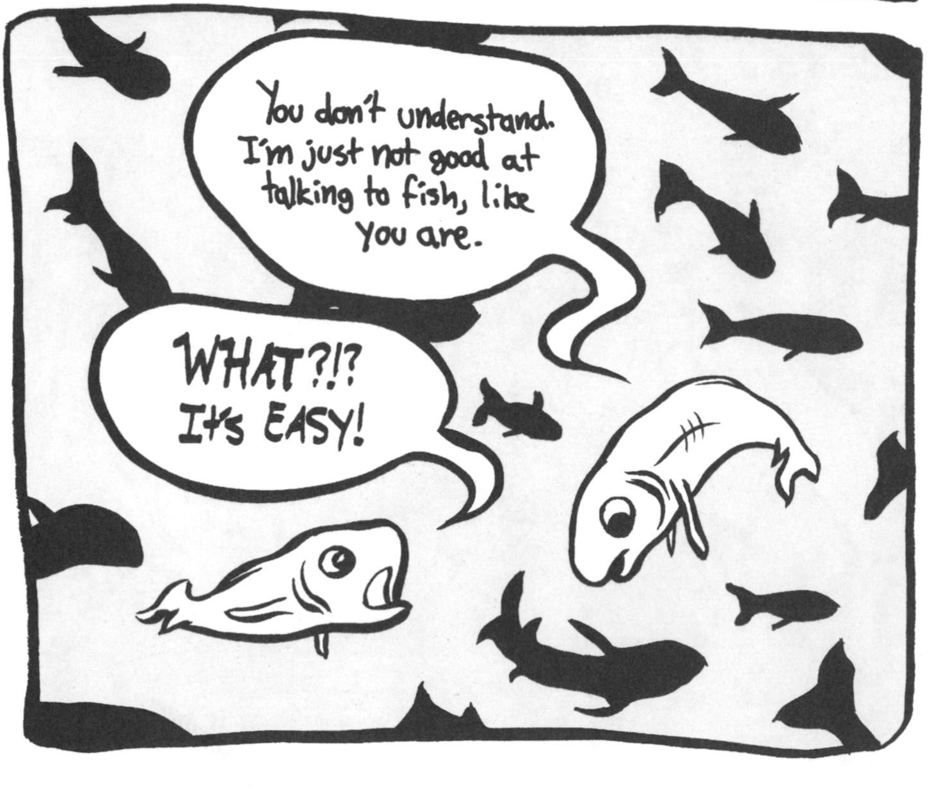
You don't understand. I'm just not good at talking to fish, like you are.
WHAT?!? It's EASY!

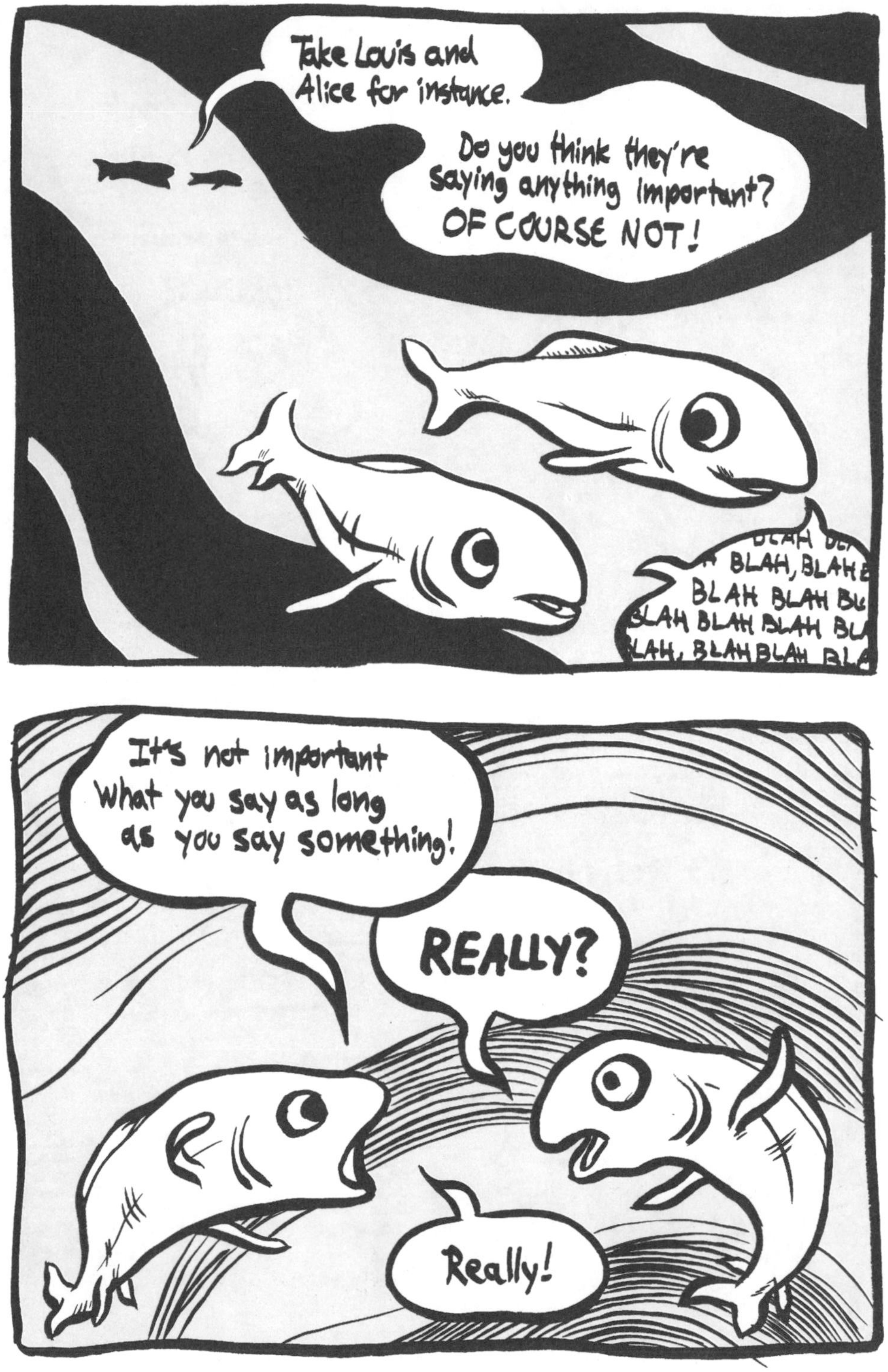
Take Louis and Alice for instance.
Do you think they're saying anything important? OF COURSE NOT!
BLAH, BLAH BLAH BLAH BLAH BLAH BLAH BLAH, BLAH BLAH
It's not important what you say as long as you say something!
REALLY?
Really!

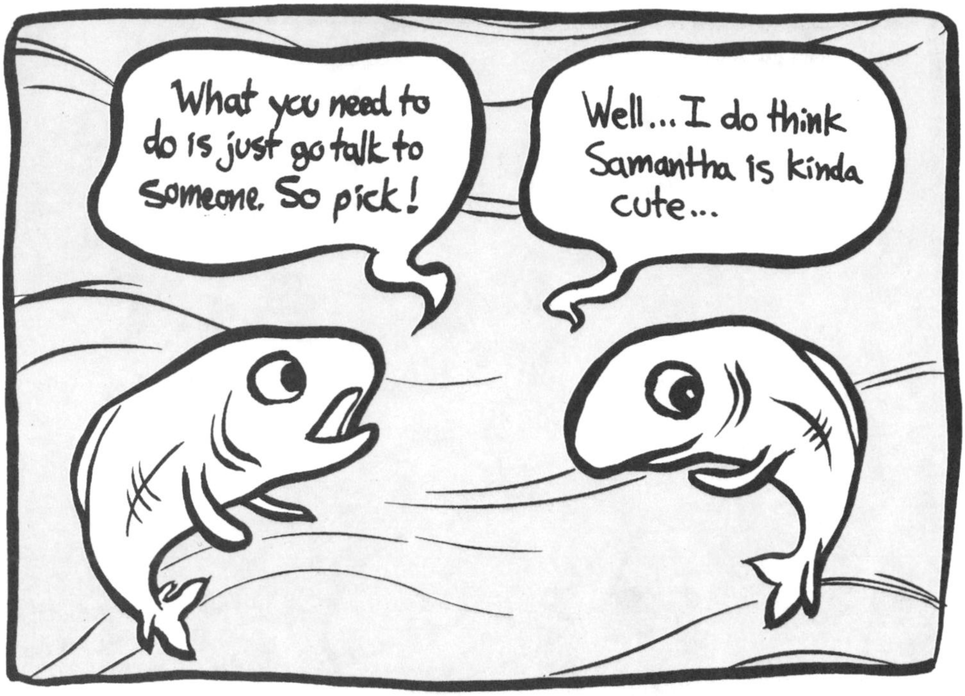
What you need to do is just go talk to someone. So pick!
Well... I do think Samantha is kinda cute...

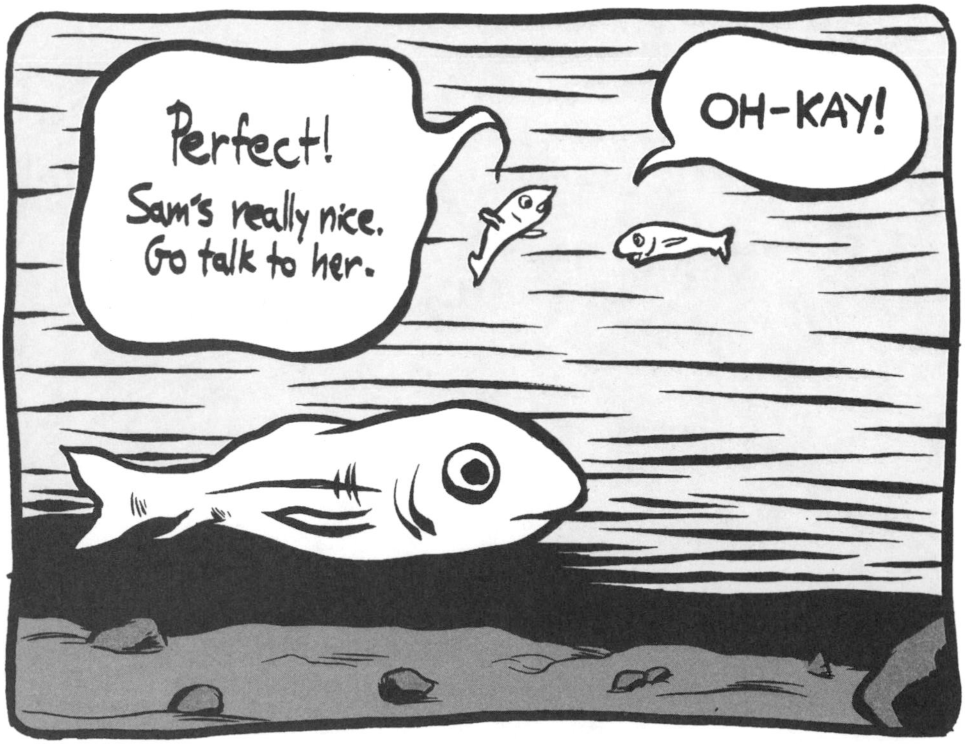
Perfect! Sam's really nice. Go talk to her.
OH-KAY!

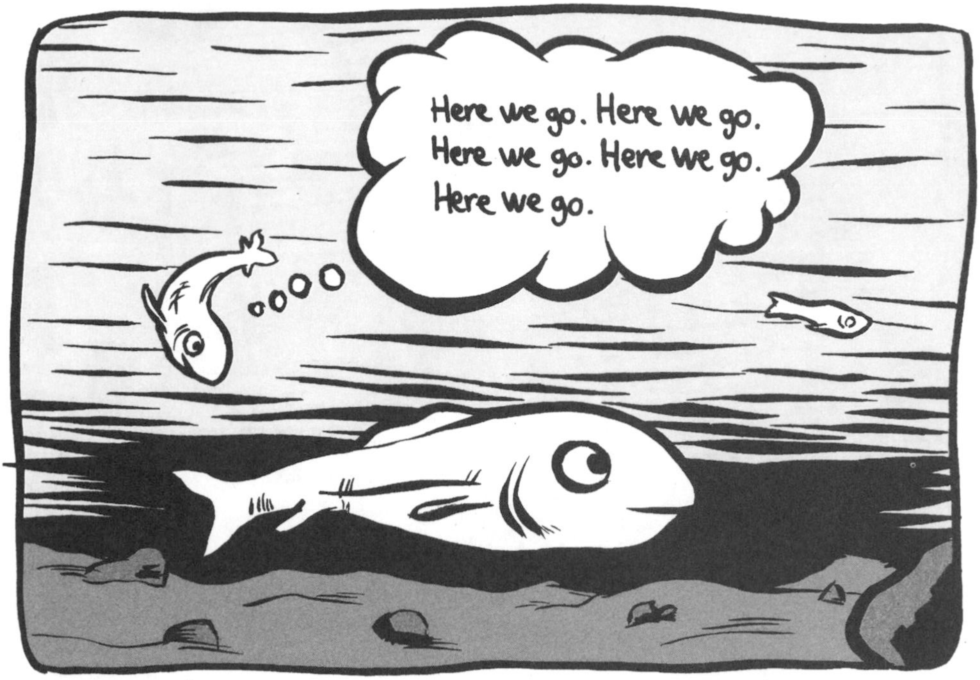
Here we go. Here we go.
Here we go. Here we go.
Here we go.

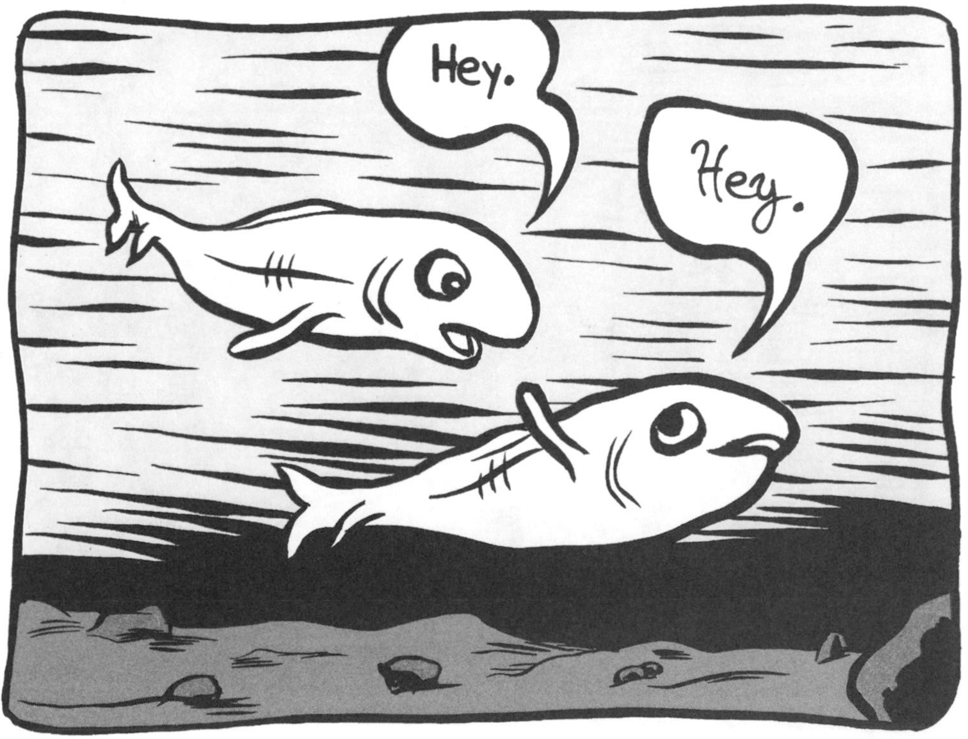
Hey.
Hey.

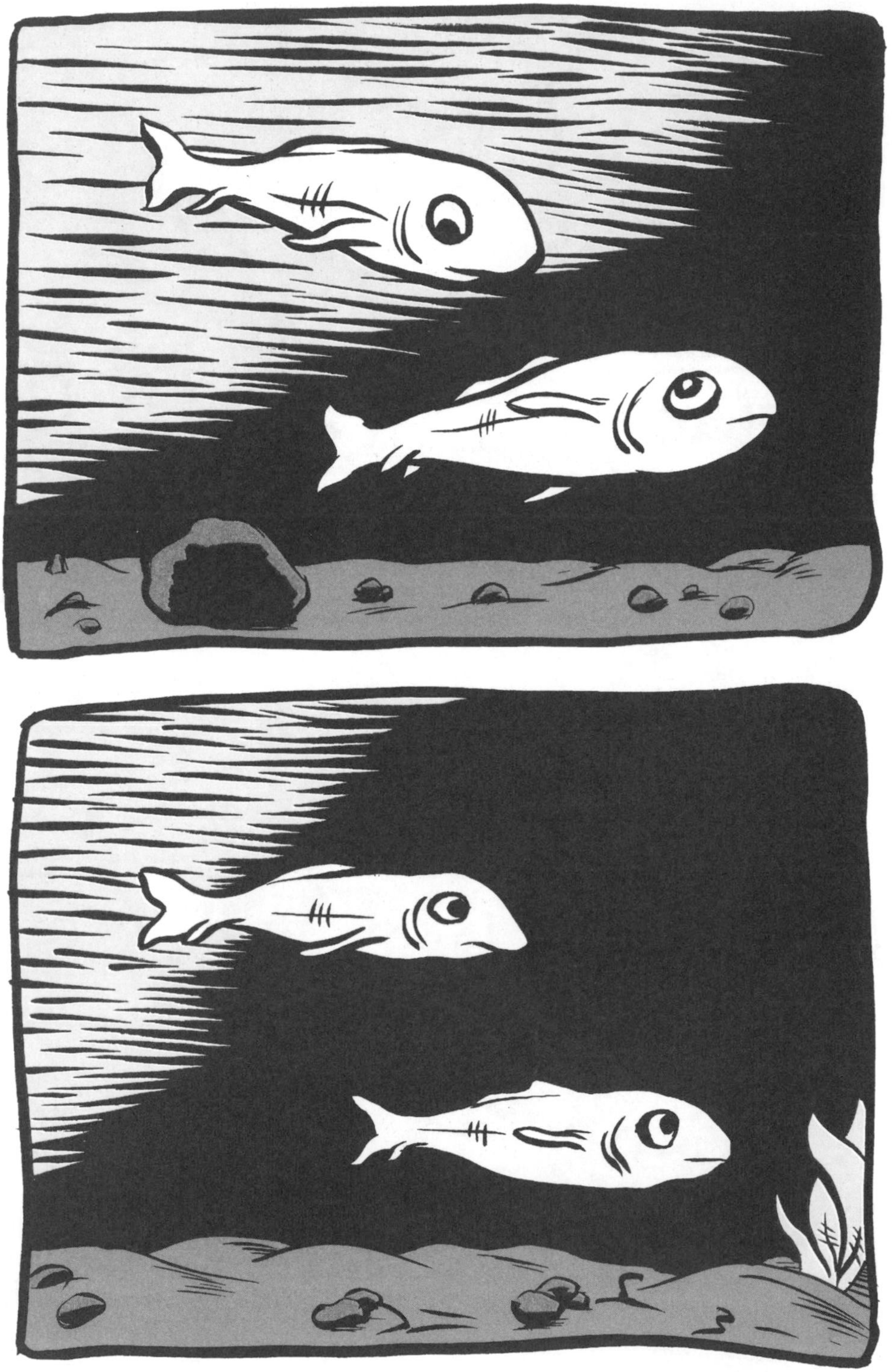

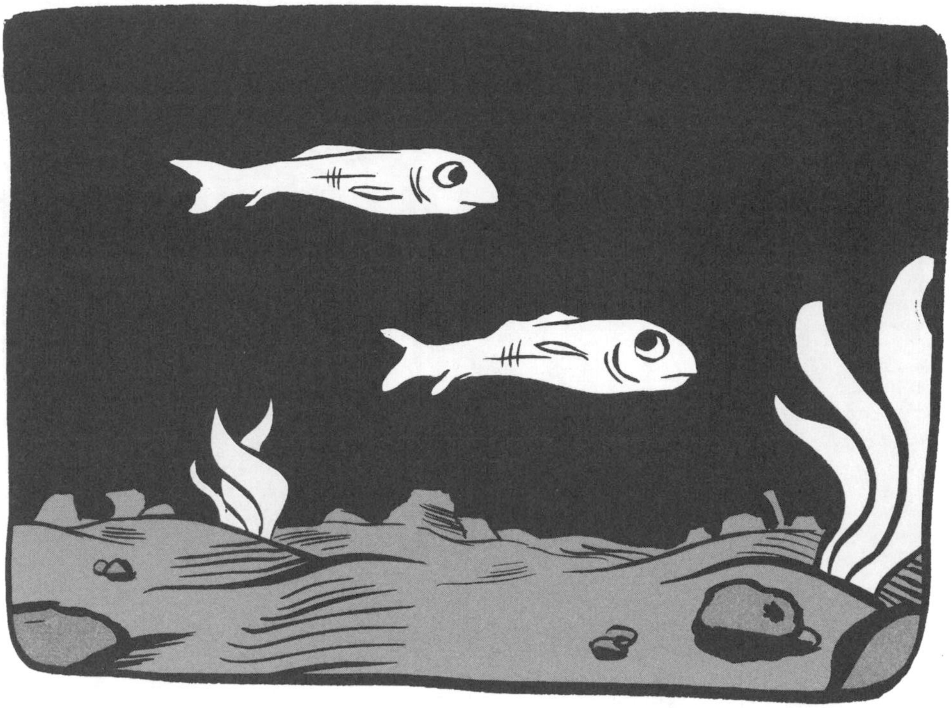

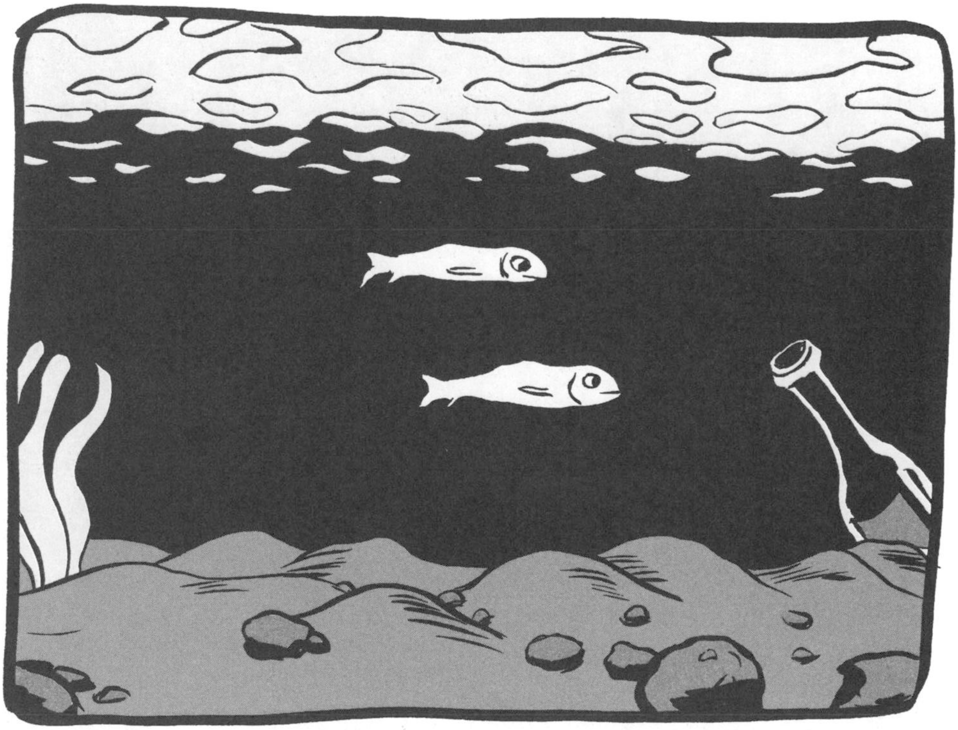

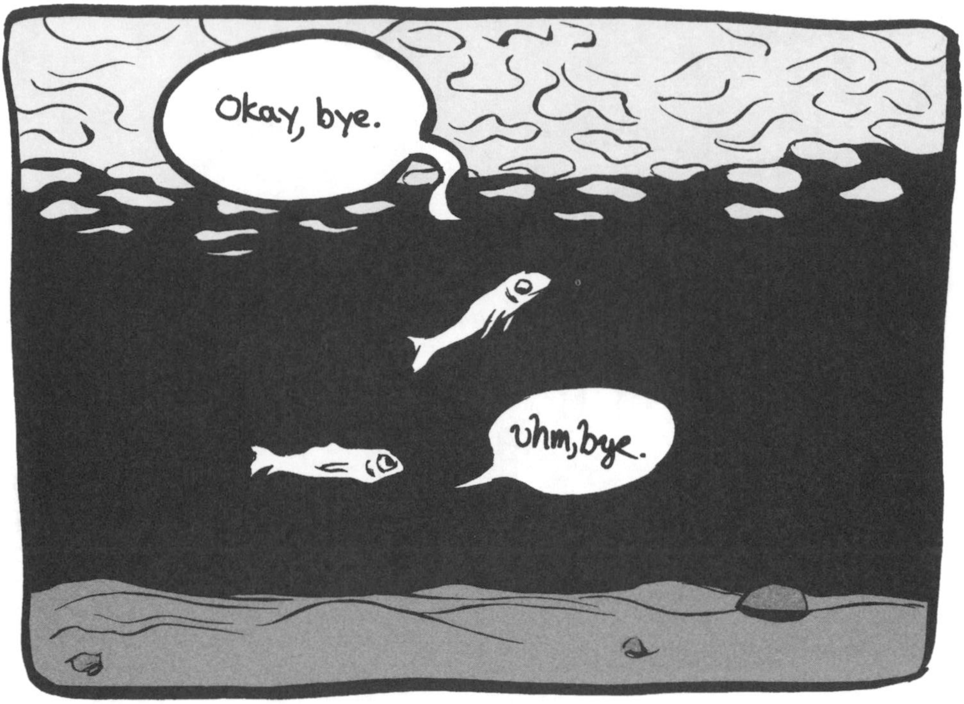
Okay, bye.
uhm, bye.

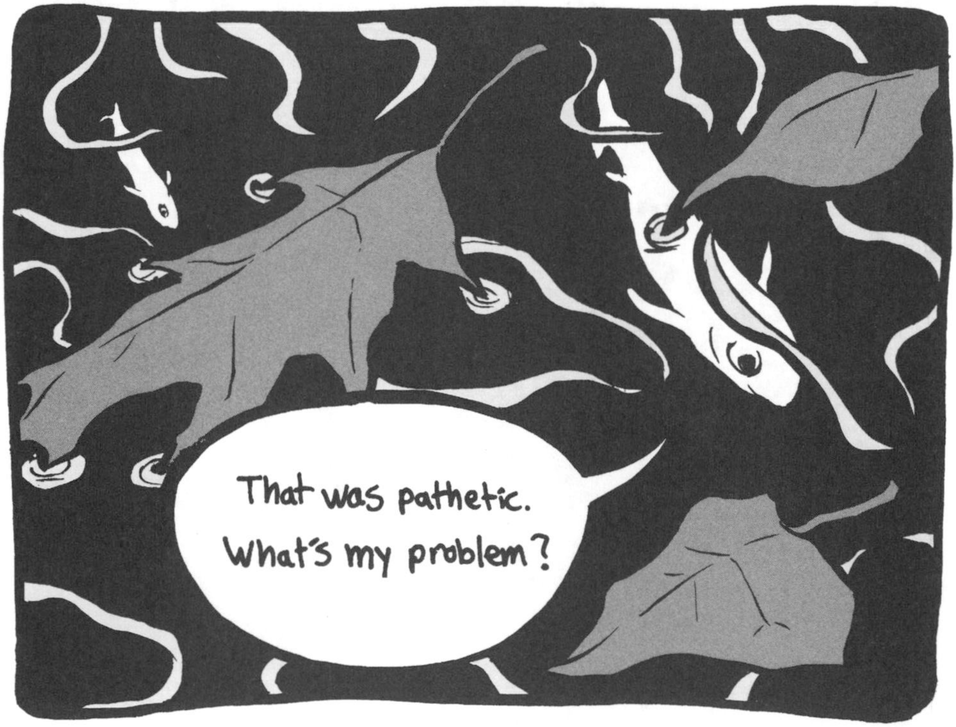
That was pathetic. What's my problem?

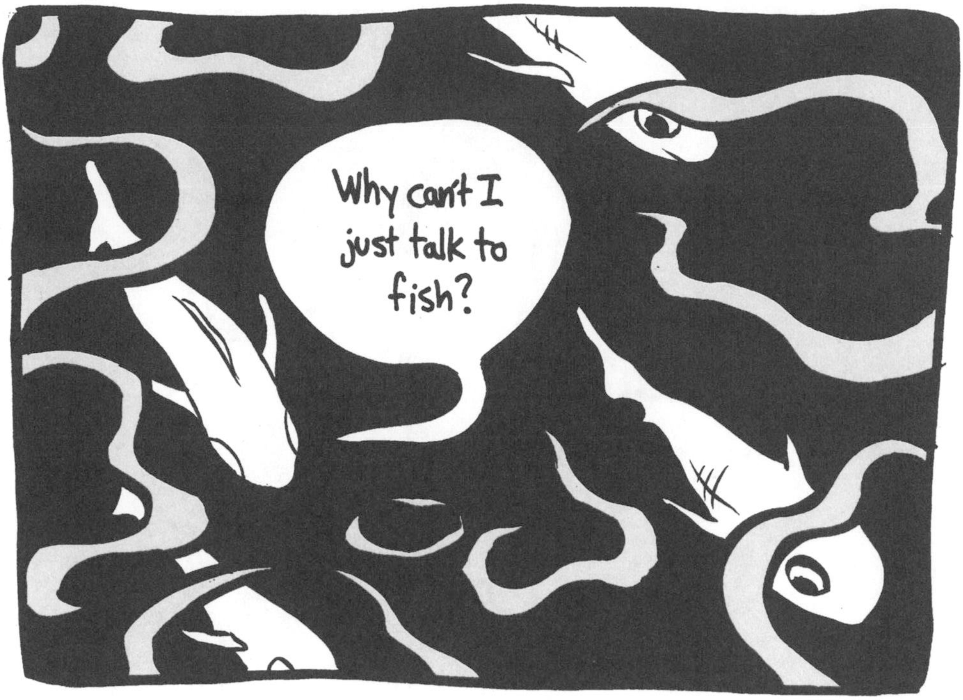
Why can't I just talk to fish?

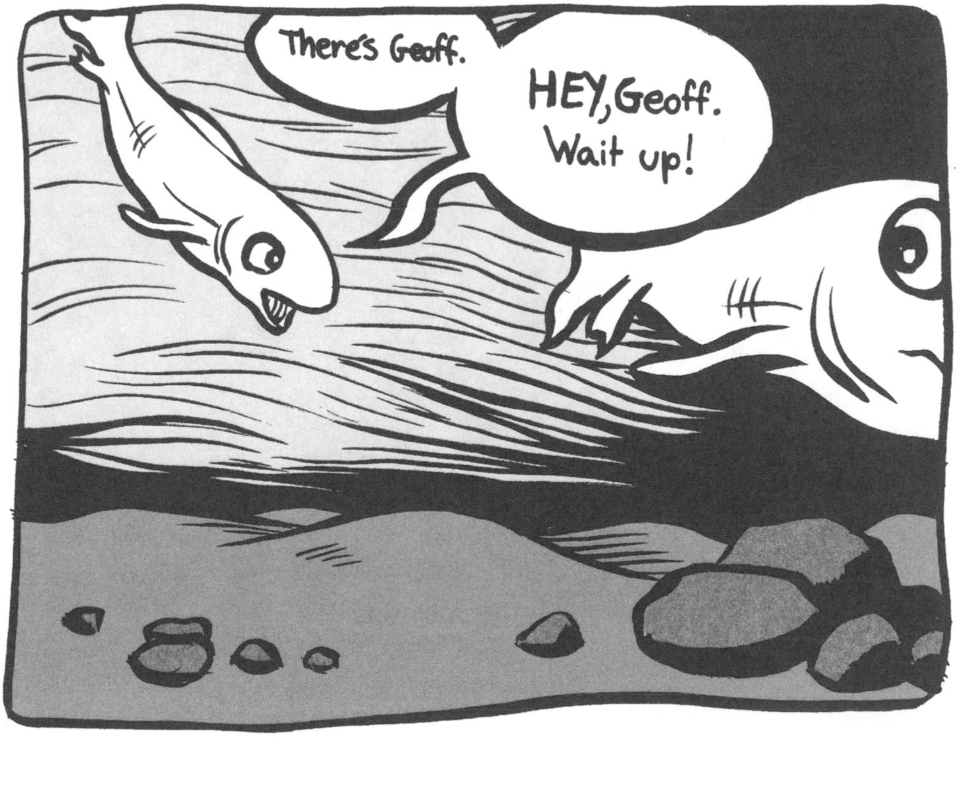
There's Geoff.
HEY, Geoff. Wait up!

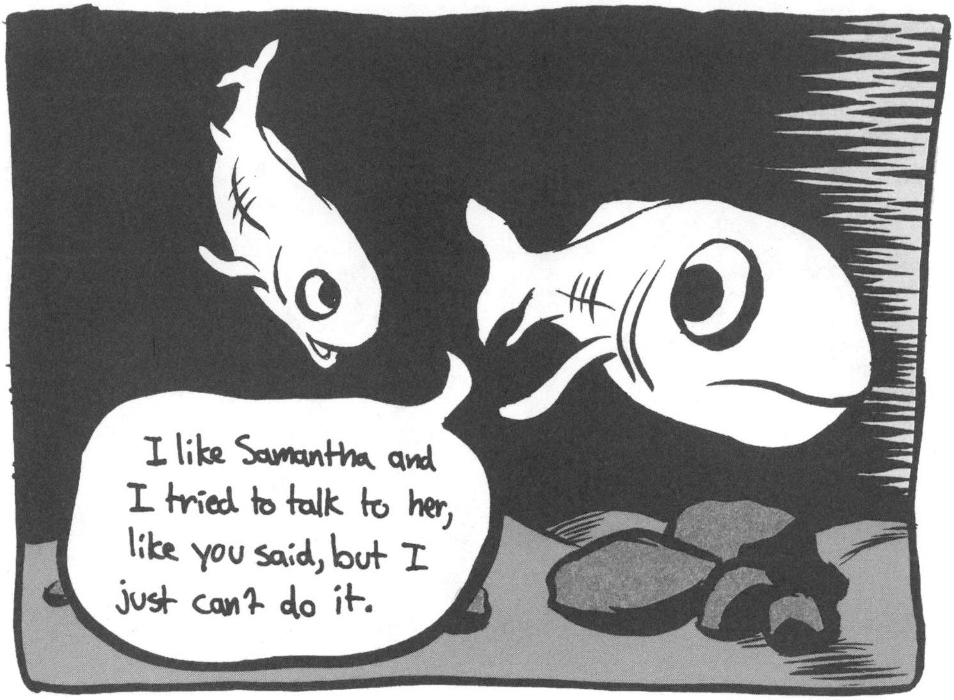
I like Samantha and I tried to talk to her, like you said, but I just can't do it.

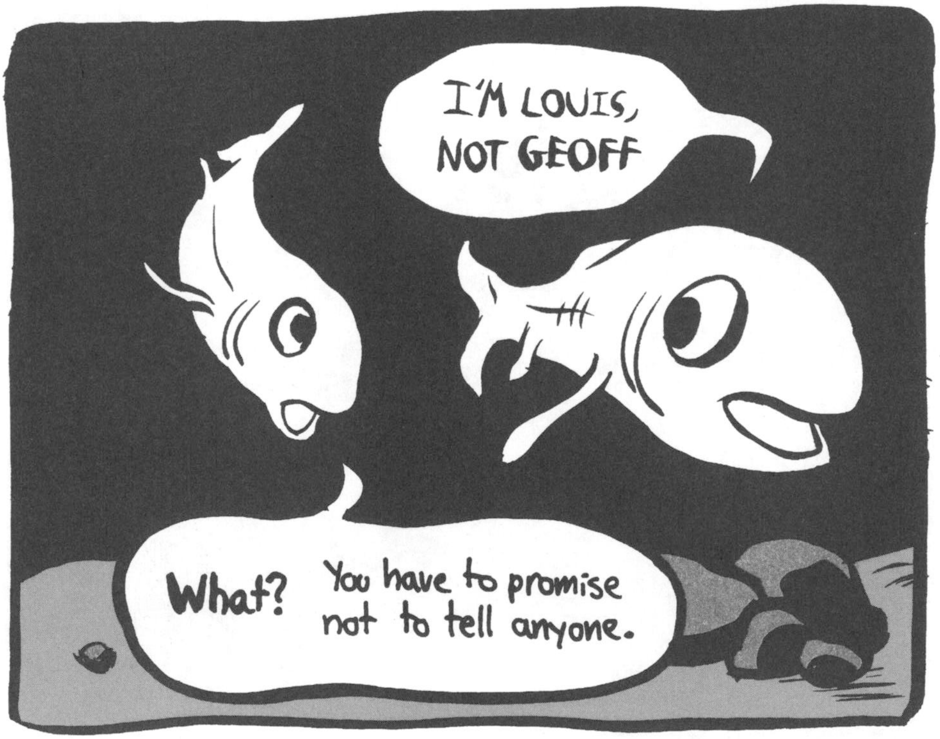
I'M LOUIS, NOT GEOFF
What?
You have to promise not to tell anyone.

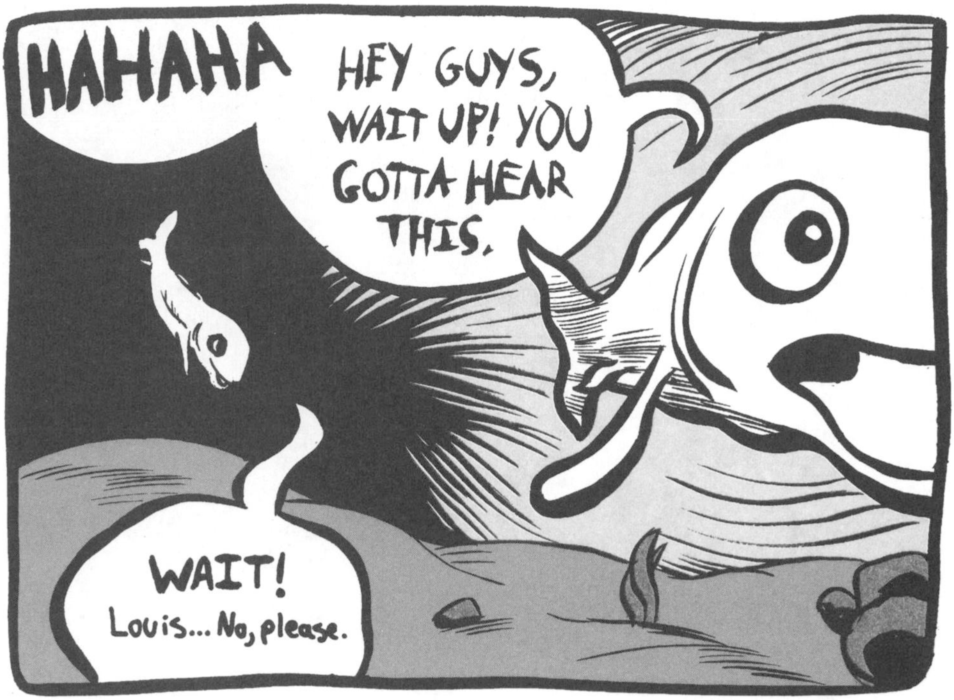
HAHAHA
HEY GUYS, WAIT UP! YOU GOTTA HEAR THIS.
WAIT! Louis... No, please.

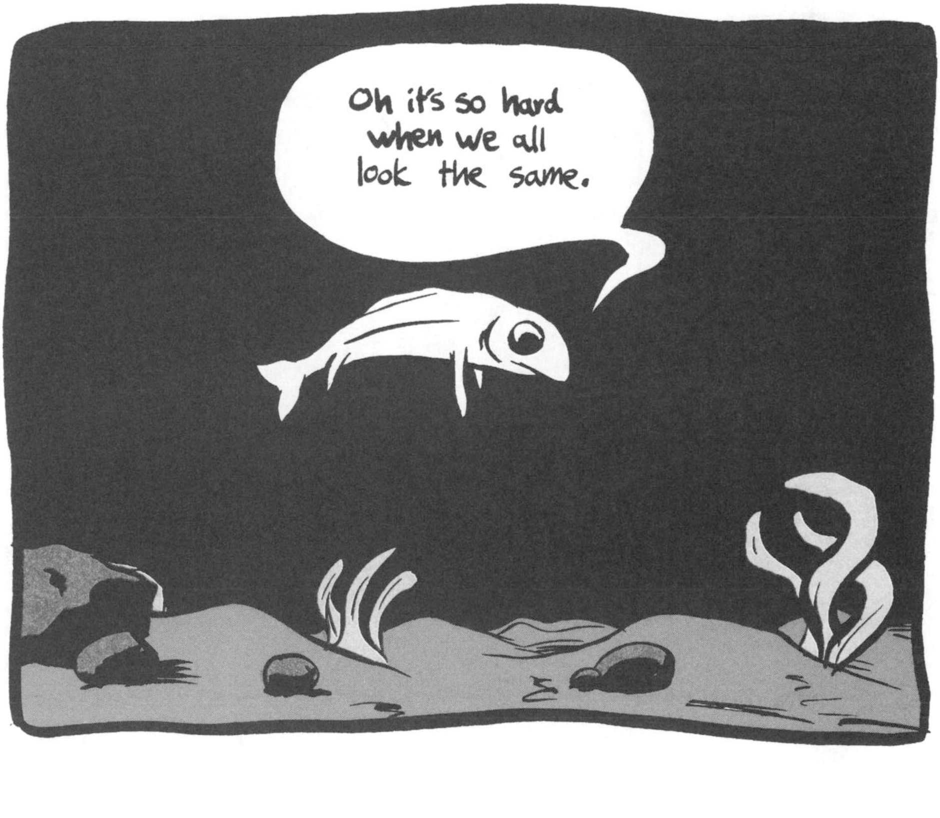
Oh it's so hard when we all look the same.

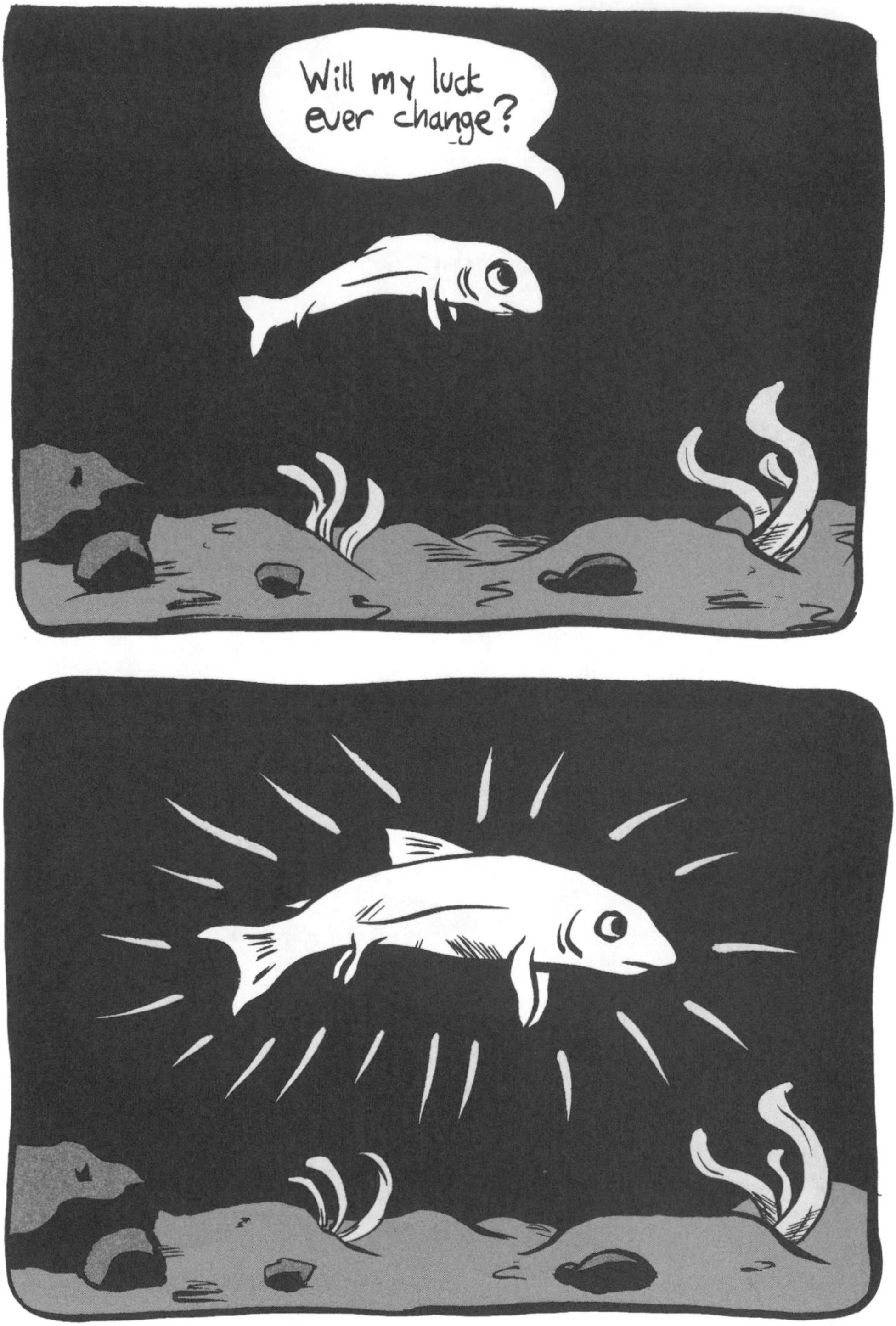
Will my luck ever change?

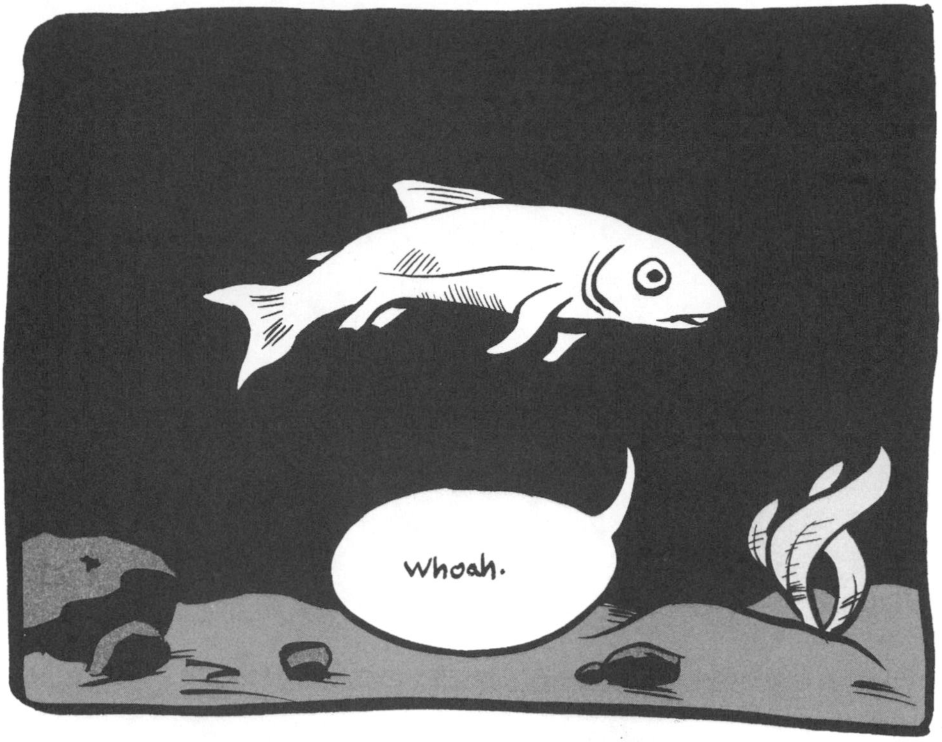
Whoah.

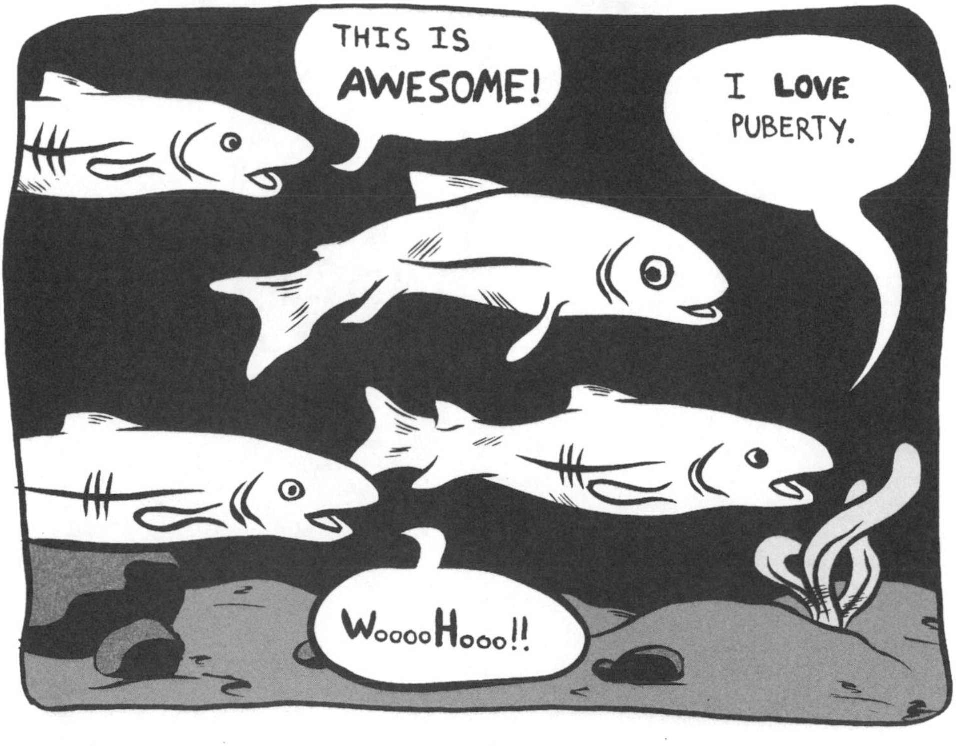
THIS IS AWESOME!
I LOVE PUBERTY.
WooooHooo!!

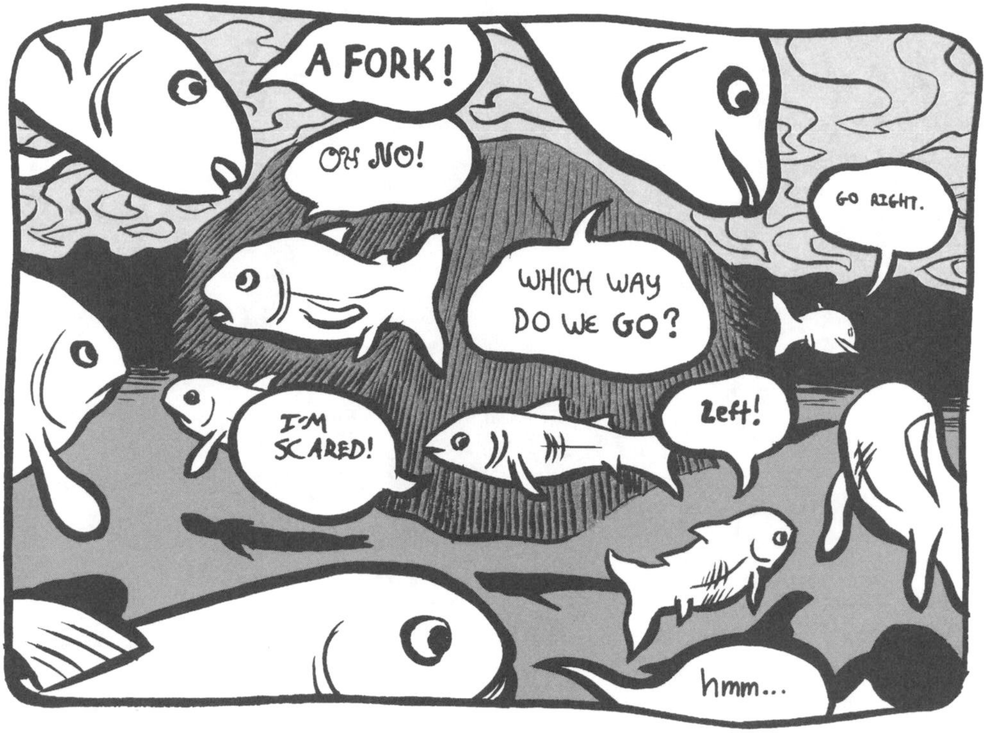
A FORK!
OH NO!
GO RIGHT.
WHICH WAY DO WE GO?
I'M SCARED!
Left!
hmm...

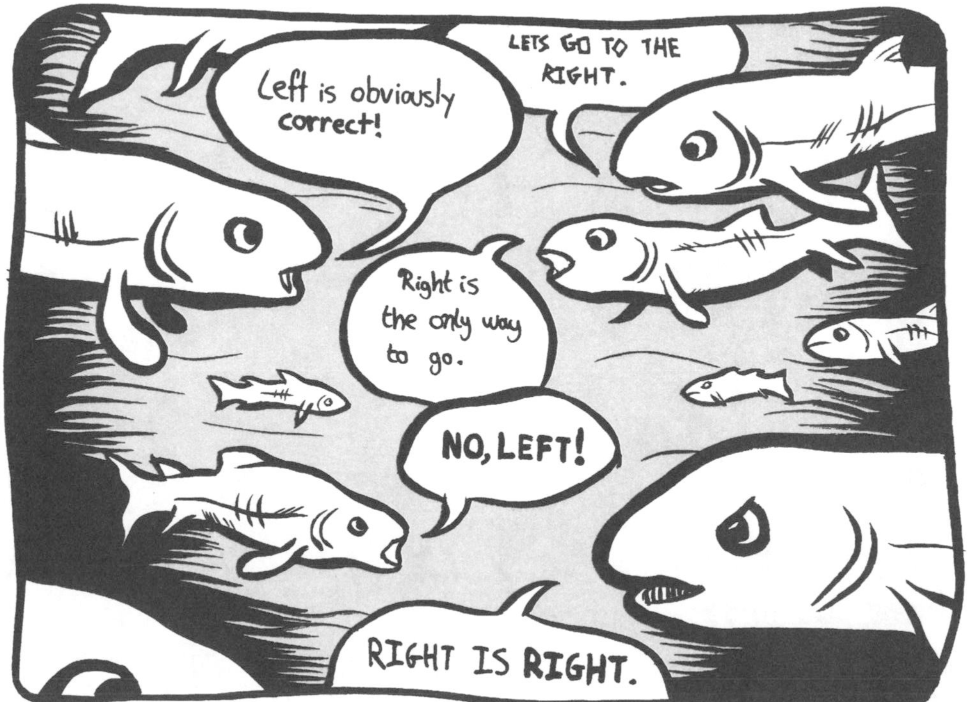
Left is obviously correct!
LETS GO TO THE RIGHT.
Right is the only way to go.
NO, LEFT!
RIGHT IS RIGHT.

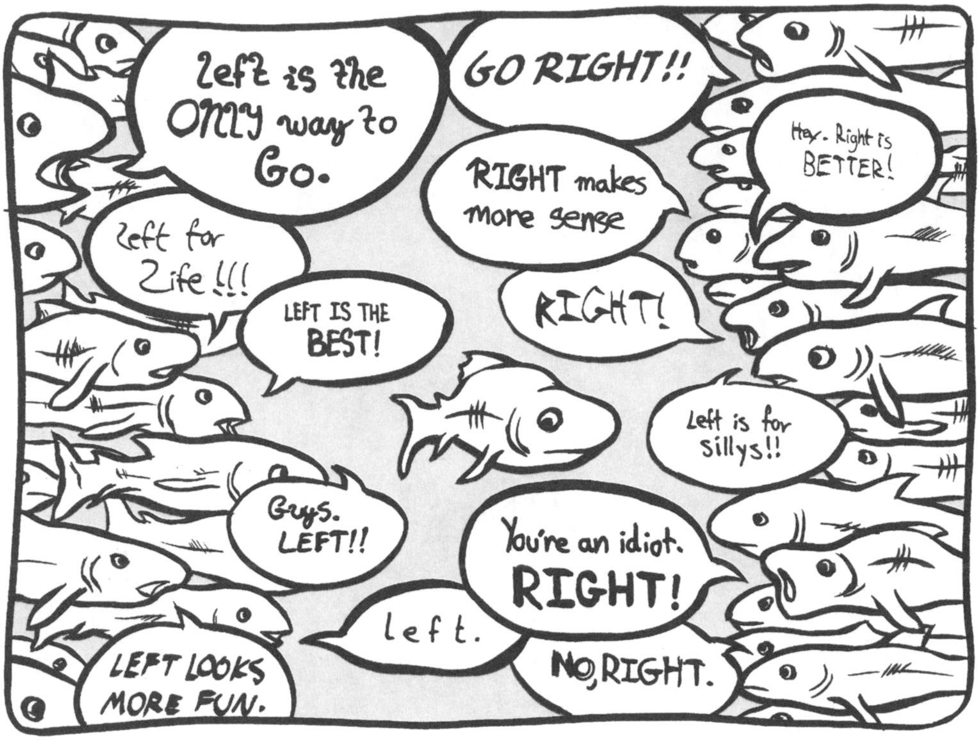
Left is the ONLY way to Go.
GO RIGHT!!
Hey. Right is BETTER!
RIGHT makes more sense
Left for Life!!!
LEFT IS THE BEST!
RIGHT!
Left is for sillys!!
Guys. LEFT!!
You're an idiot. RIGHT!
left.
LEFT LOOKS MORE FUN.
NO, RIGHT.

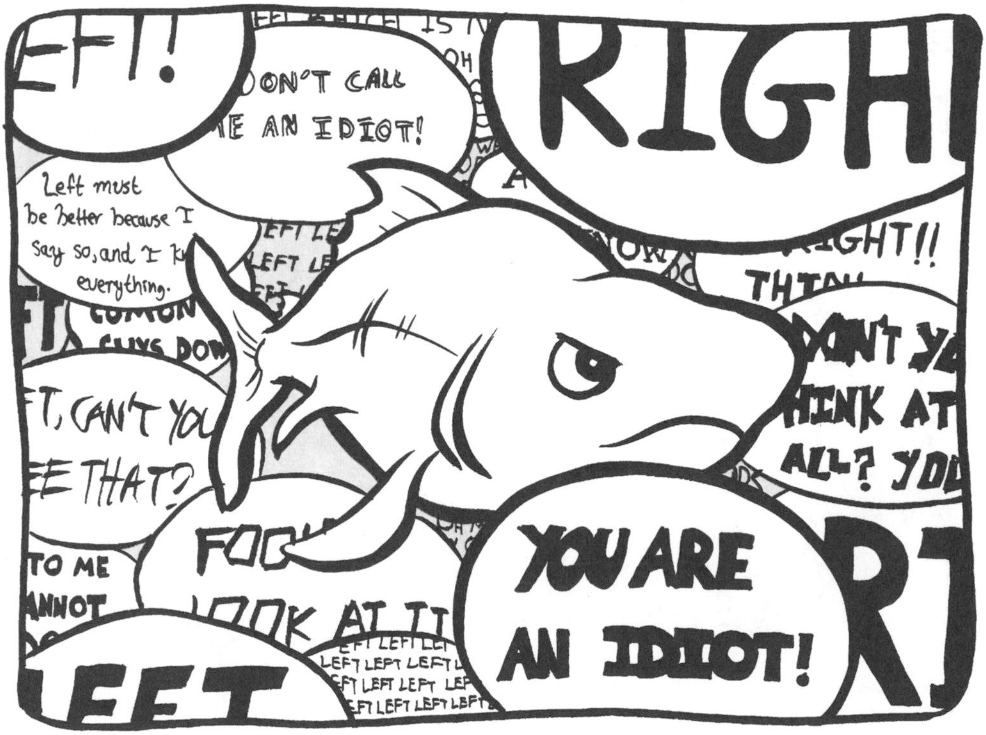
Left must be better because I say so, and I
everything.
YOU ARE AN IDIIOT!

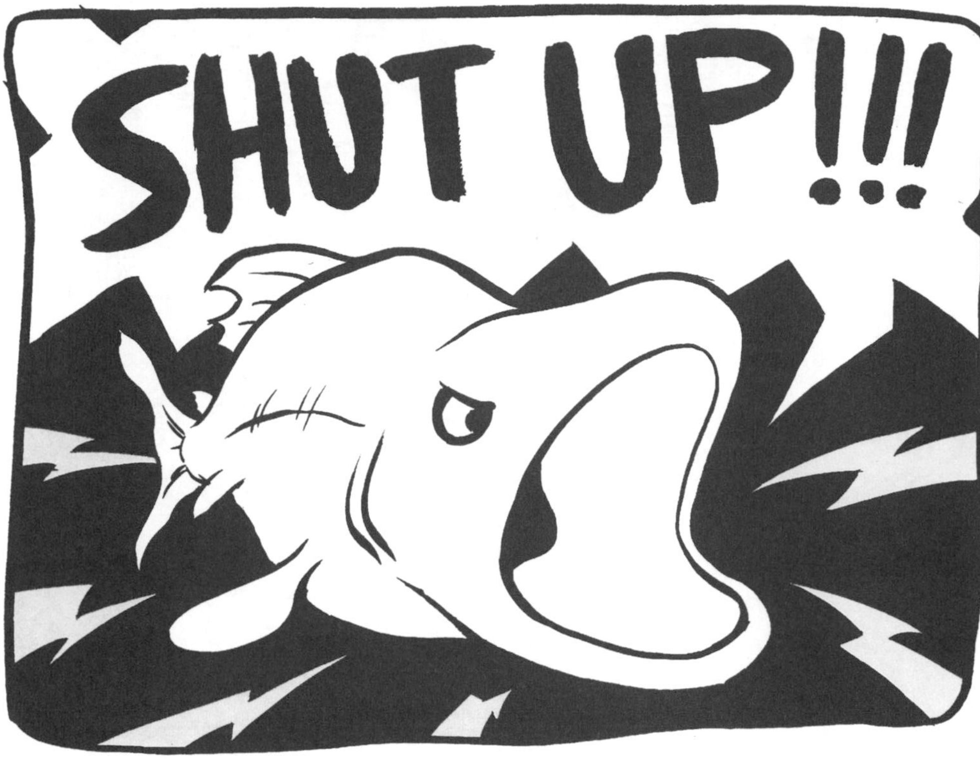
SHUT UP!!!

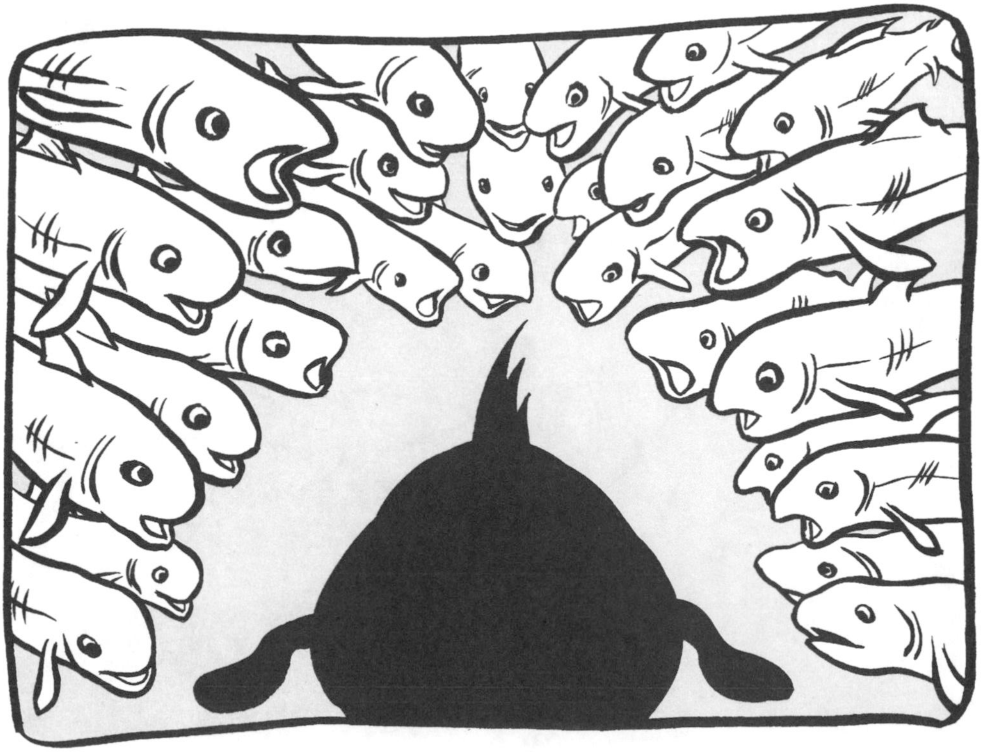

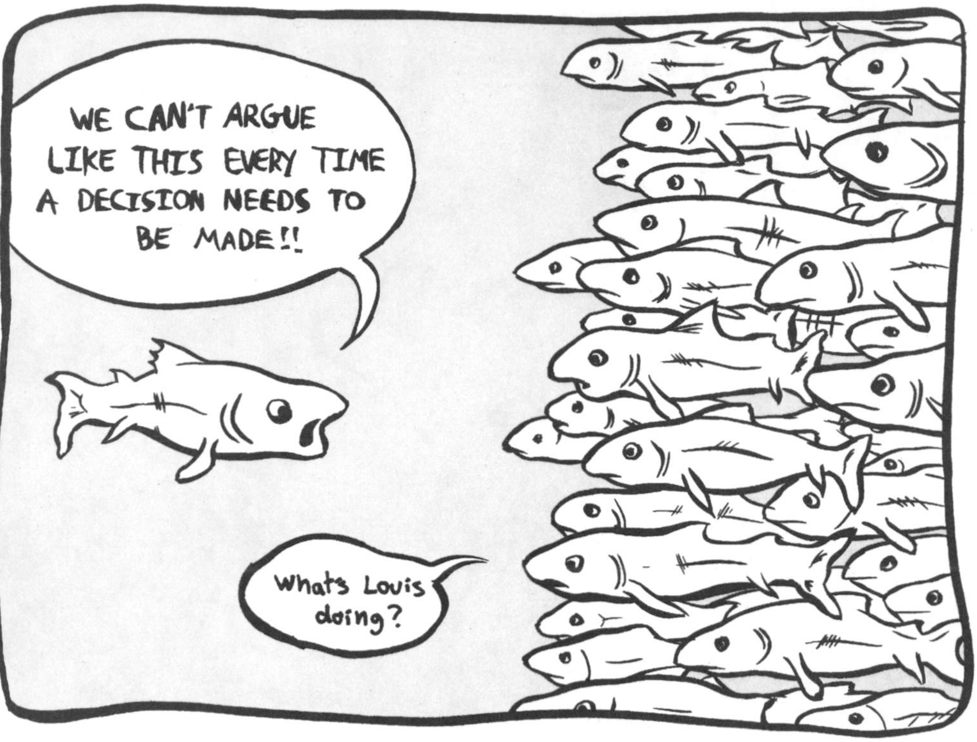
WE CAN'T ARGUE LIKE THIS EVERY TIME A DECISION NEEDS TO BE MADE!!
Whats Louis doing?

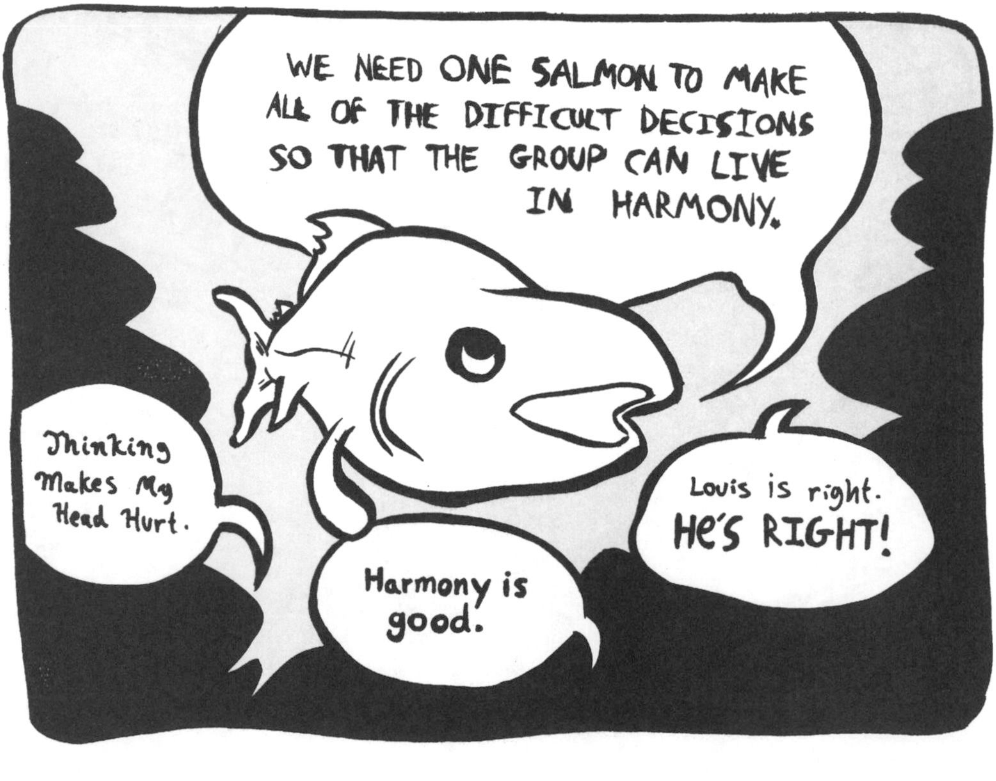
WE NEED ONE SALMON TO MAKE ALL OF THE DIFFICULT DECISIONS SO THAT THE GROUP CAN LIVE IN HARMONY.
Thinking Makes My Head Hurt.
Harmony is good.
Louis is right. HE'S RIGHT!

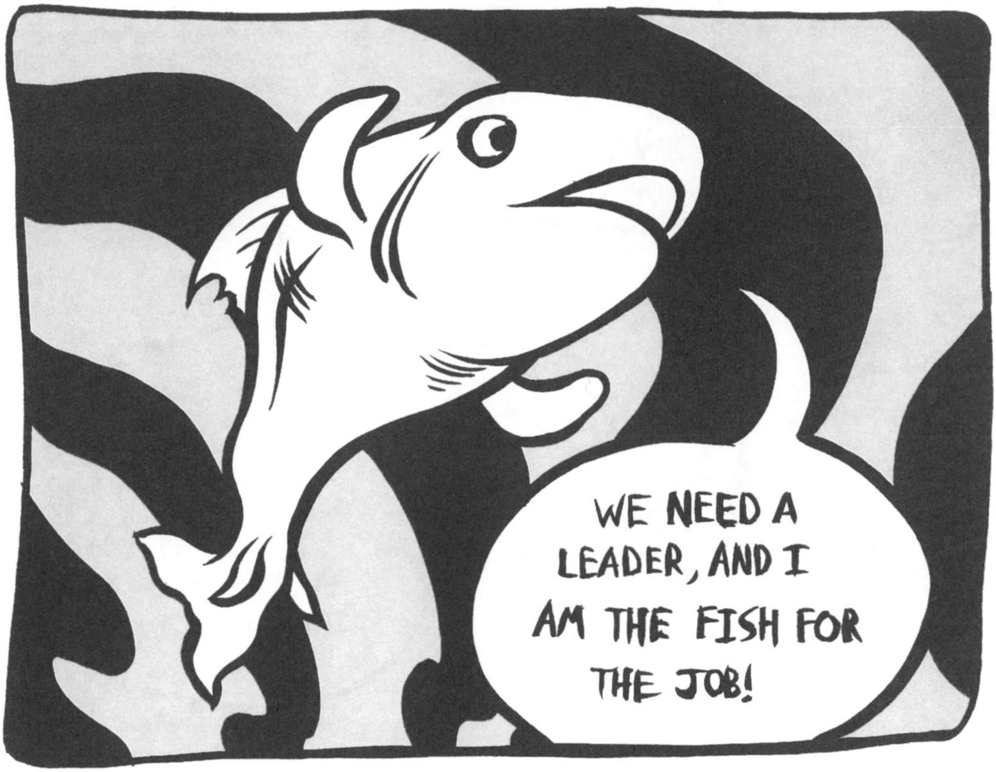
WE NEED A LEADER, AND I AM THE FISH FOR THE JOB!

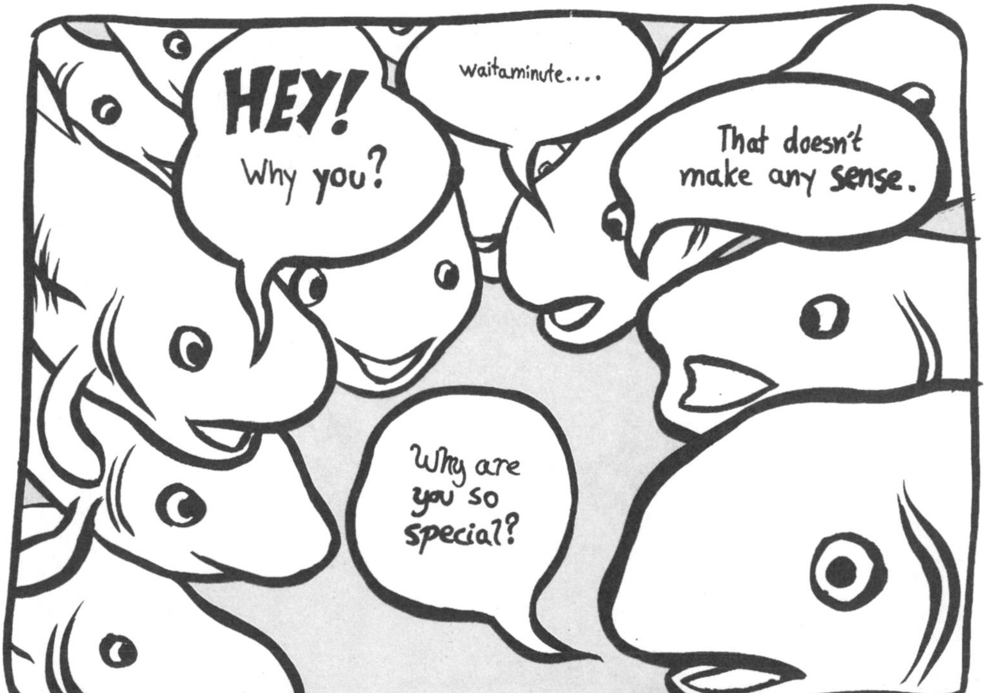
HEY! Why you?
waitaminute....
That doesn't make any sense.
Why are you so special??

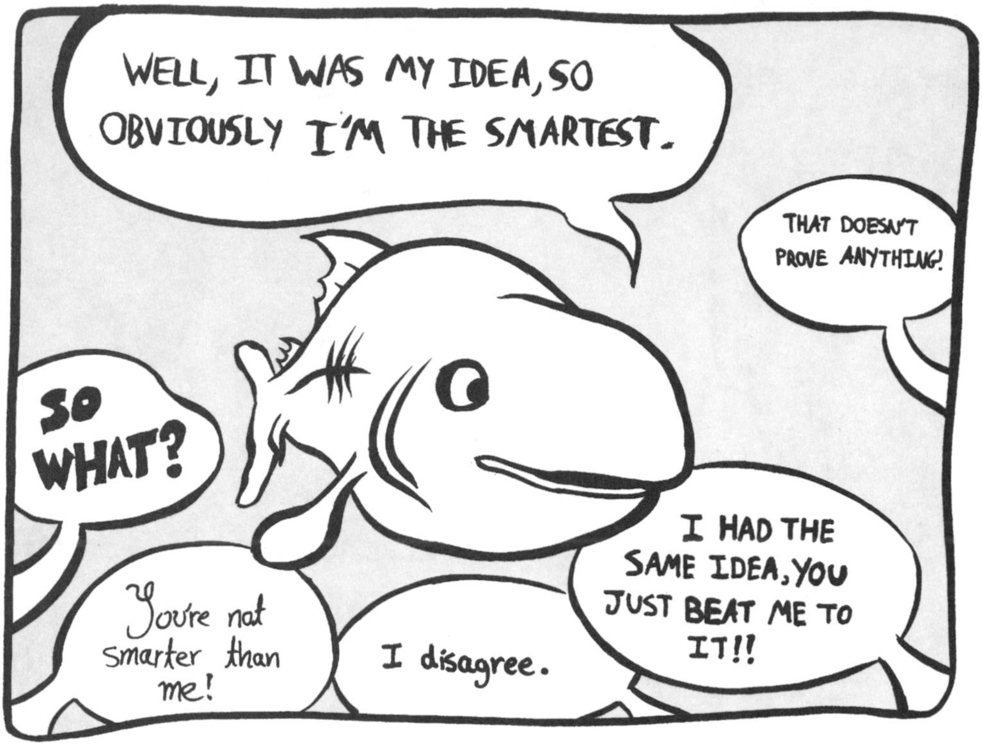
WELL, IT WAS MY IDEA, SO OBVIOUSLY I'M THE SMARTEST.
THAT DOESN'T PROVE ANYTHING!
SO WHAT?
You're not smarter than me!
I disagree.
I HAD THE SAME IDEA, YOU JUST BEAT ME TO IT!!

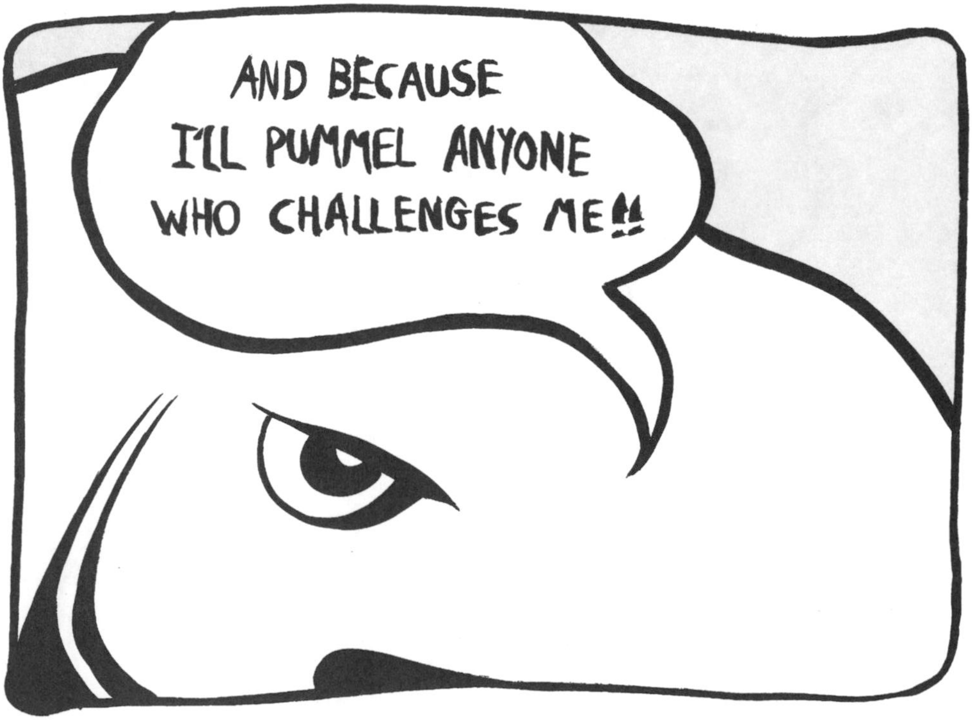
AND BECAUSE I'LL PUMMEL ANYONE WHO CHALLENGES ME!!

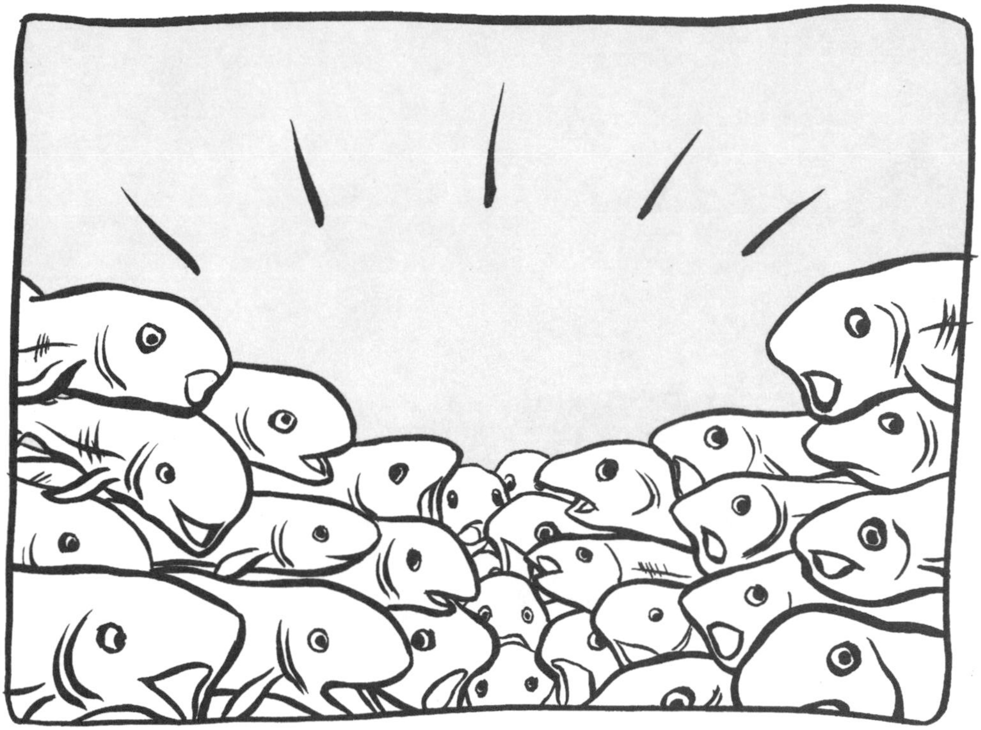

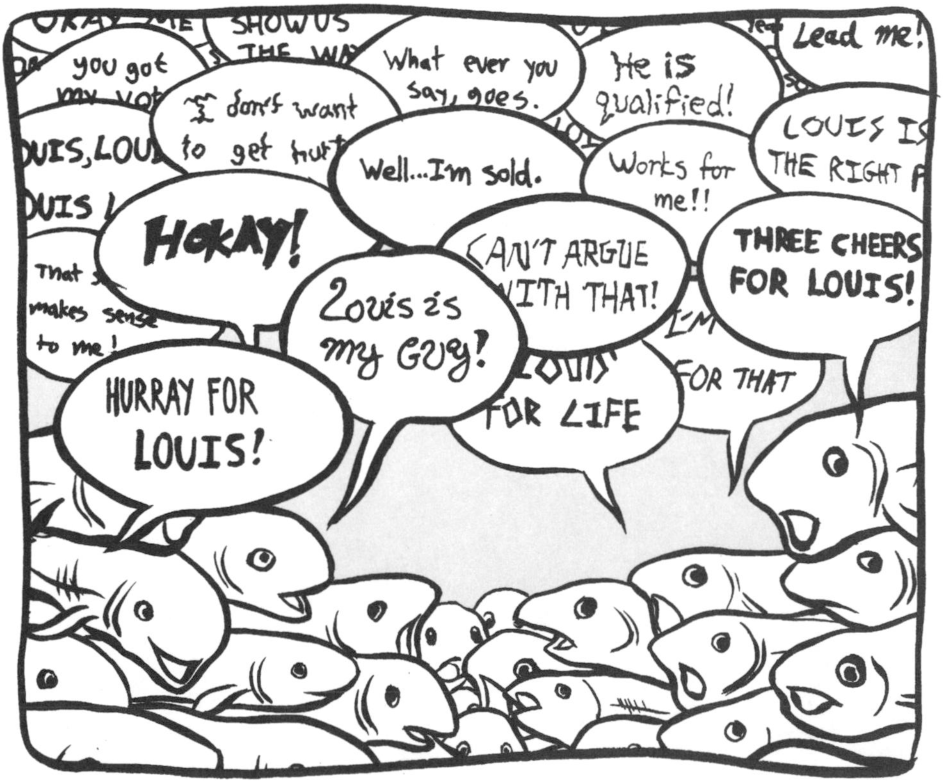
What ever you say, goes.
He is qualified!
Lead me!
Well...I'm sold.
Works for me!!
HOKAY!
CAN'T ARGUE WITH THAT!
THREE CHEERS FOR LOUIS!
Louis is my GUY!
HURRAY FOR LOUIS!

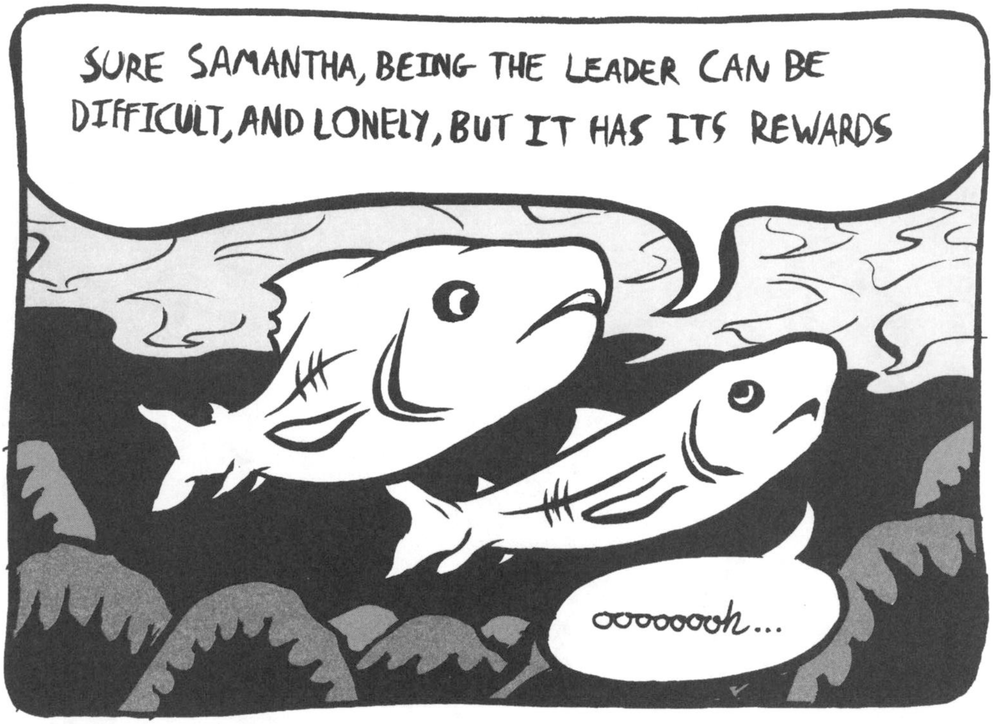
SURE SAMANTHA, BEING THE LEADER CAN BE DIFFICULT, AND LONELY, BUT IT HAS ITS REWARDS
oooooooh...

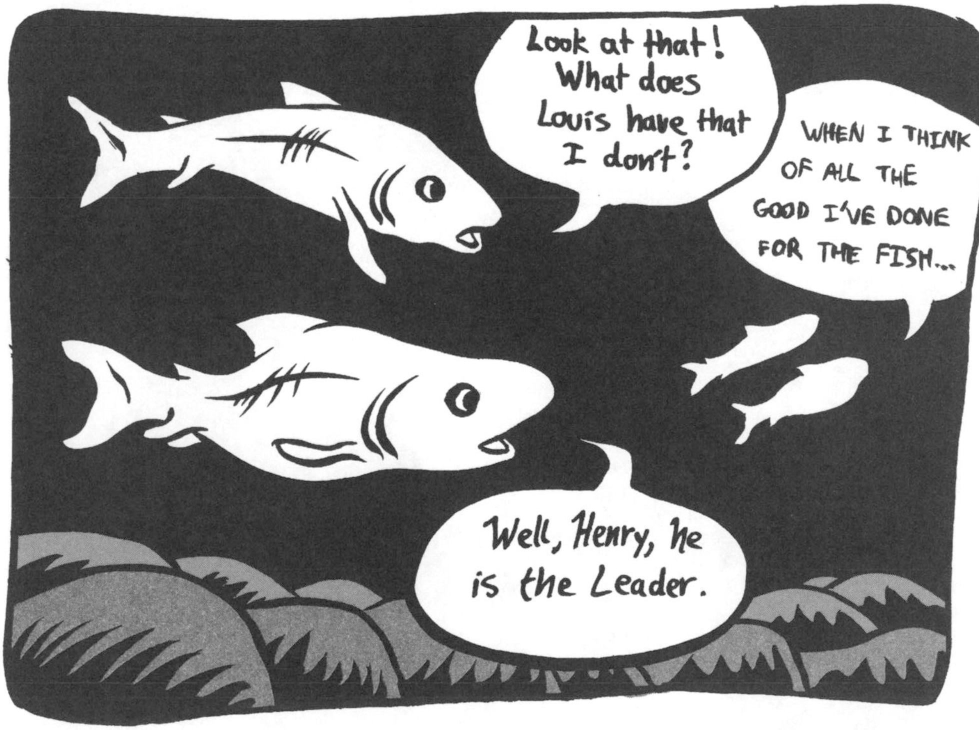
Look at that! What does Louis have that I don't?
WHEN I THINK OF ALL THE GOOD I'VE DONE FOR THE FISH...
Well, Henry, he is the Leader.

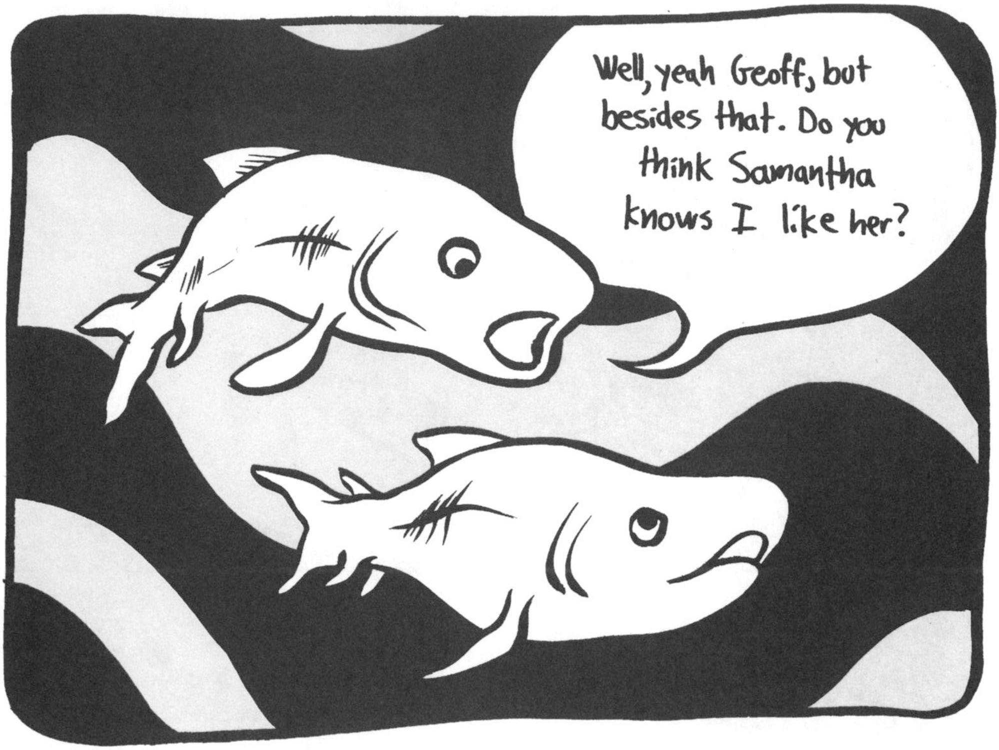
Well, yeah Geoff, but besides that. Do you think Samantha knows I like her?

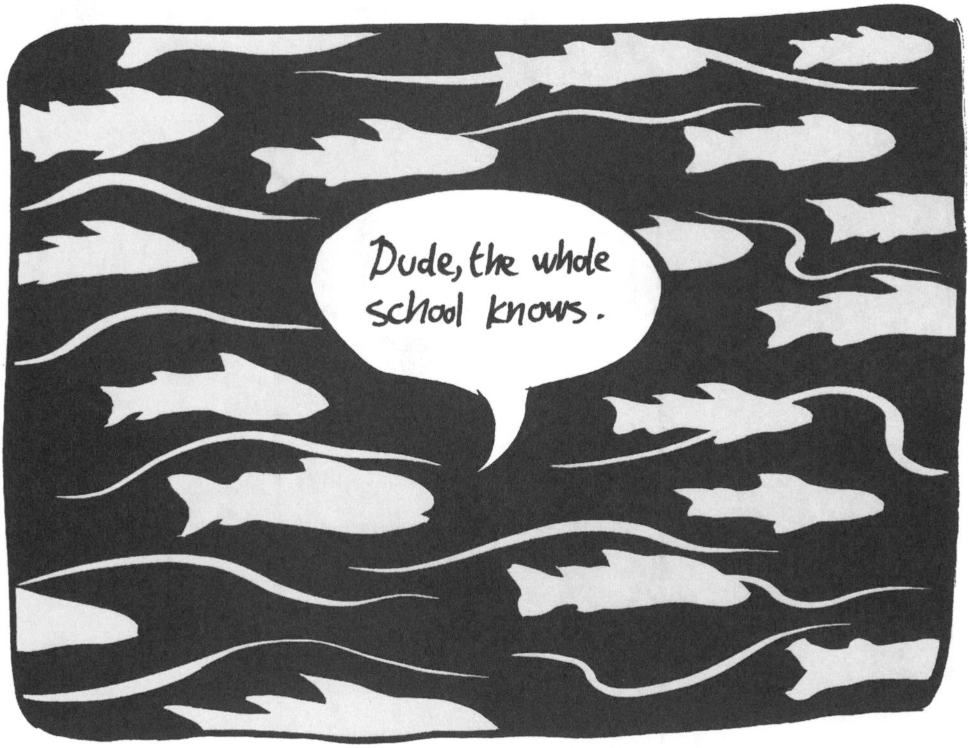
Dude, the whole school knows.

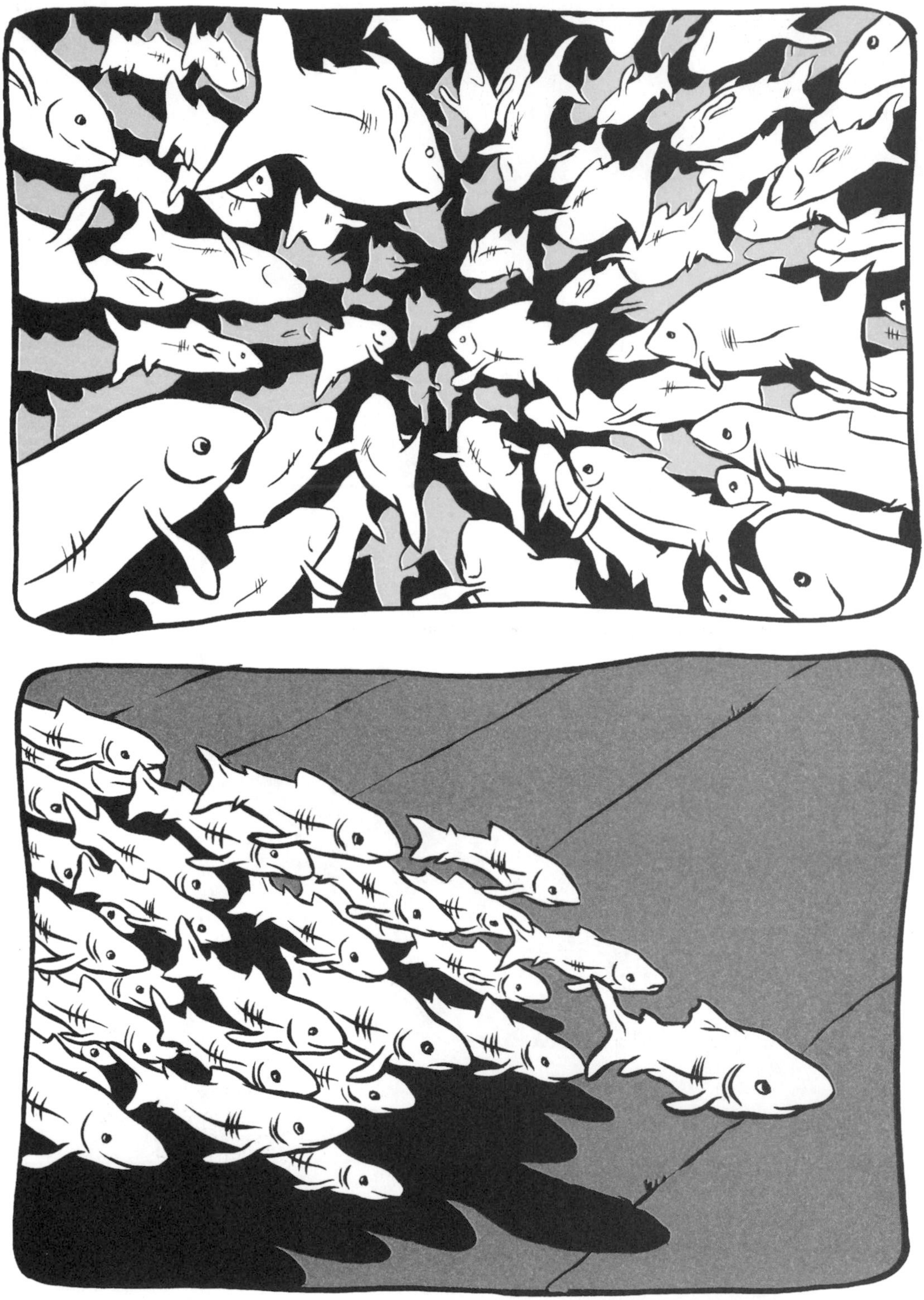

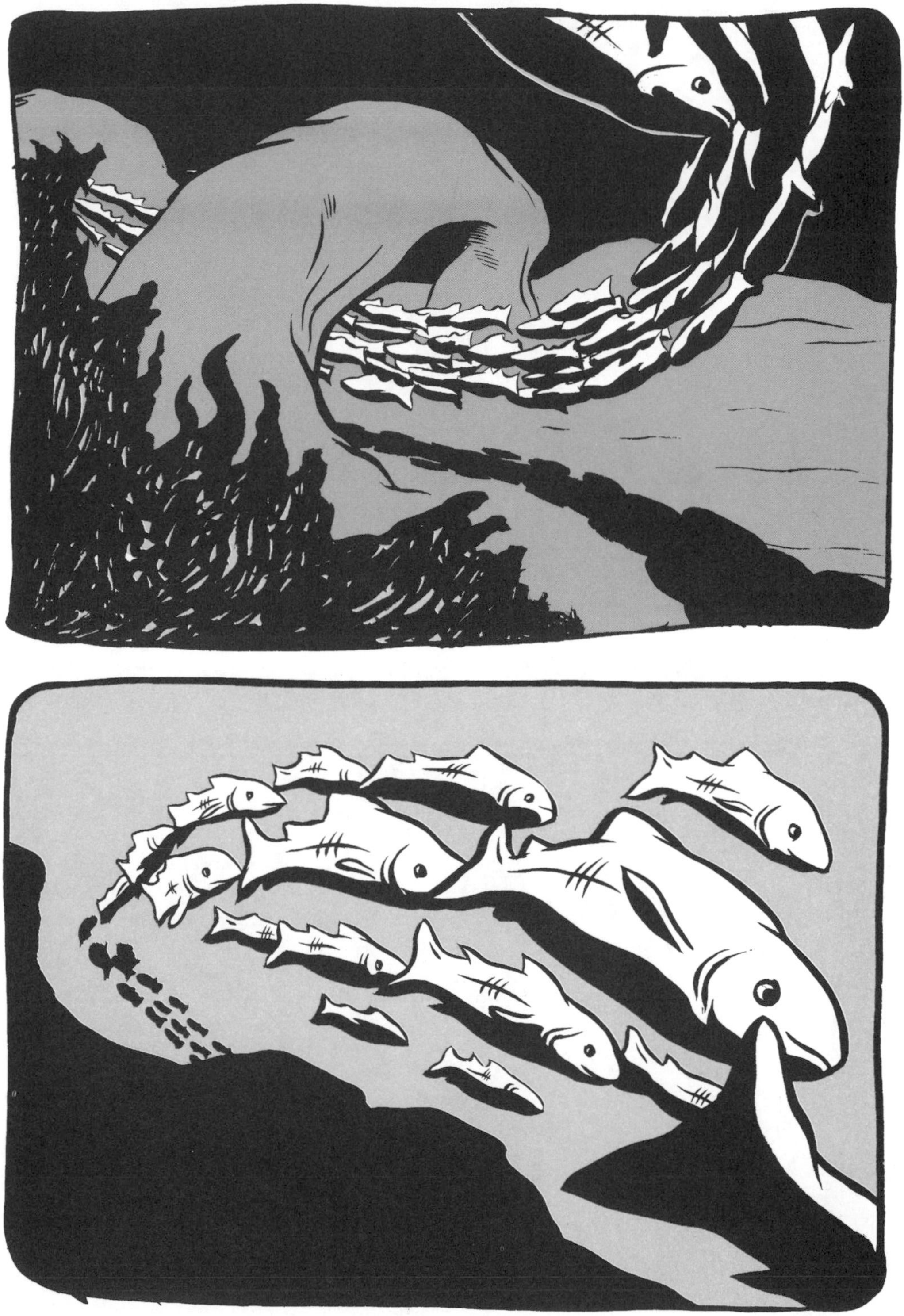

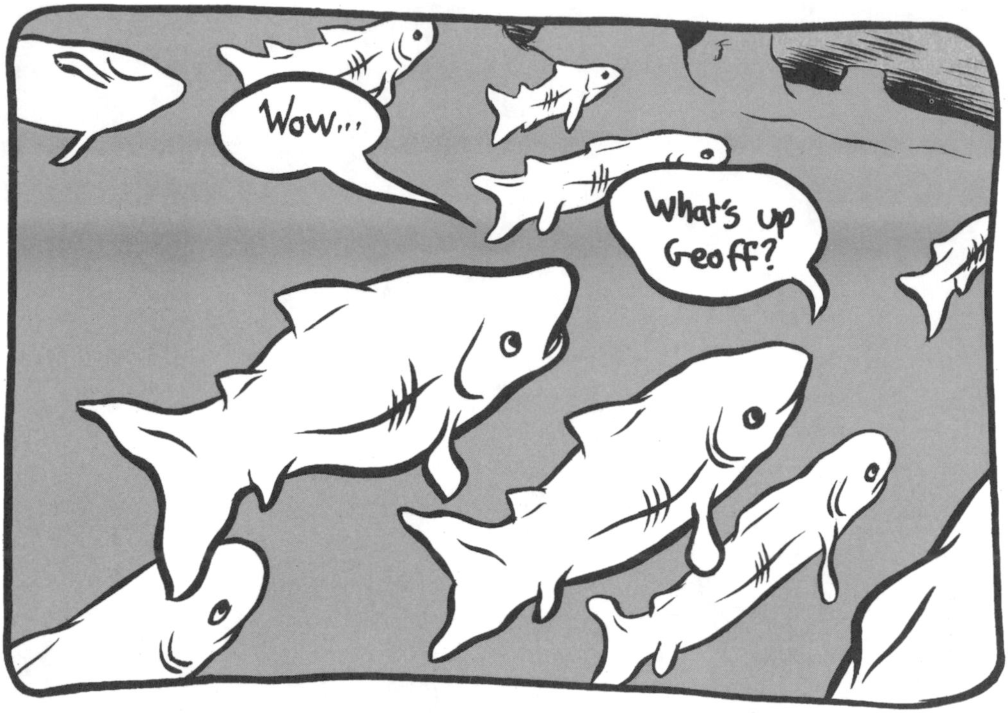
Wow...
What's up Geoff?

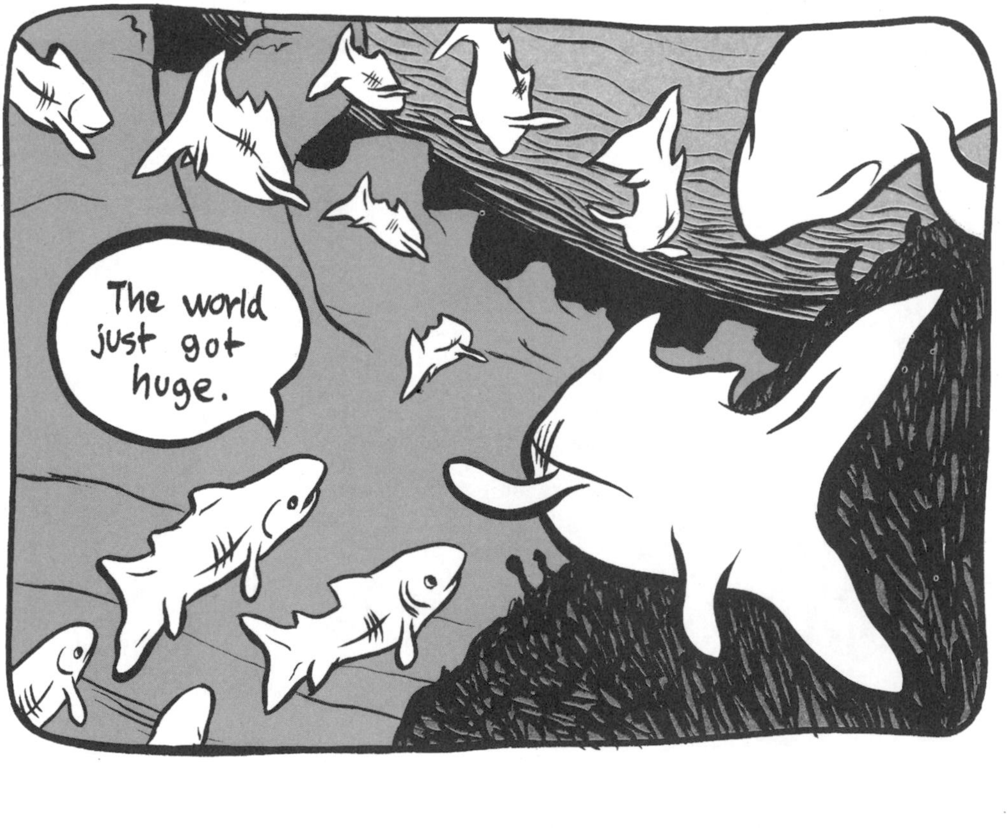
The world just got huge.

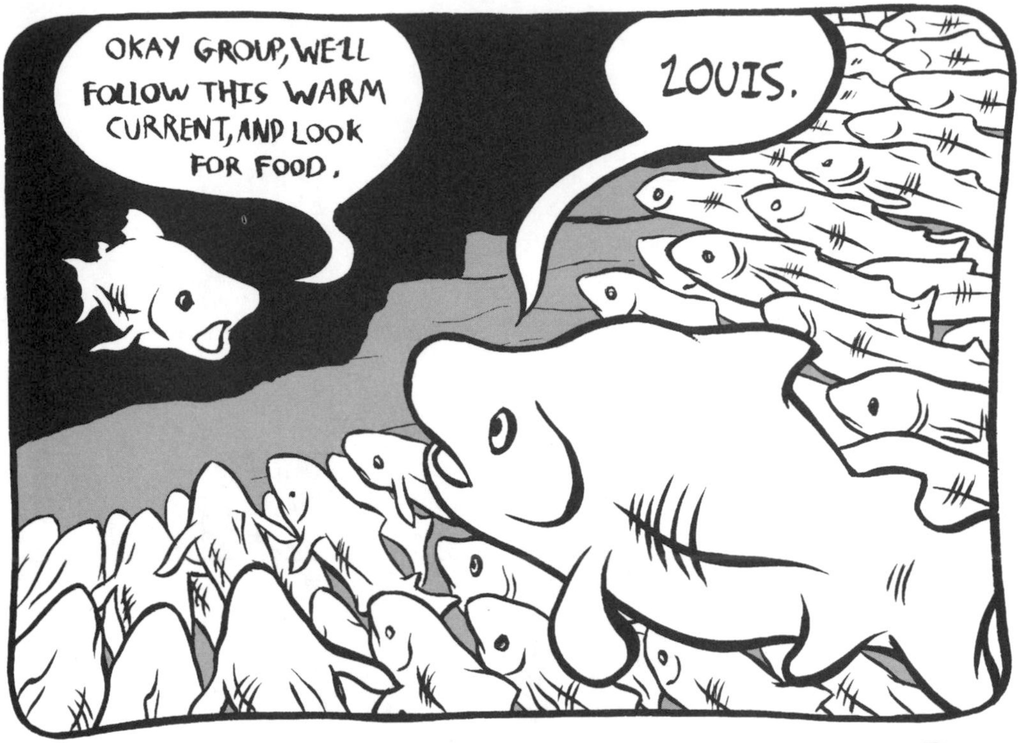
OKAY GROUP, WE'LL FOLLOW THIS WARM CURRENT, AND LOOK FOR FOOD.
LOUIS.
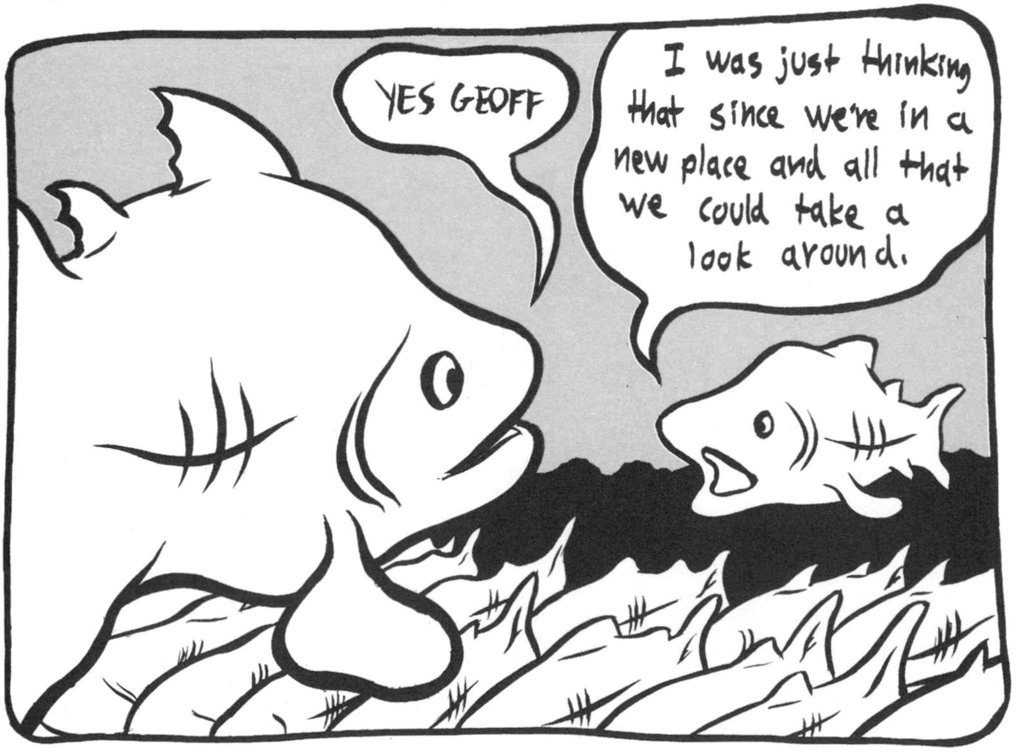
YES GEOFF
I was just thinking that since we're in a new place and all that we could take a look around.

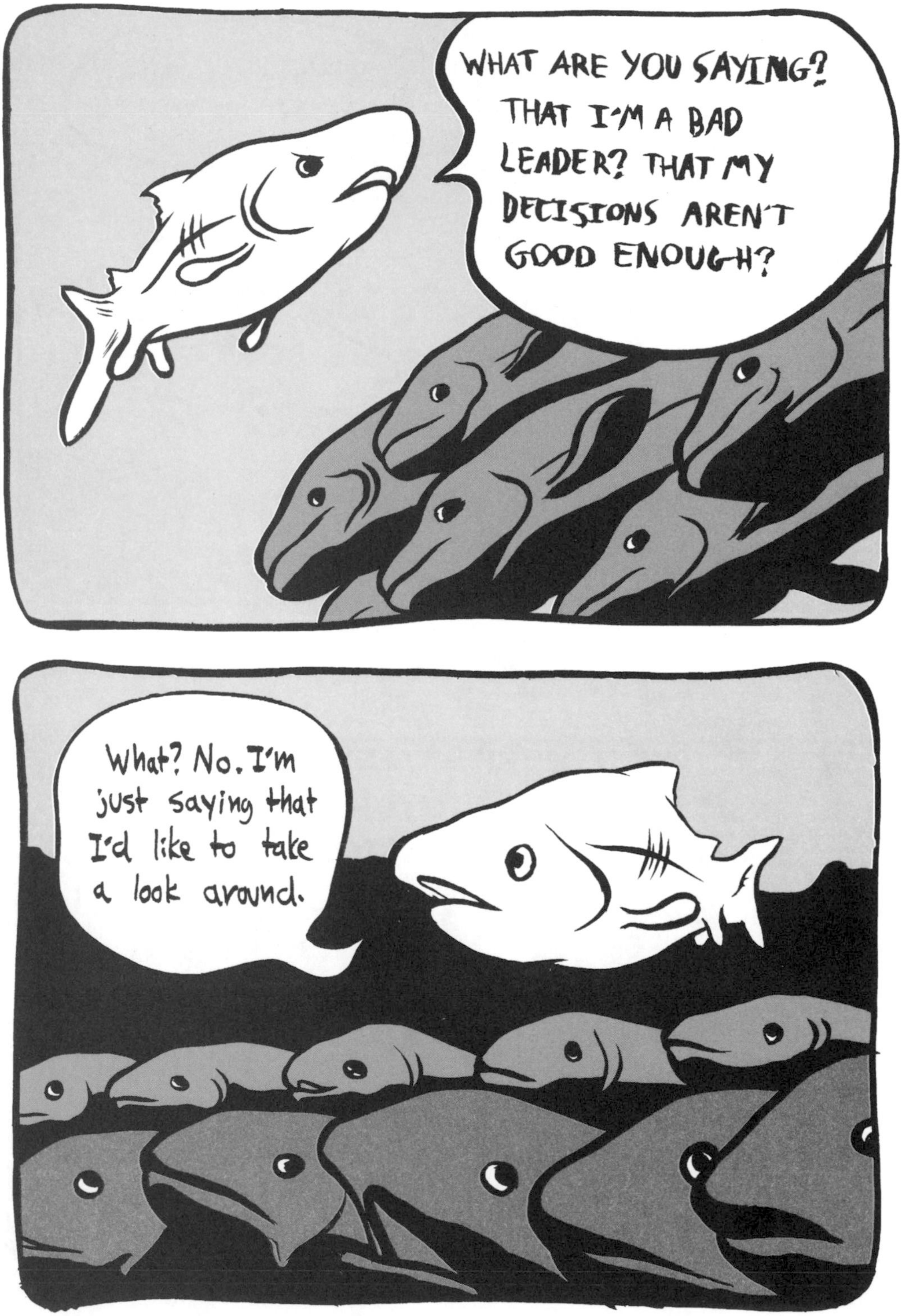
WHAT ARE YOU SAYING? THAT I'M A BAD LEADER? THAT MY DECISIONS AREN'T GOOD ENOUGH?
What? No. I'm just saying that I'd like to take a look around.

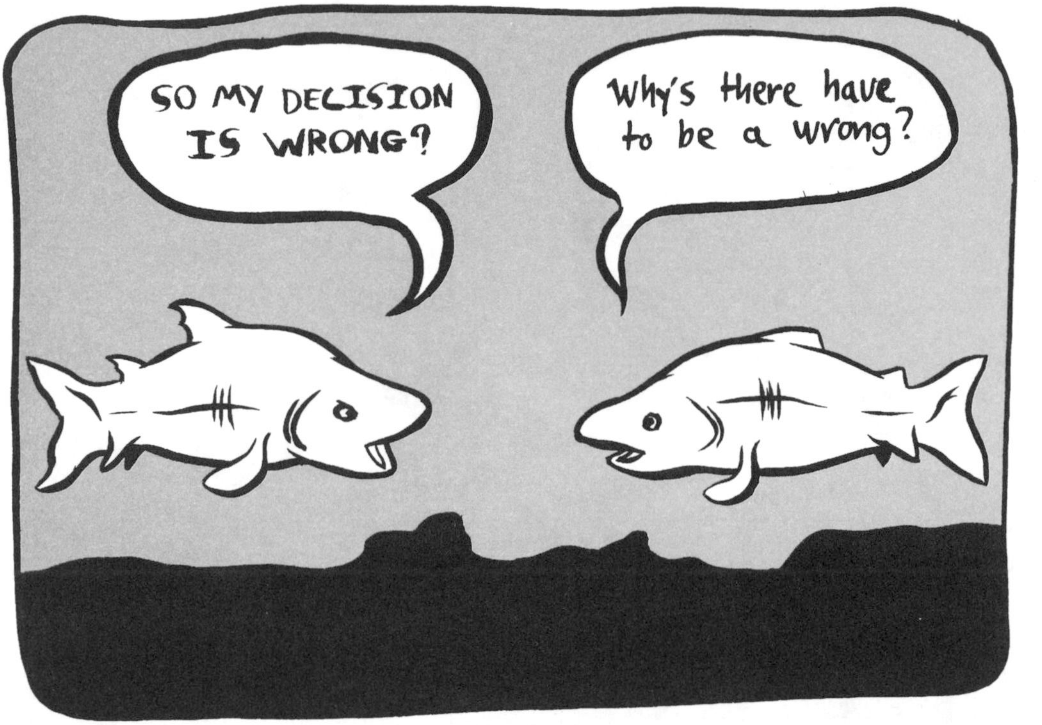
SO MY DECISION IS WRONG?
Why's there have to be a wrong?

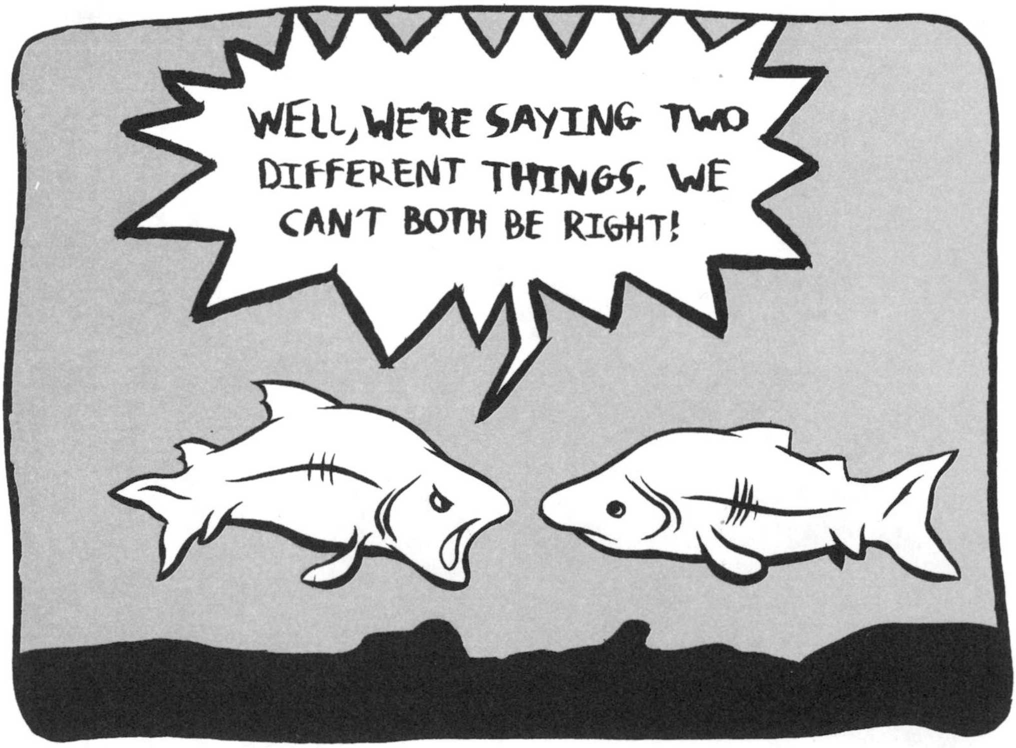
WELL, WE'RE SAYING TWO DIFFERENT THINGS. WE CAN'T BOTH BE RIGHT!

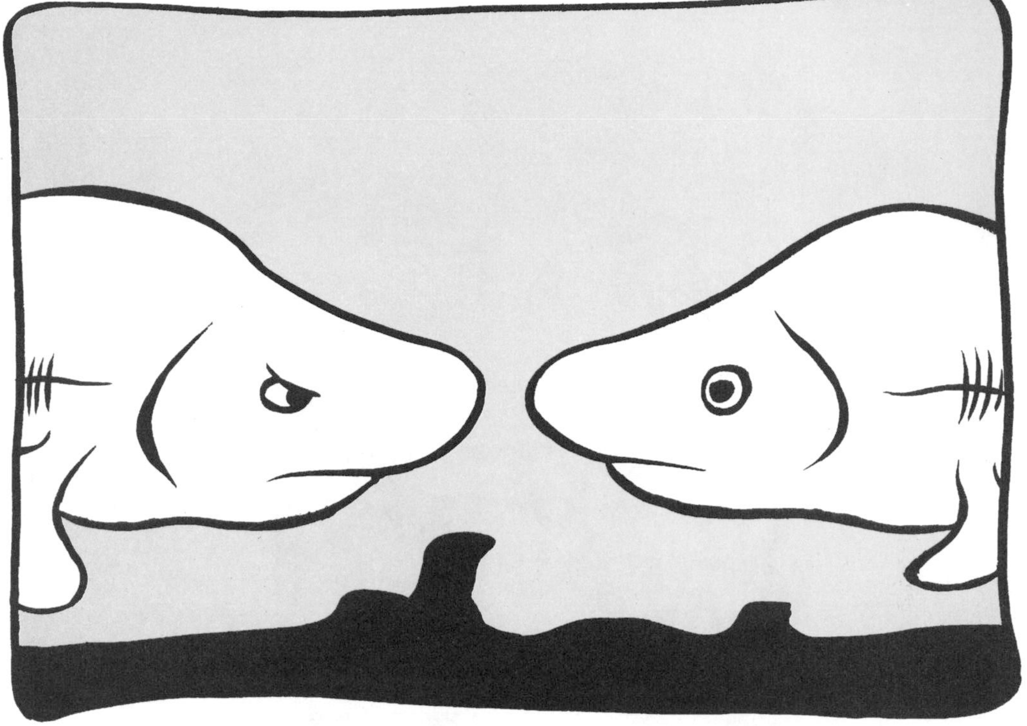

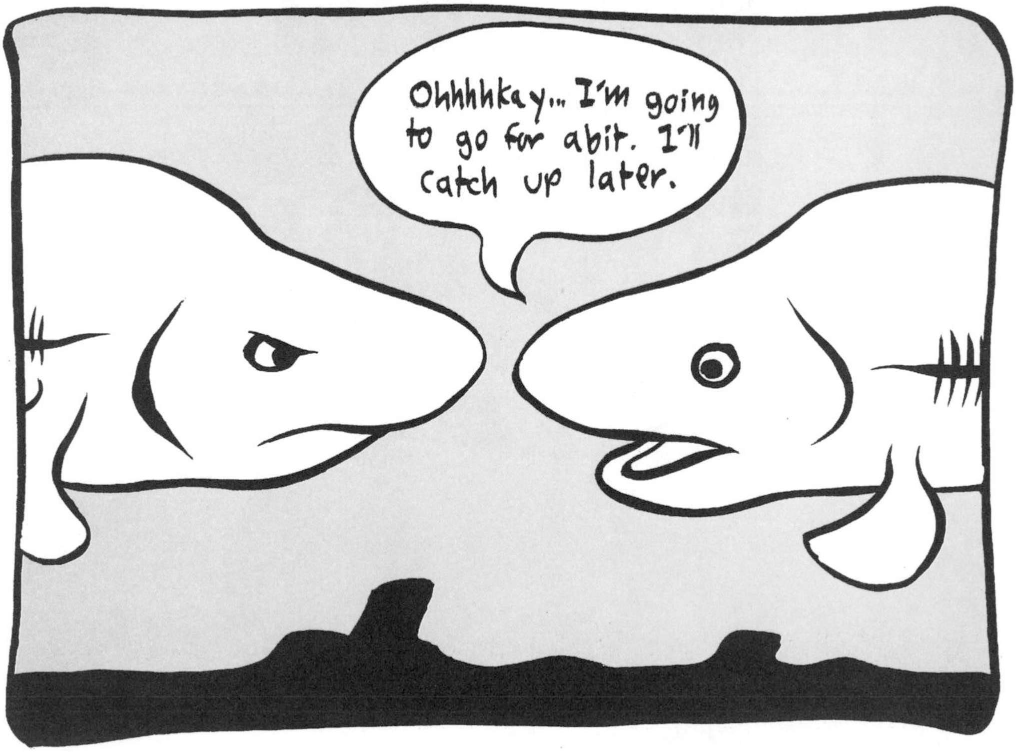
Ohhhhkay... I'm going to go for abit. I'll catch up later.

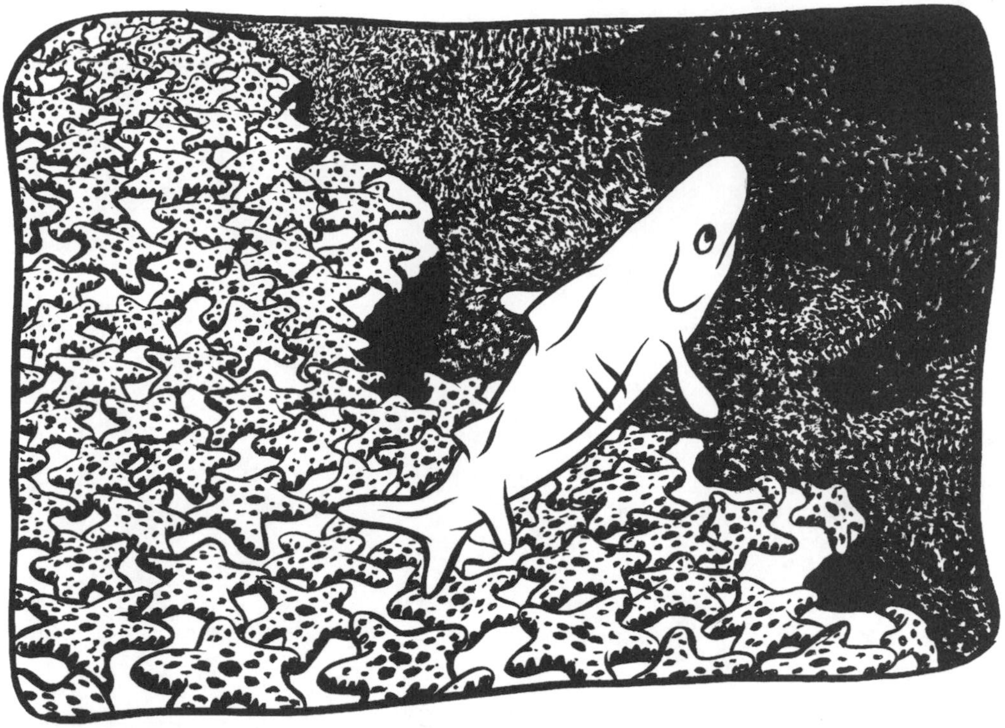

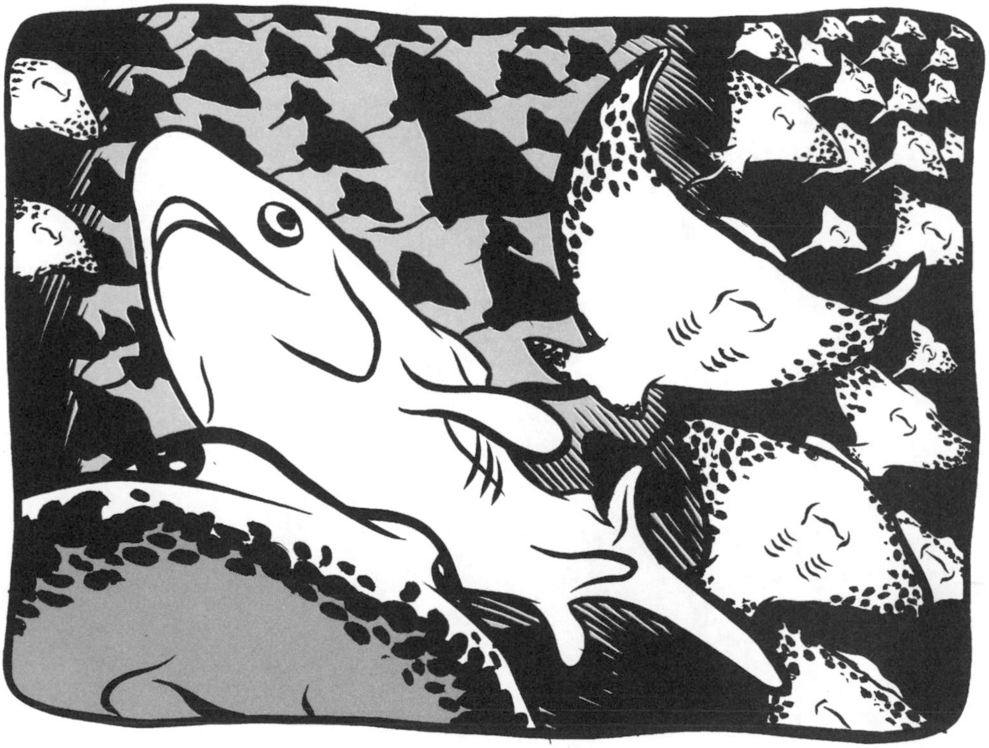

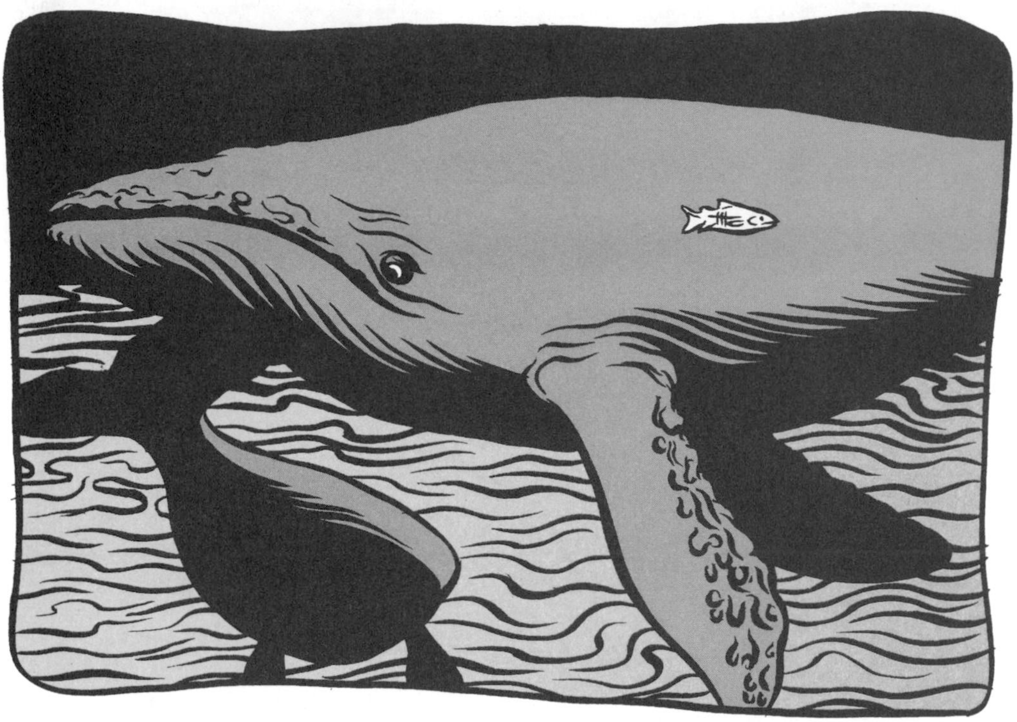

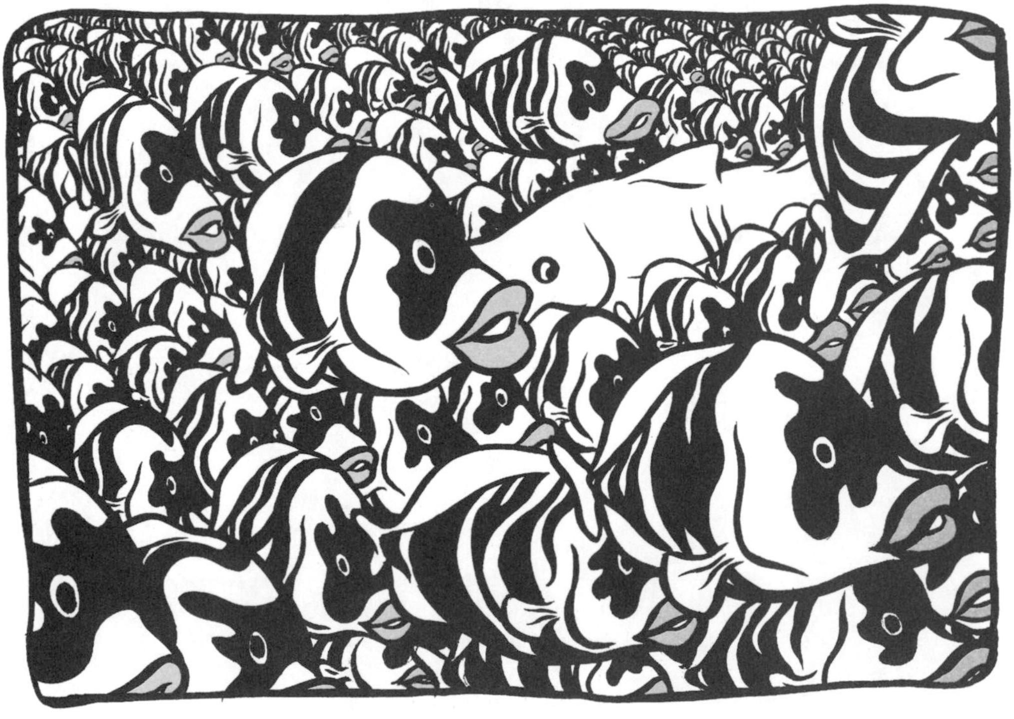

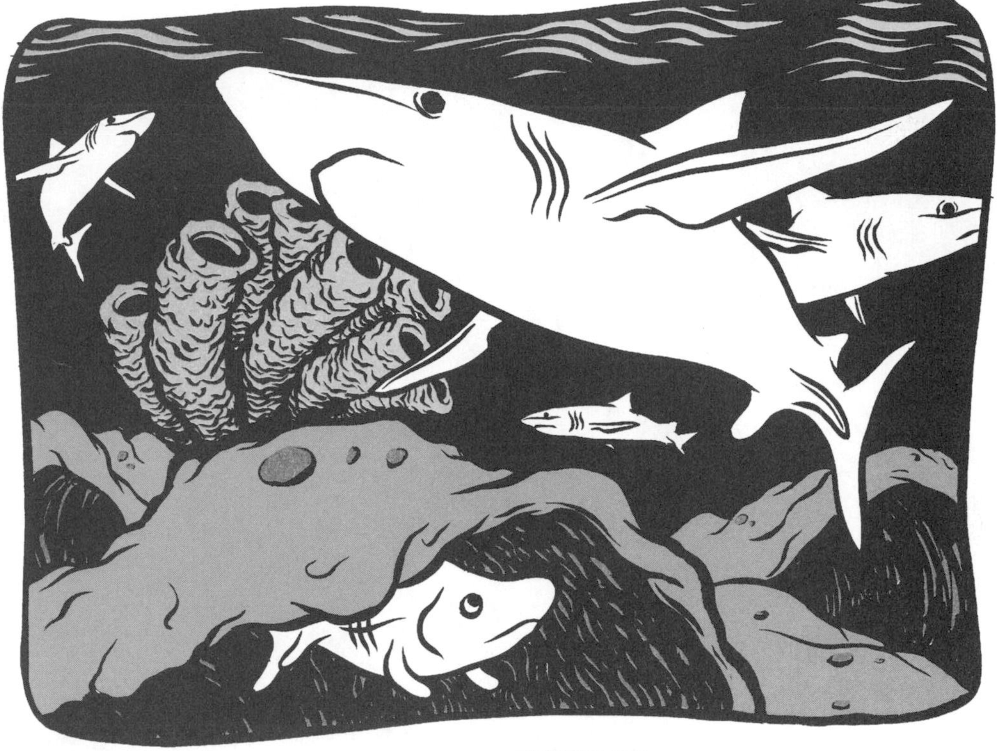

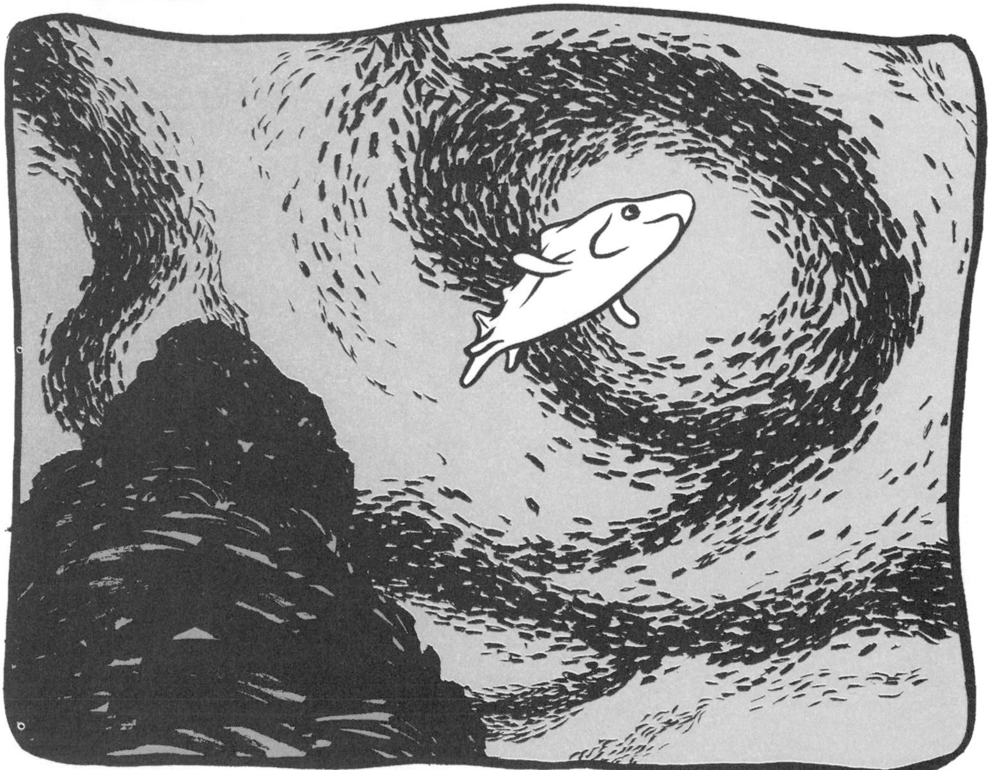

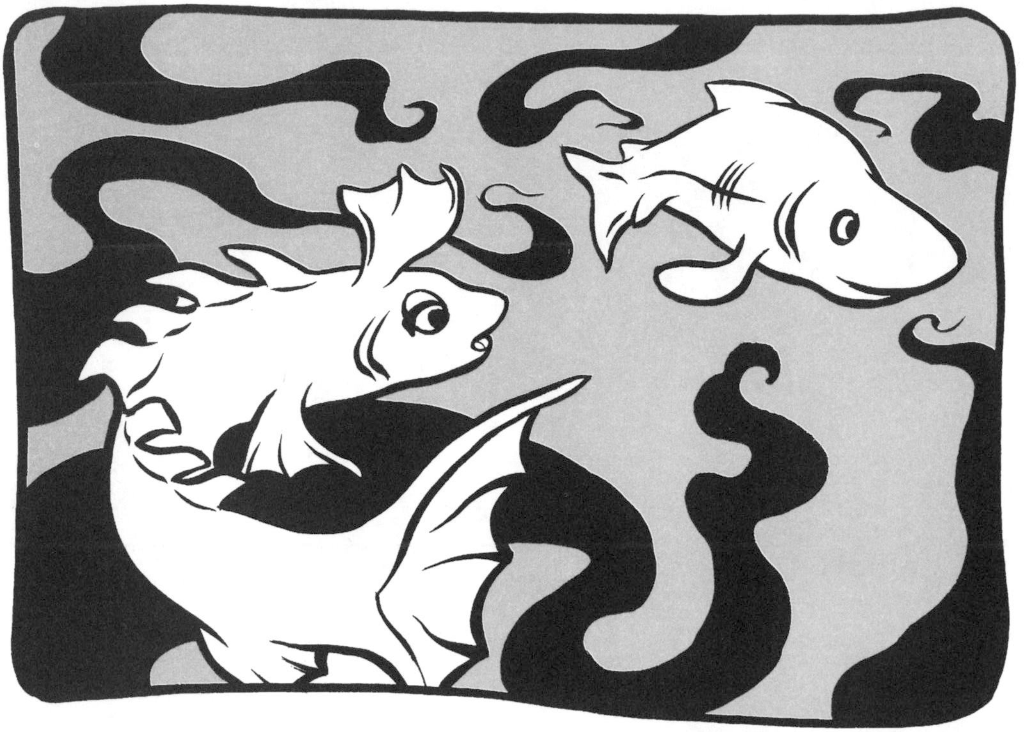

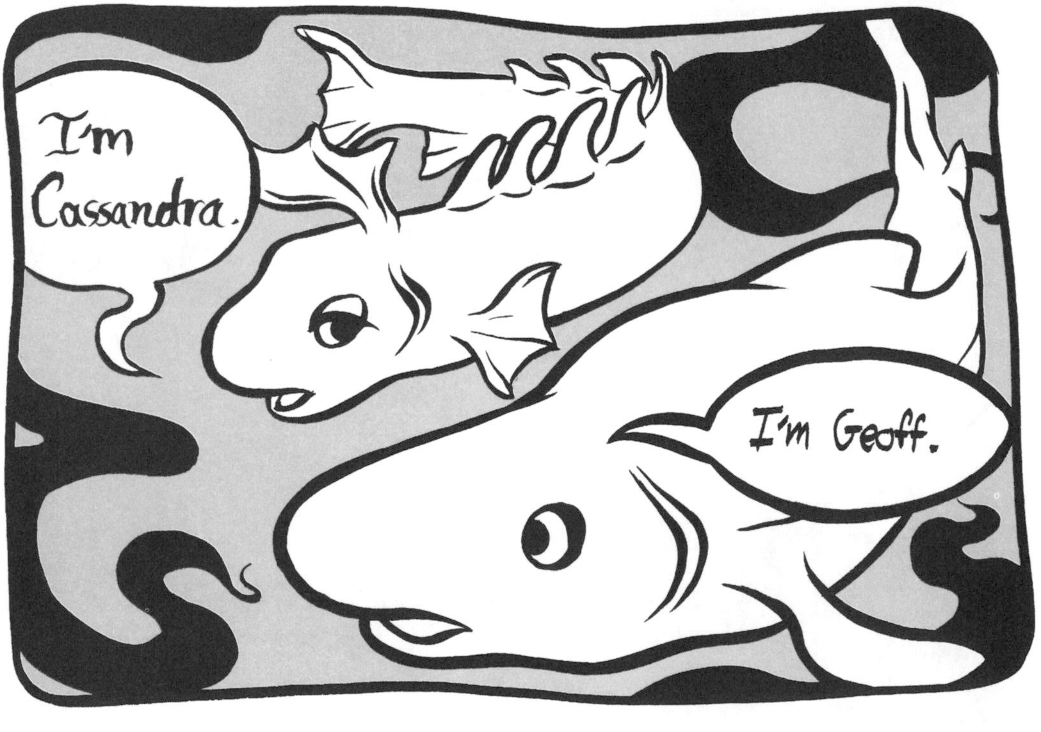
I'm Cassandra.
I'm Geoff.

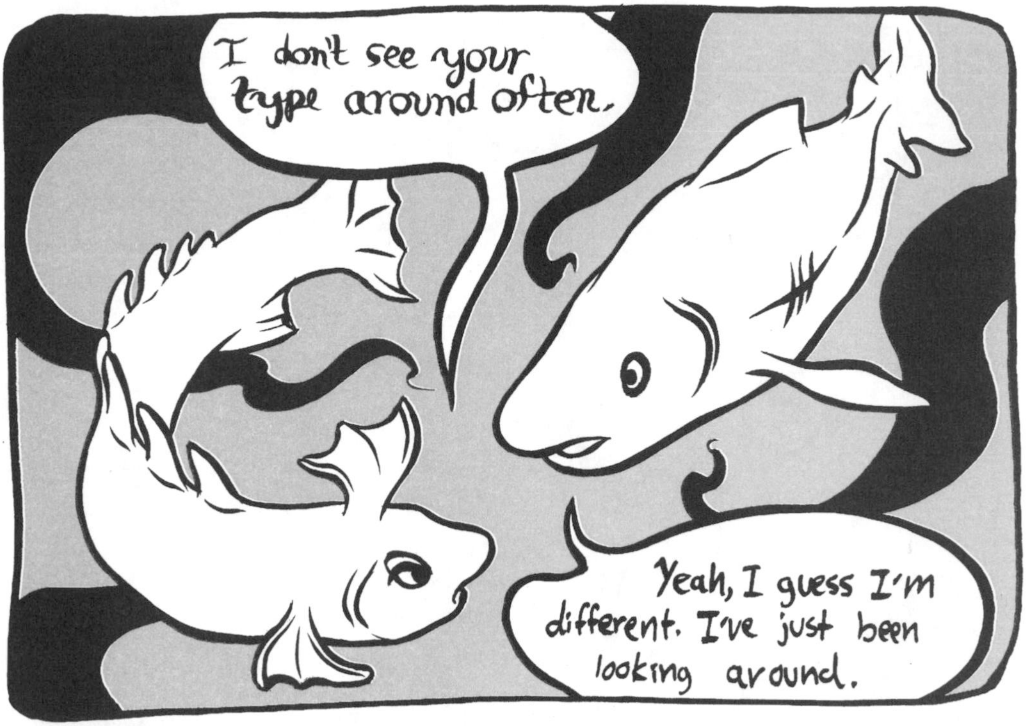
I don't see your type around often.
Yeah, I guess I'm different. I've just been looking around.

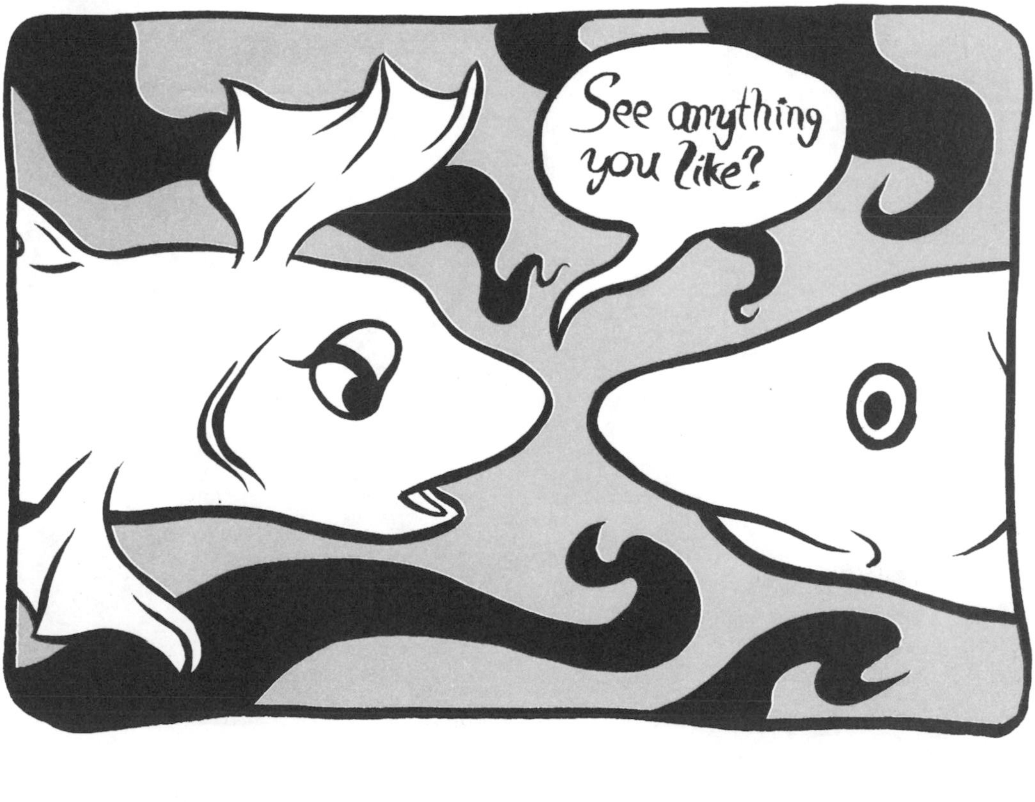
See anything you like?

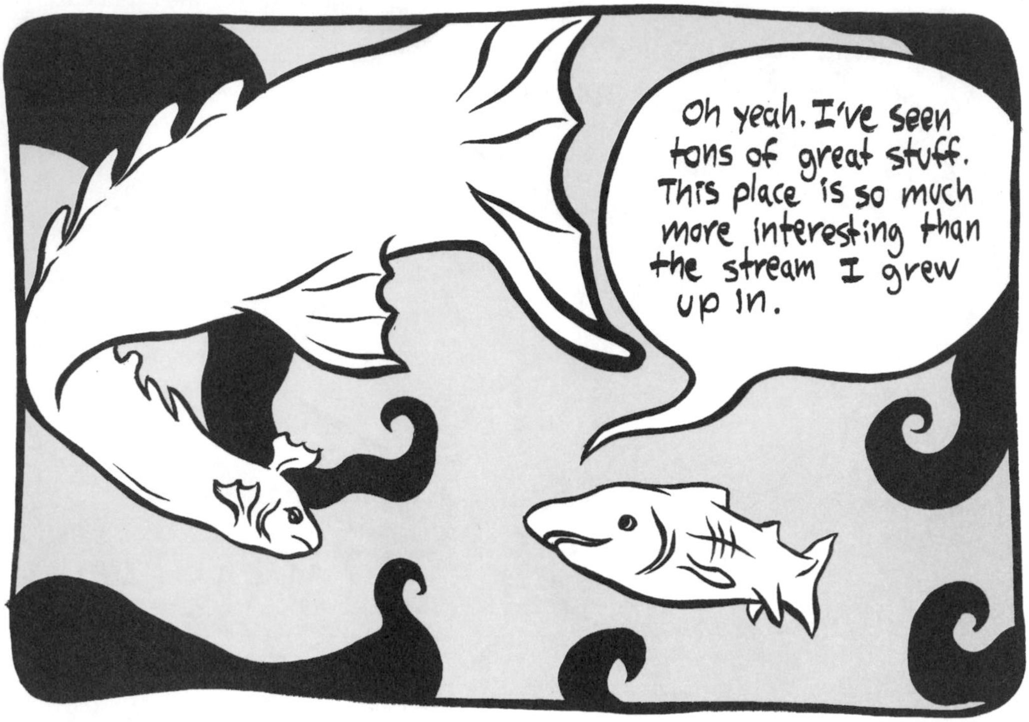
Oh yeah. I've seen tons of great stuff. This place is so much more interesting than the stream I grew up in.

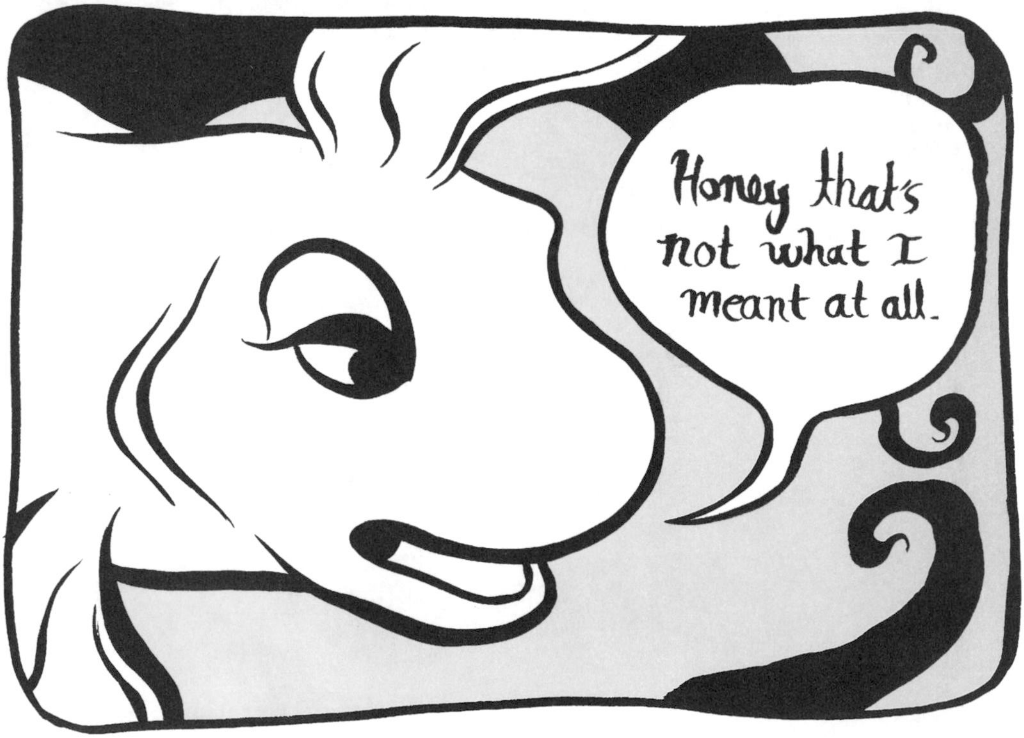
Honey that's not what I meant at all.

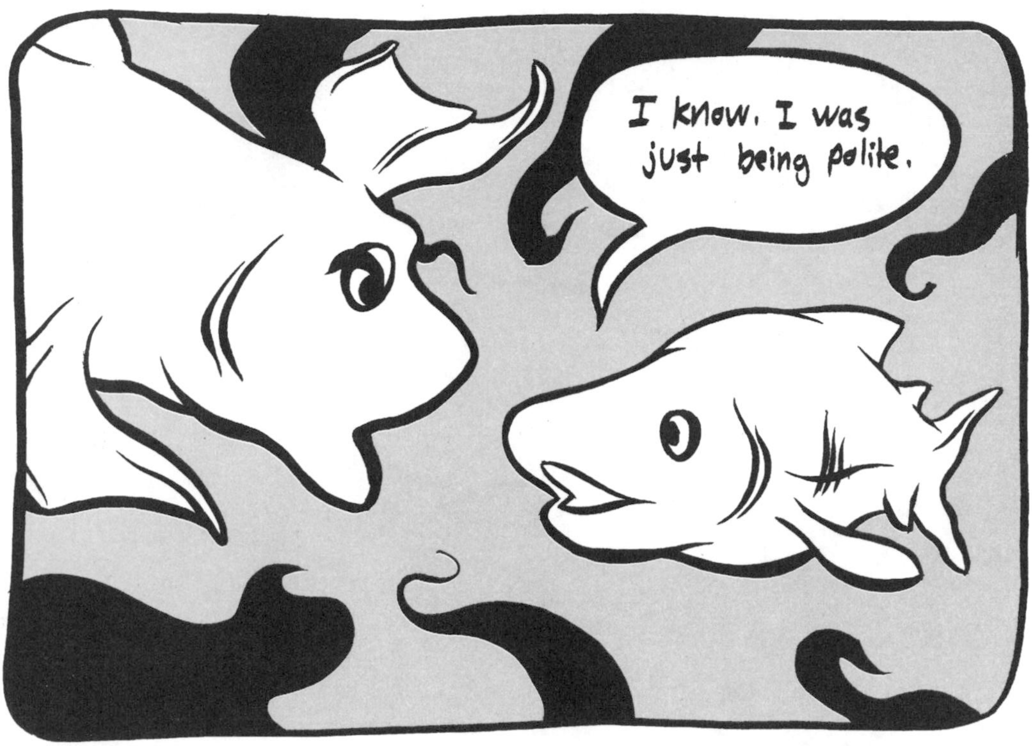
I know. I was just being polite.

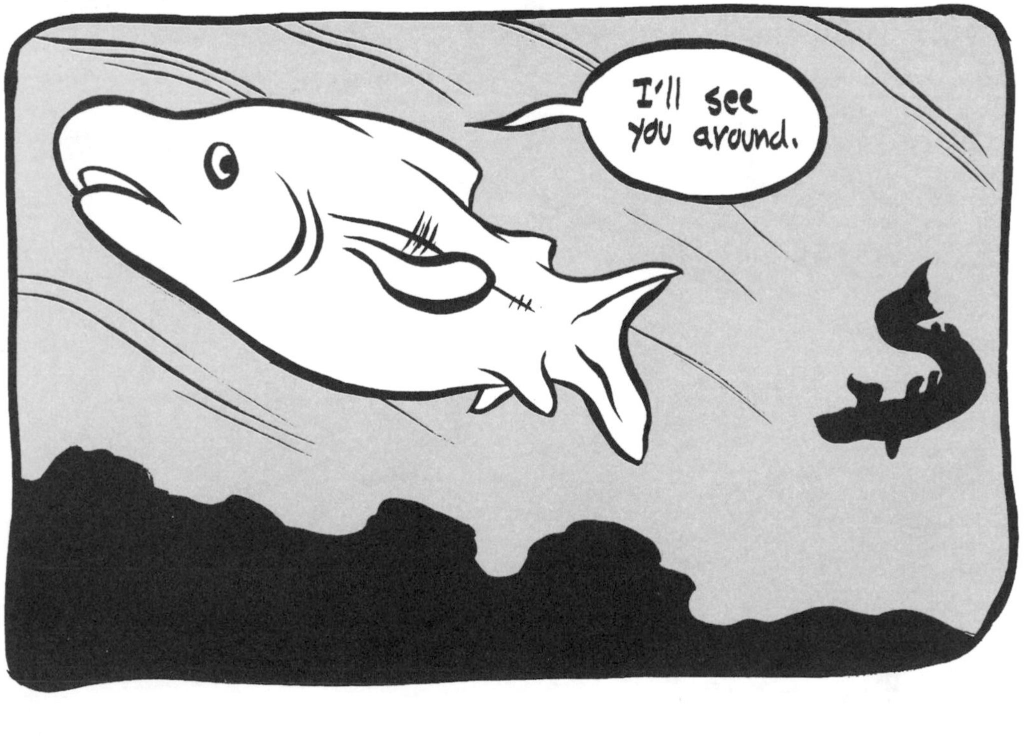
I'll see you around.

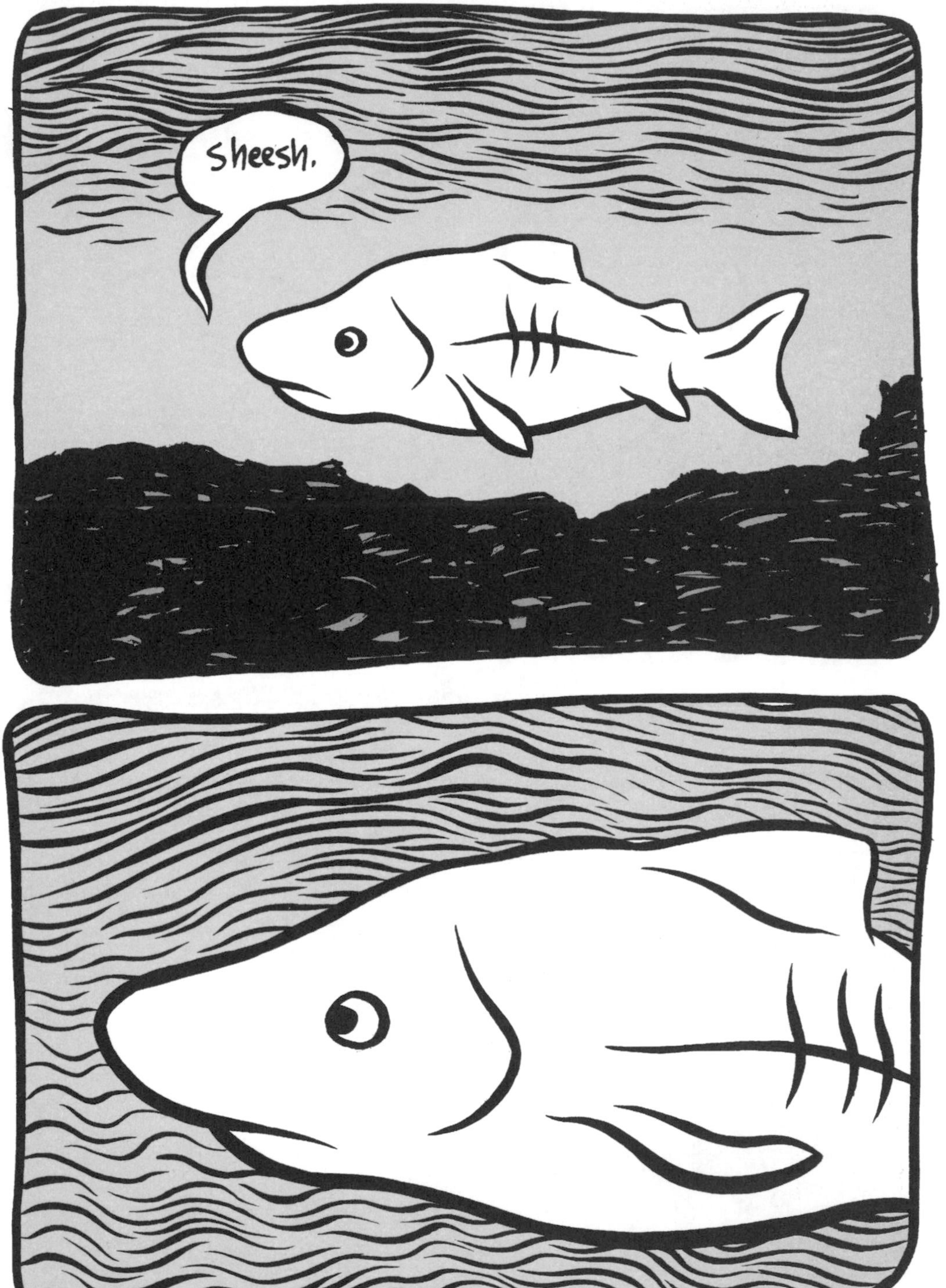
Sheesh.

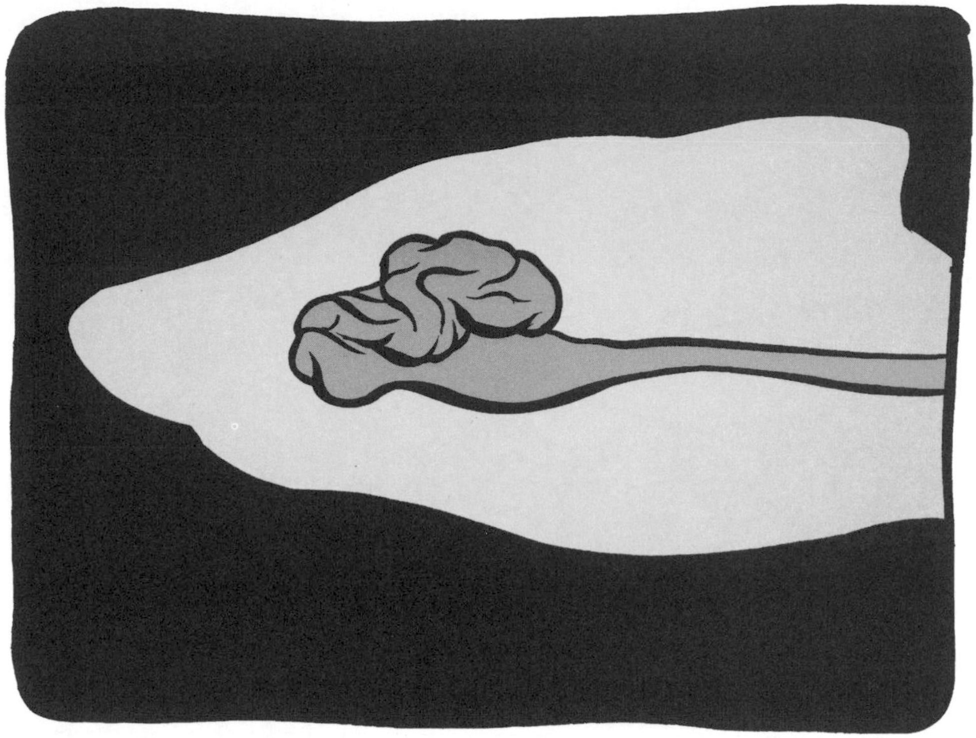

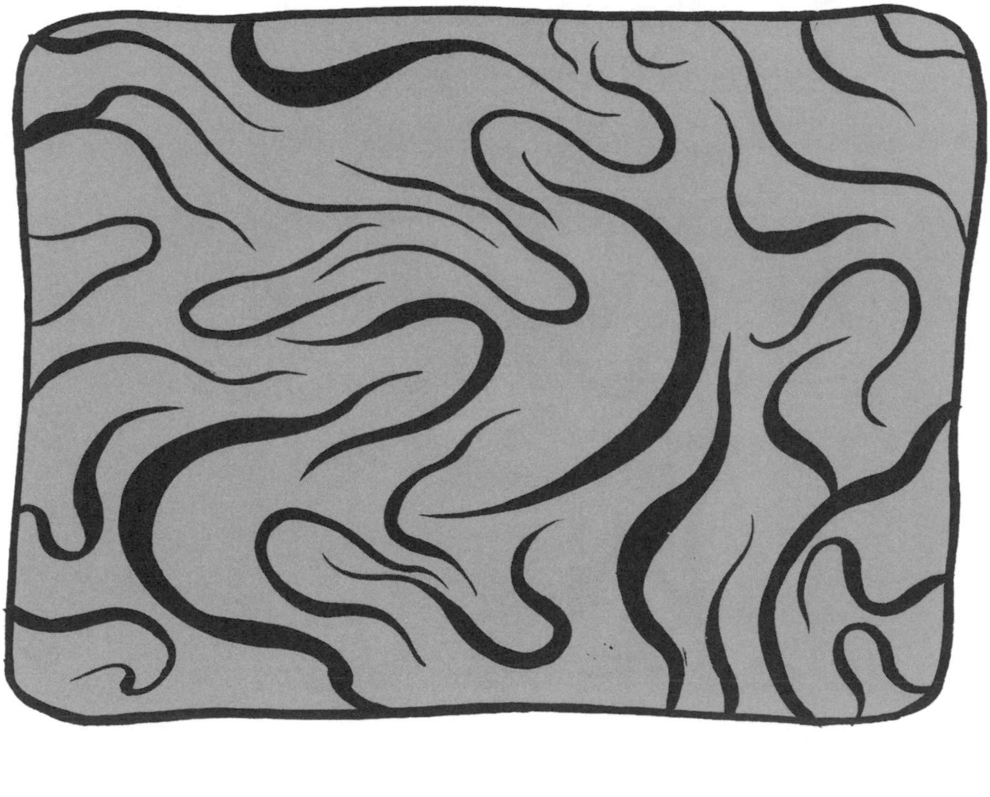

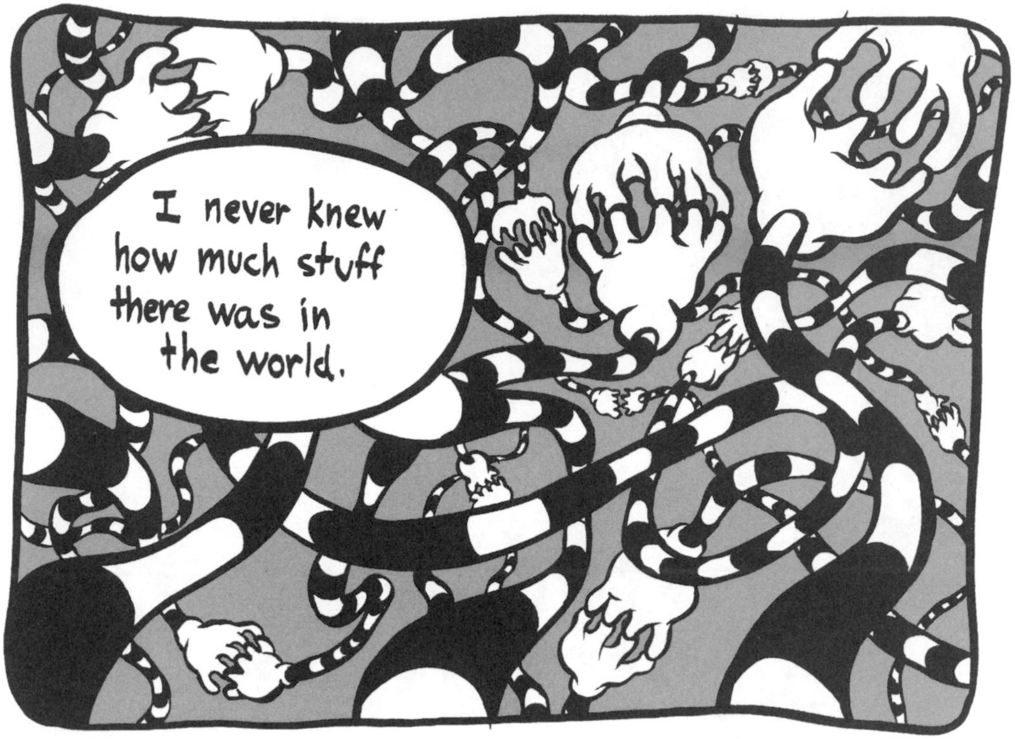
I never knew how much stuff there was in the world.

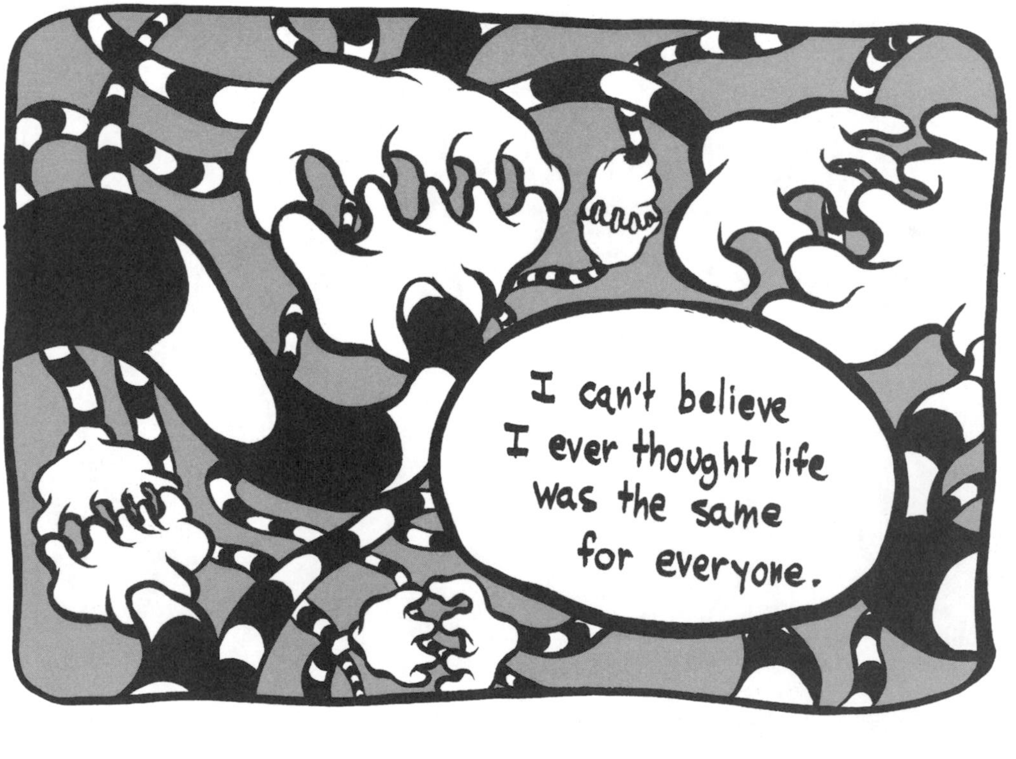
I can't believe I ever thought life was the same for everyone.

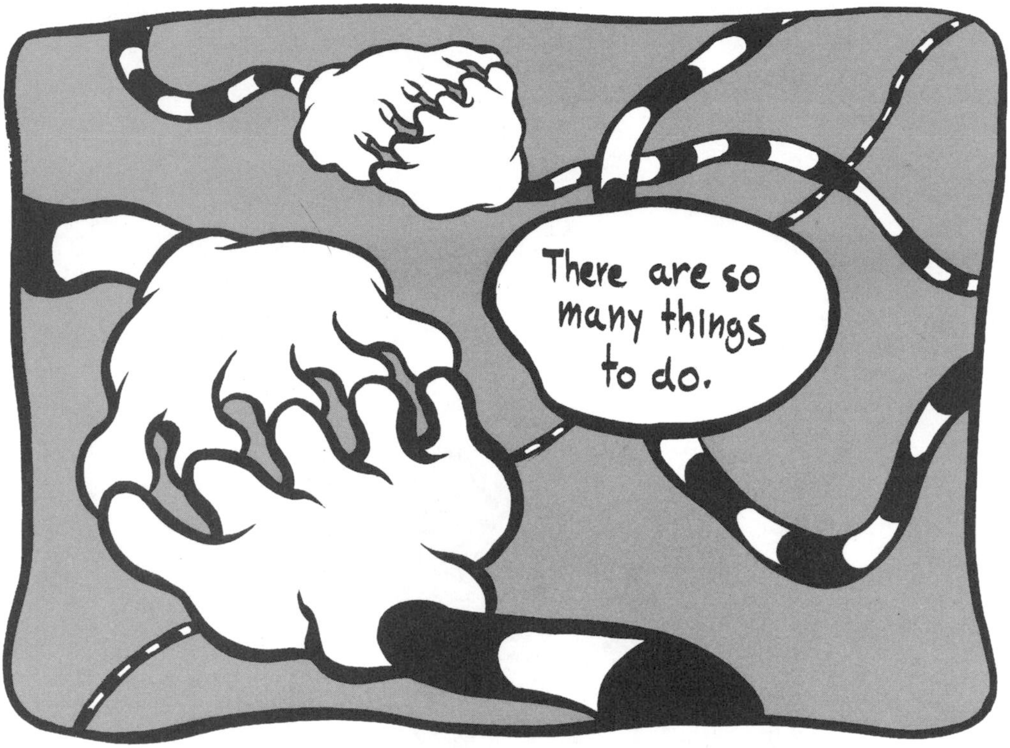
There are so many things to do.

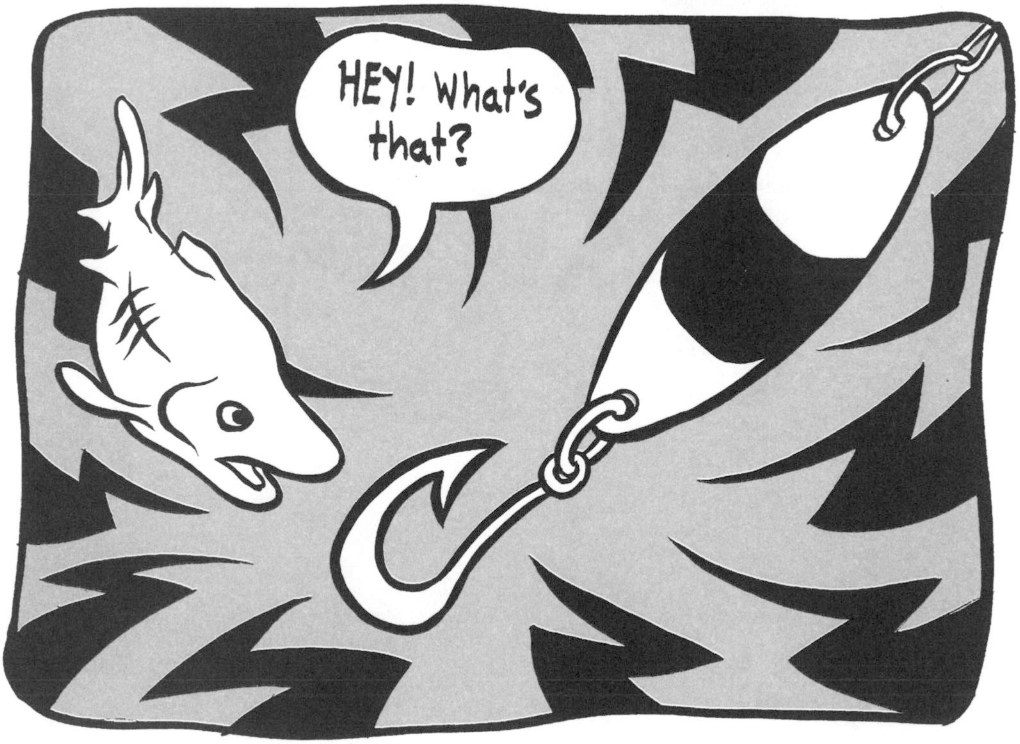
HEY! What's that?

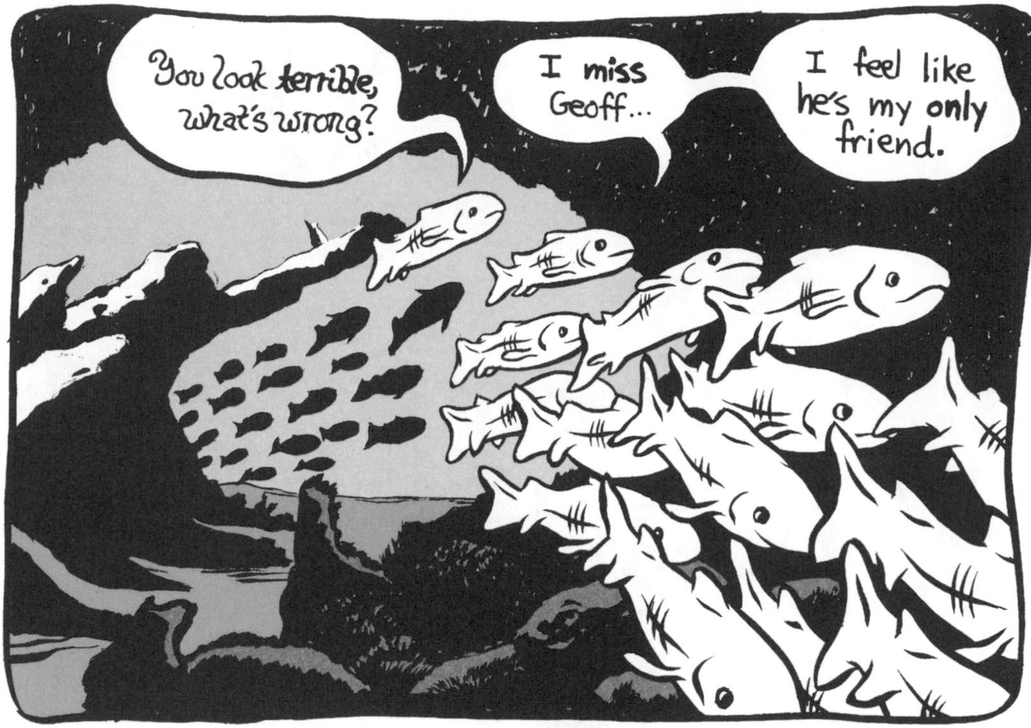
You look terrible, what's wrong?
I miss Geoff...
I feel like he's my only friend.

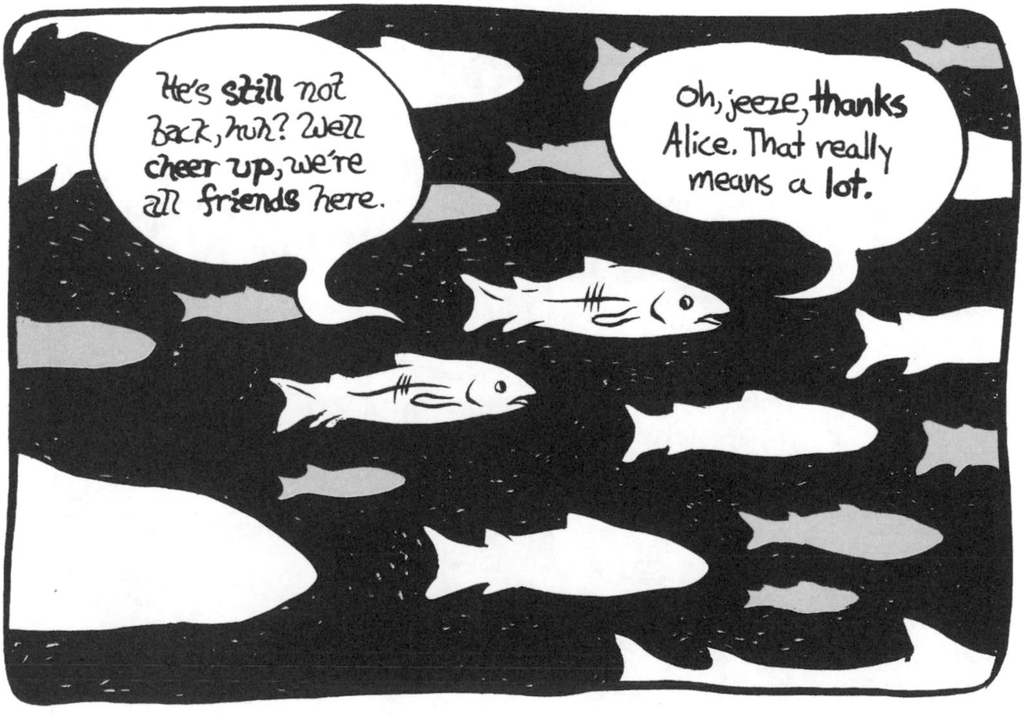
He's still not back, huh? Well cheer up, we're all friends here.
Oh, jeeze, thanks Alice. That really means a lot.

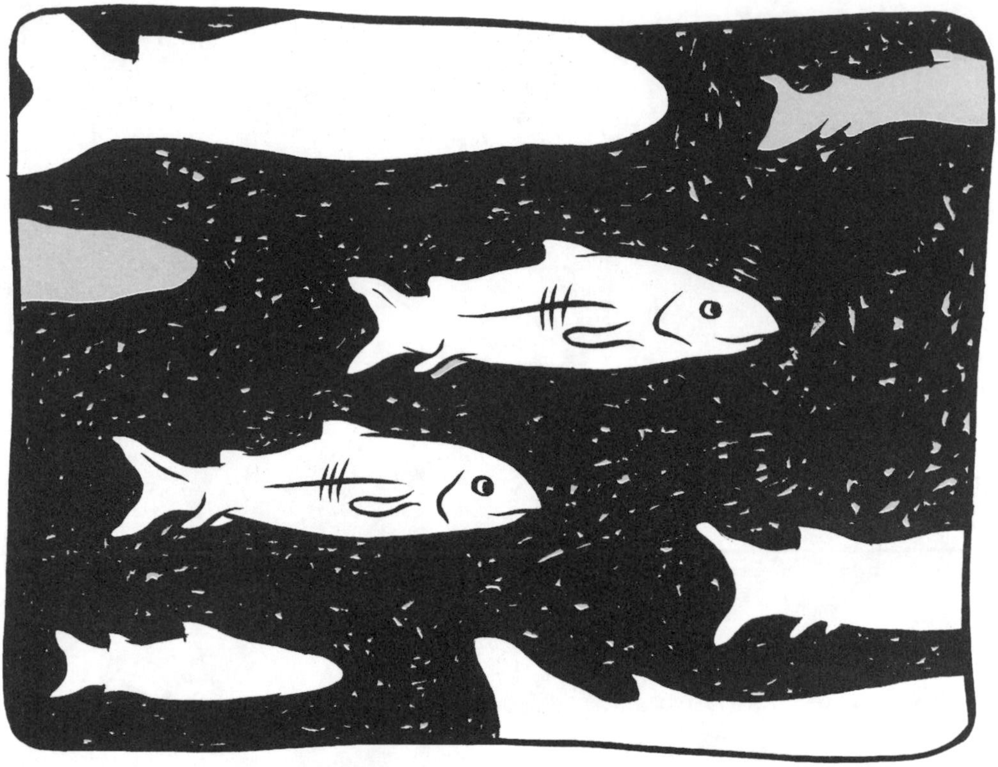

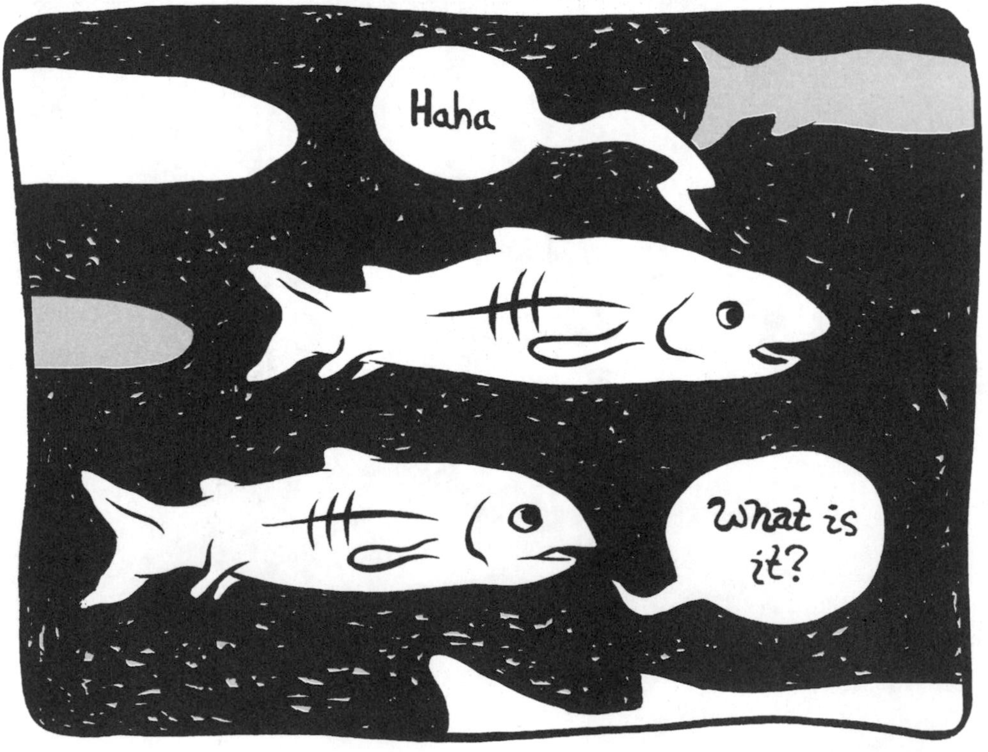
Haha
What is it?

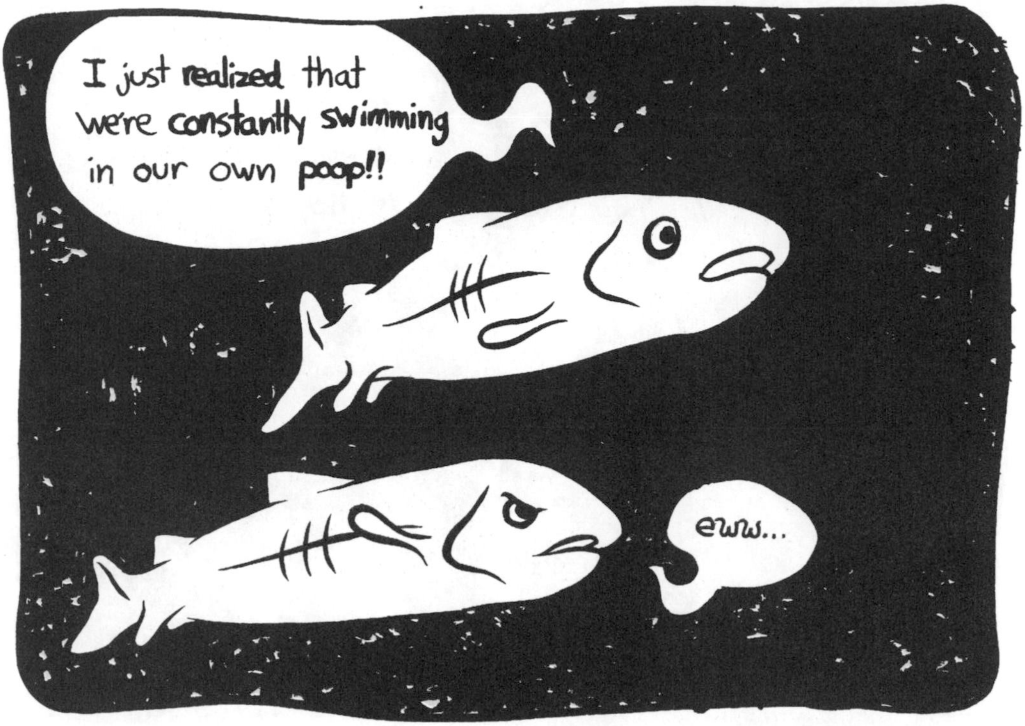
I just realized that we're constantly swimming in our own poop!!
eww...

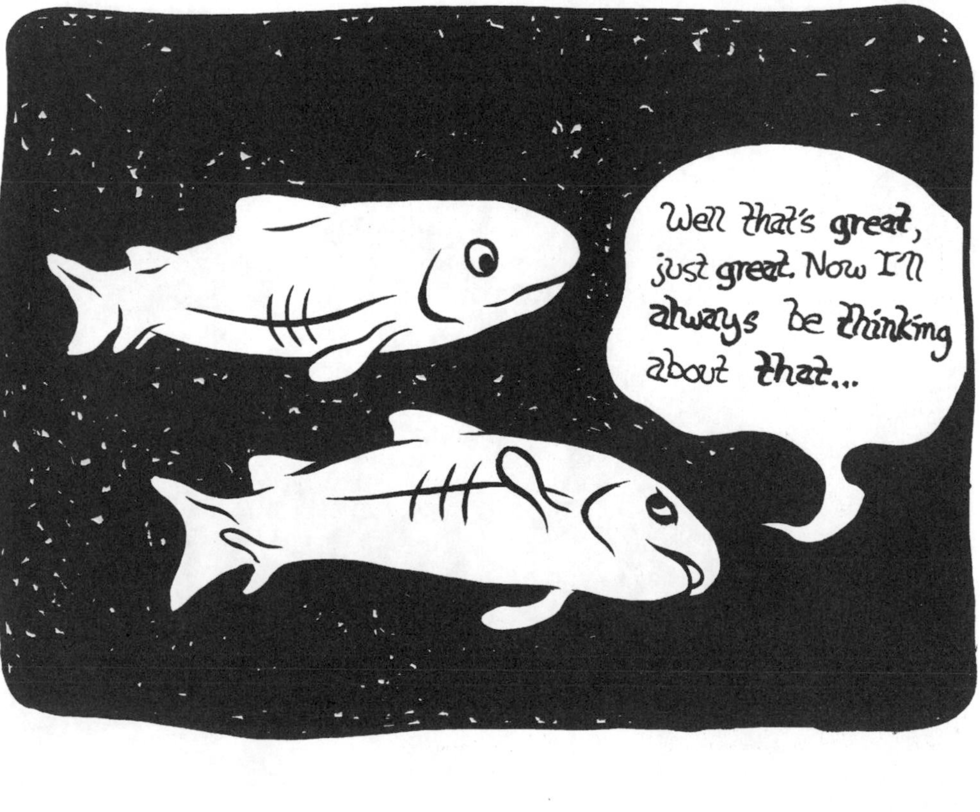
Well that's great, just great. Now I'll always be thinking about that...

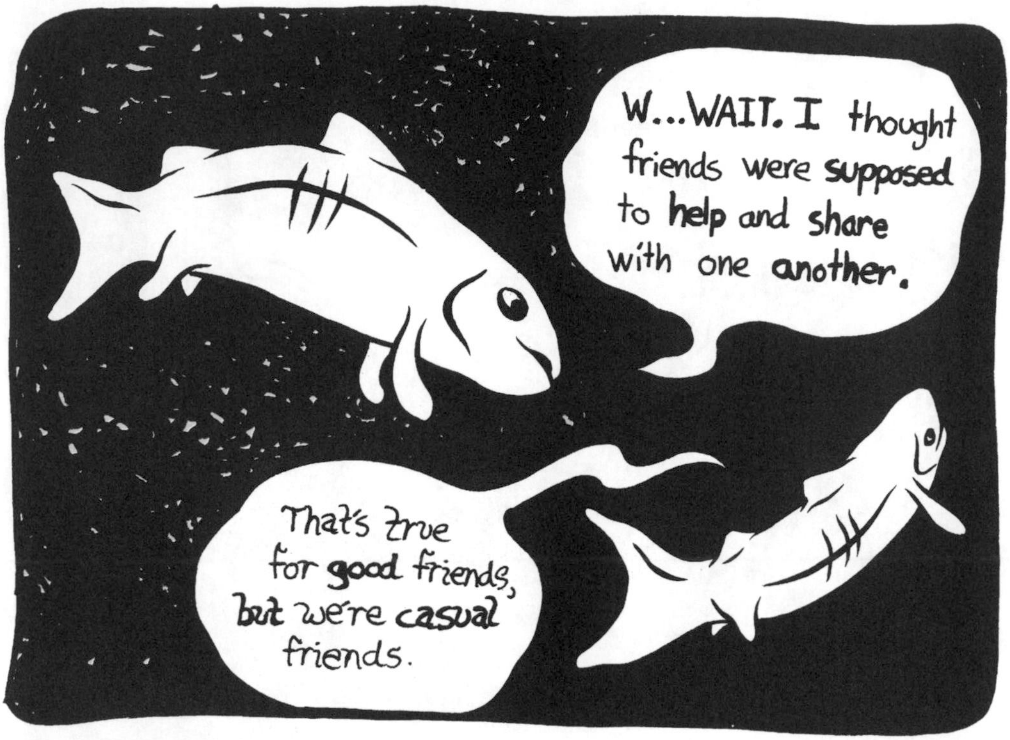
W...WAIT. I thought friends were supposed to help and share with one another.
That's true for good friends, but we're casual friends.

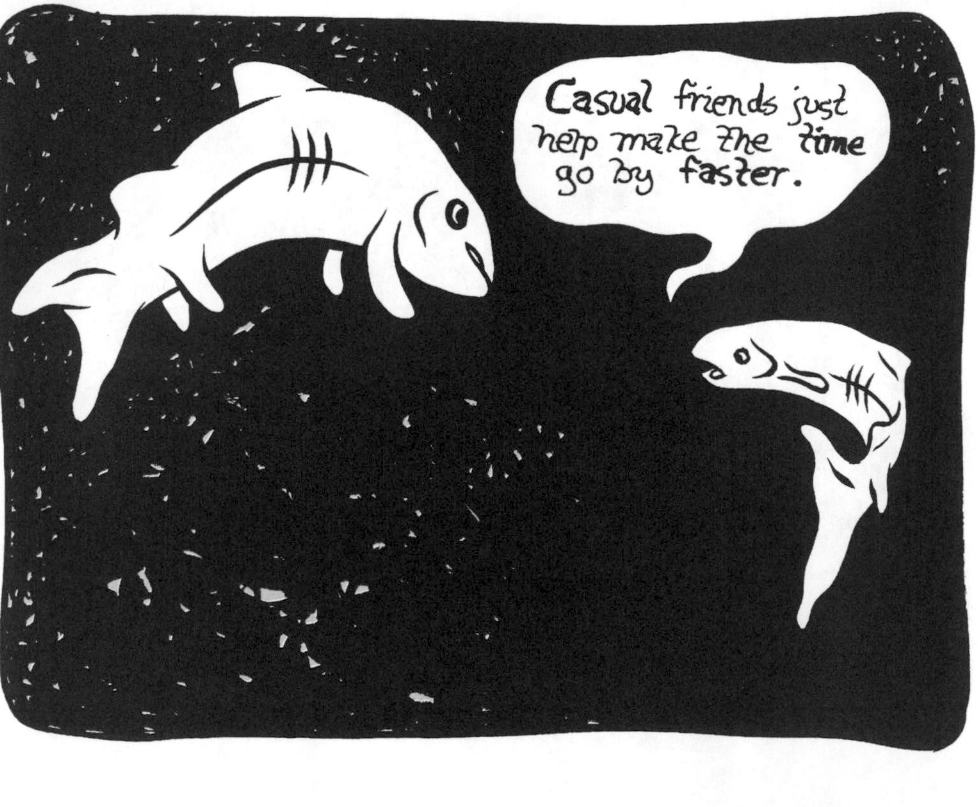
Casual friends just help make the time go by faster.

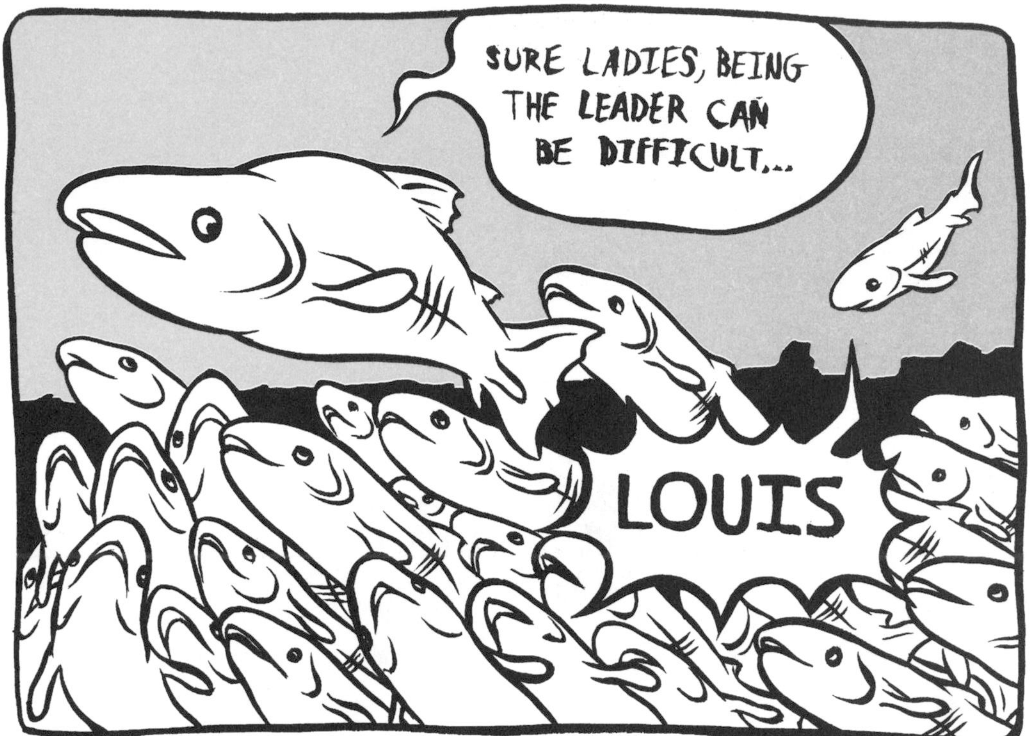
SURE LADIES, BEING THE LEADER CAN BE DIFFICULT...
LOUIS

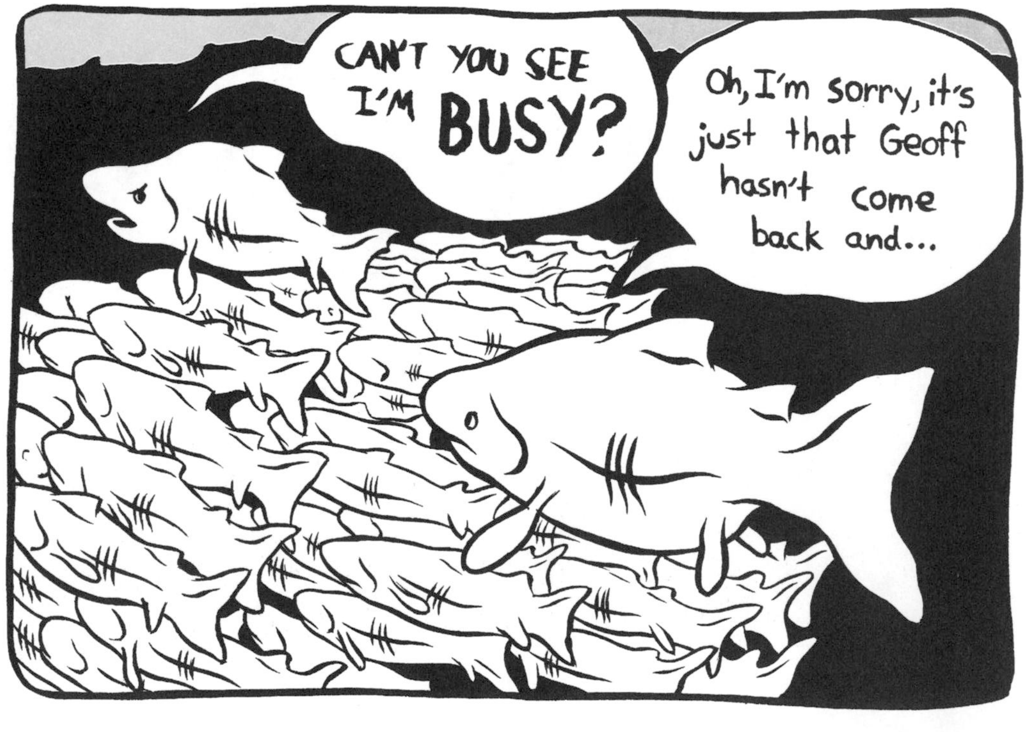
CAN'T YOU SEE I'M BUSY?
Oh, I'm sorry, it's just that Geoff hasn't come back and...

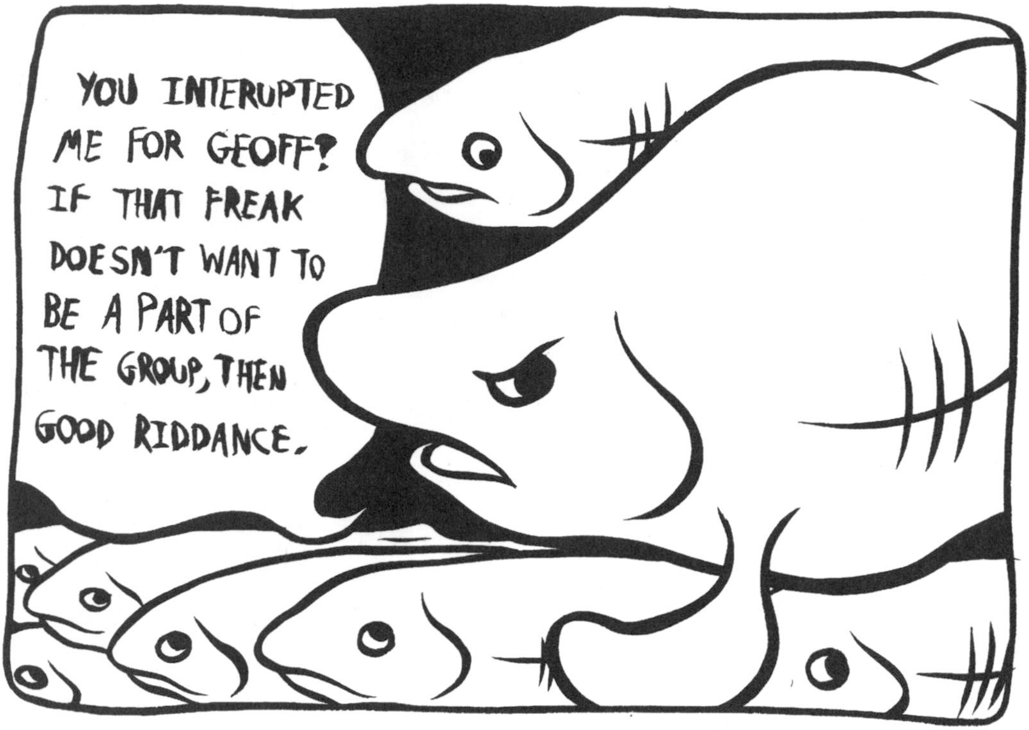
YOU INTERUPTED ME FOR GEOFF? IF THAT FREAK DOESN'T WANT TO BE A PART OF THE GROUP, THEN GOOD RIDDANCE.

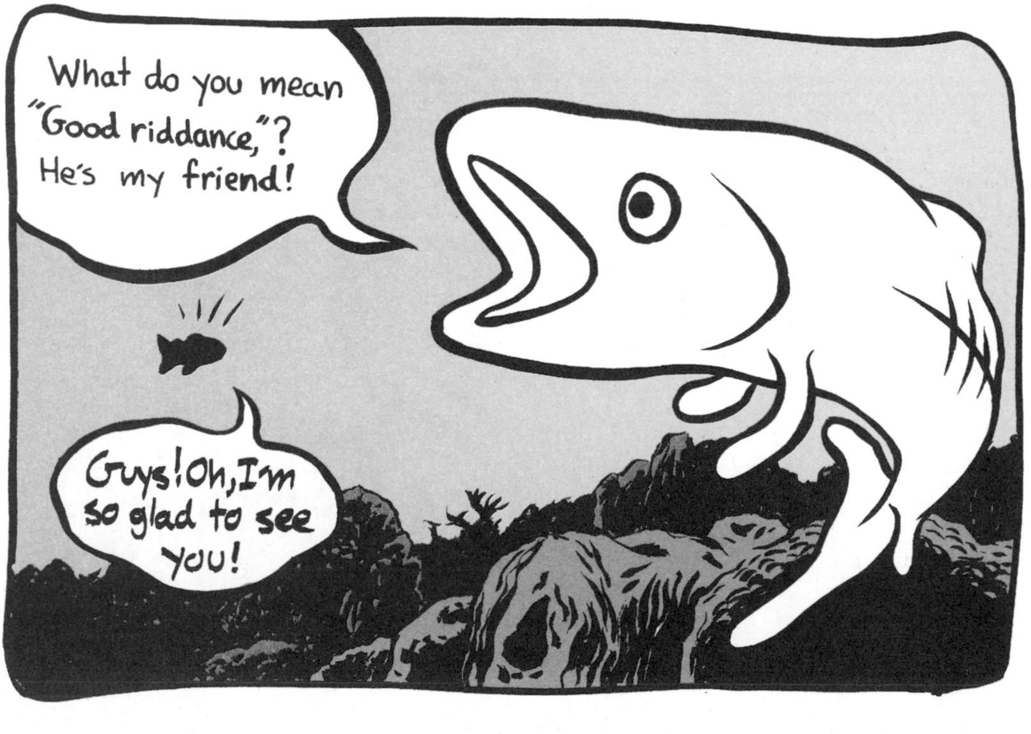
What do you mean "Good riddance,"? He's my friend!
Guys! Oh, I'm so glad to see you!

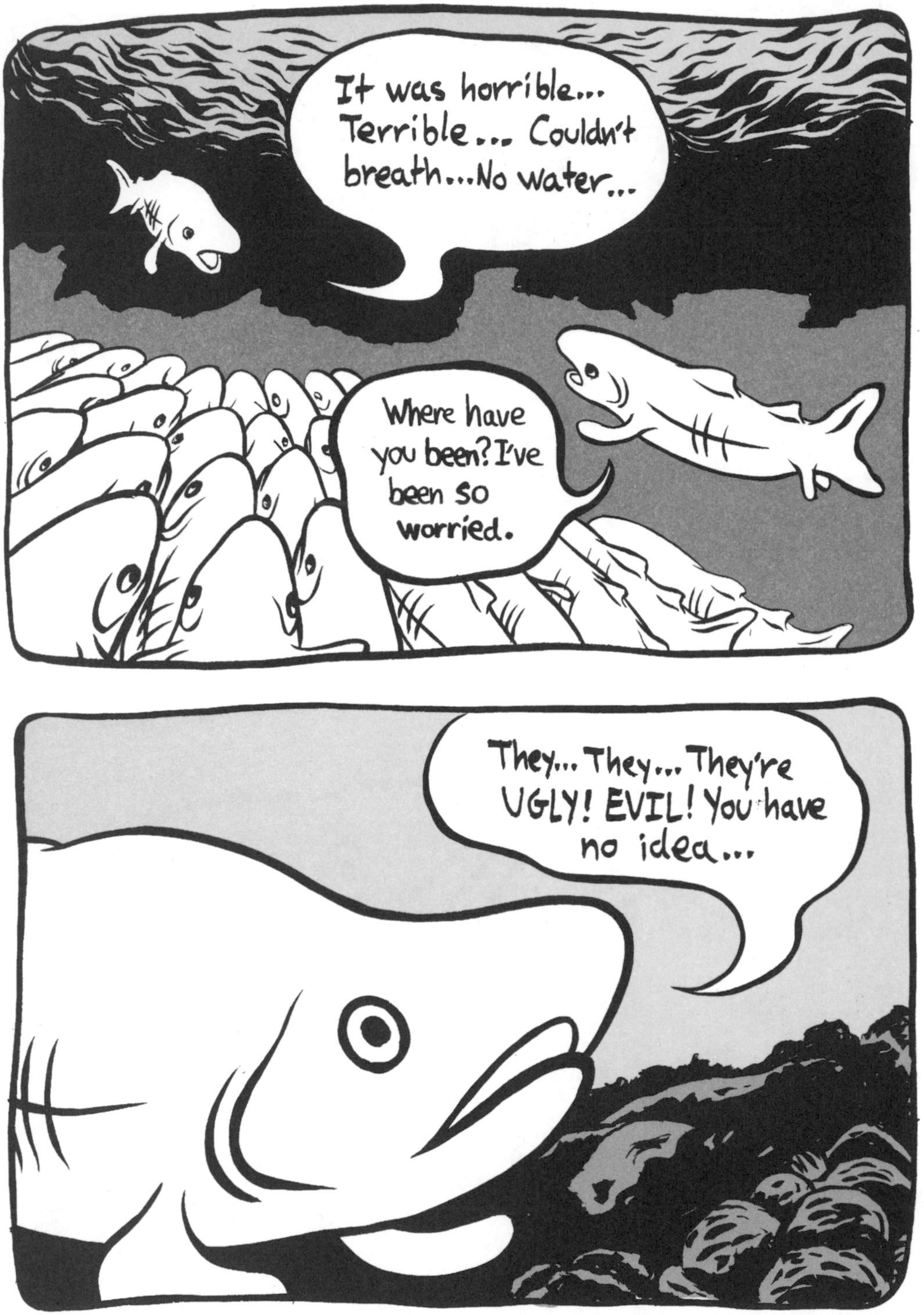
It was horrible... Terrible... Couldn't breath...No water...
Where have you been? I've been so worried.
They... They... They're UGLY! EVIL! You have no idea...

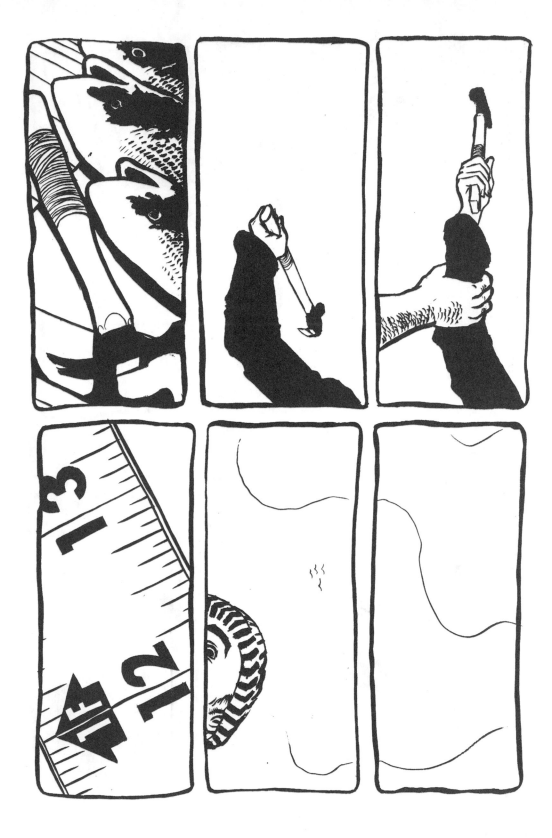

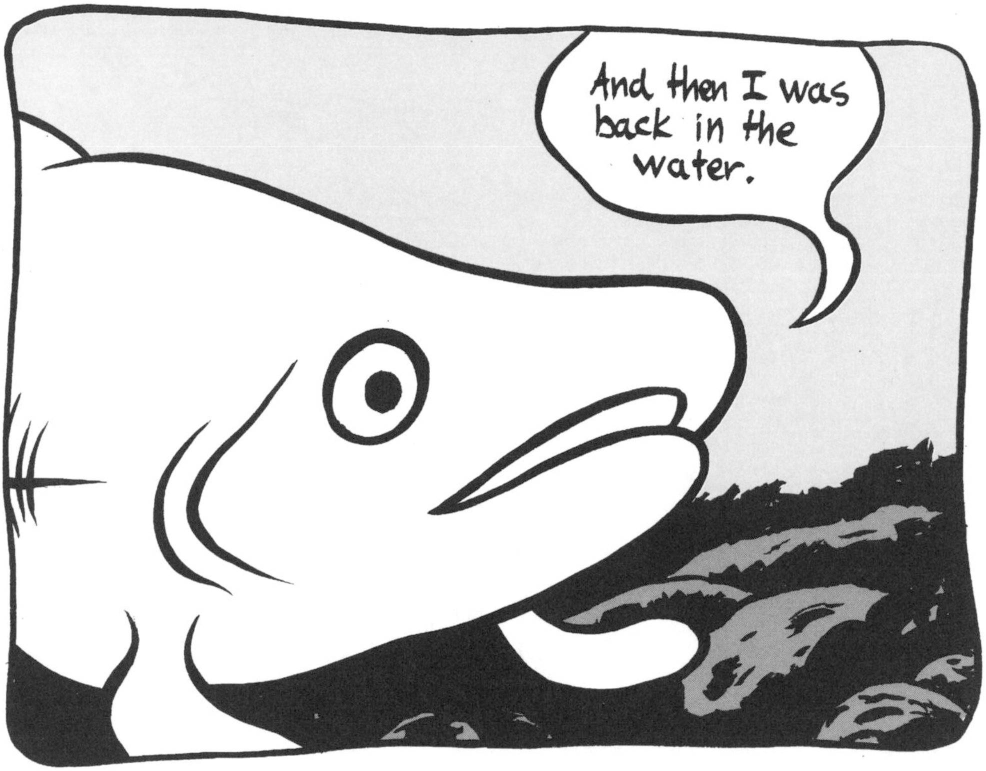
And then I was back in the water.

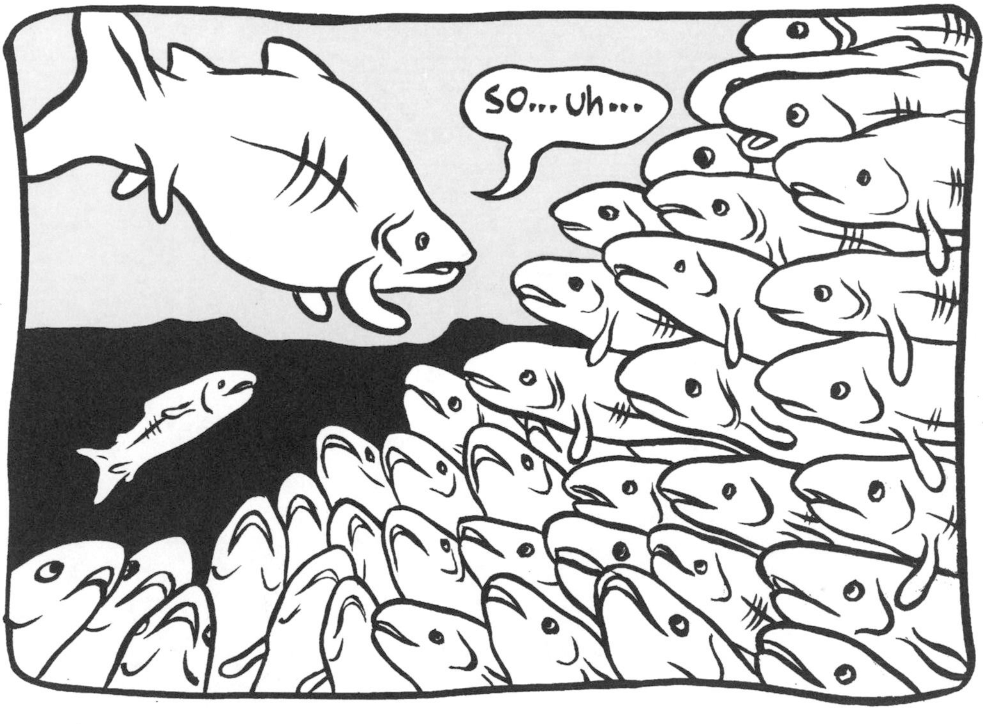
SO... uh...

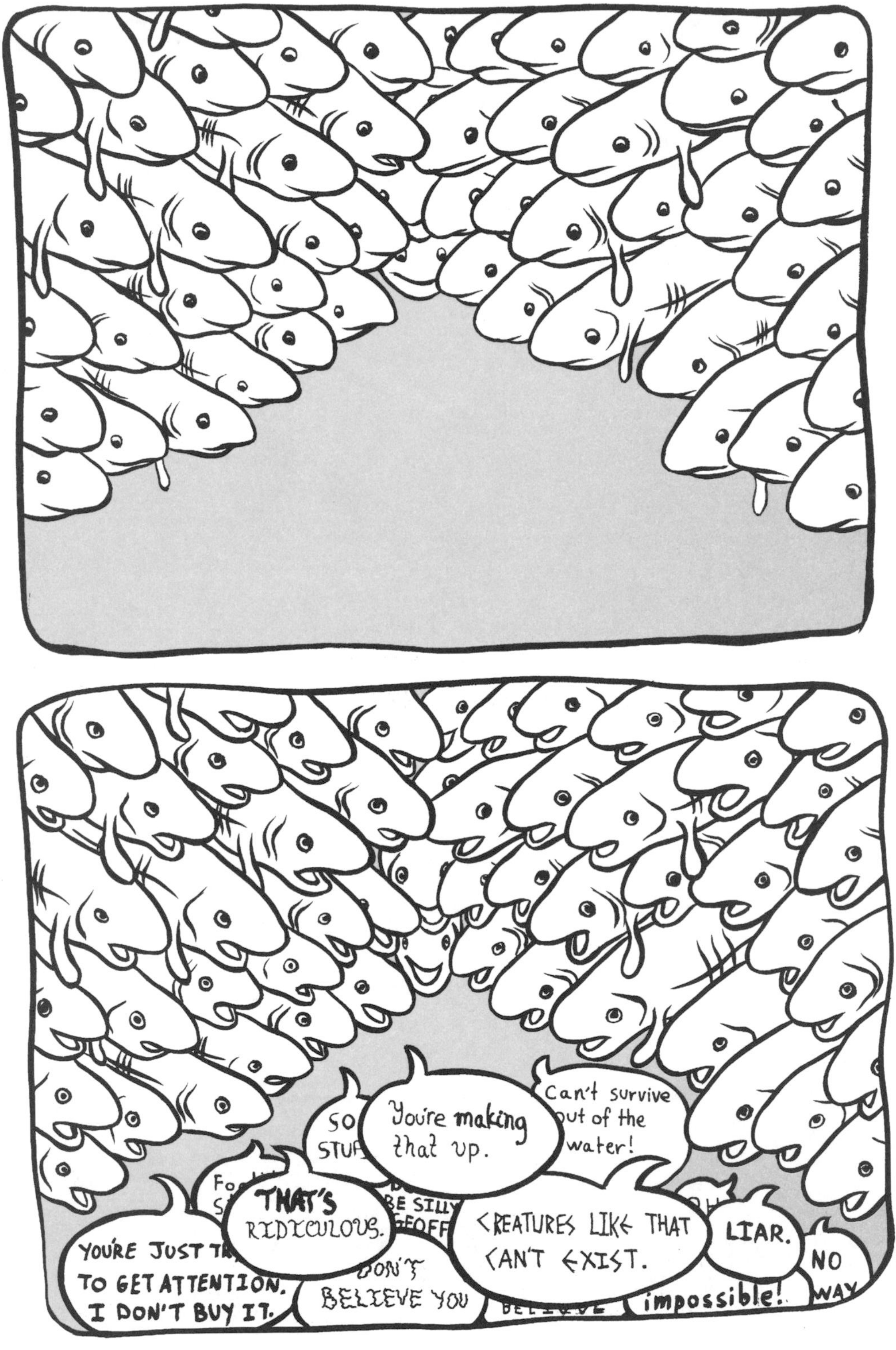
You're making that up.
Can't survive
ut of the
water!
THAT'S RIDICULOUS.
CREATURES LIKE THAT CAN'T EXIST.
LIAR.
NO WAY
YOU'RE JUST
TO GET ATTENTION. I DON'T BUY IT.
BELIEVE YOU
impossible!

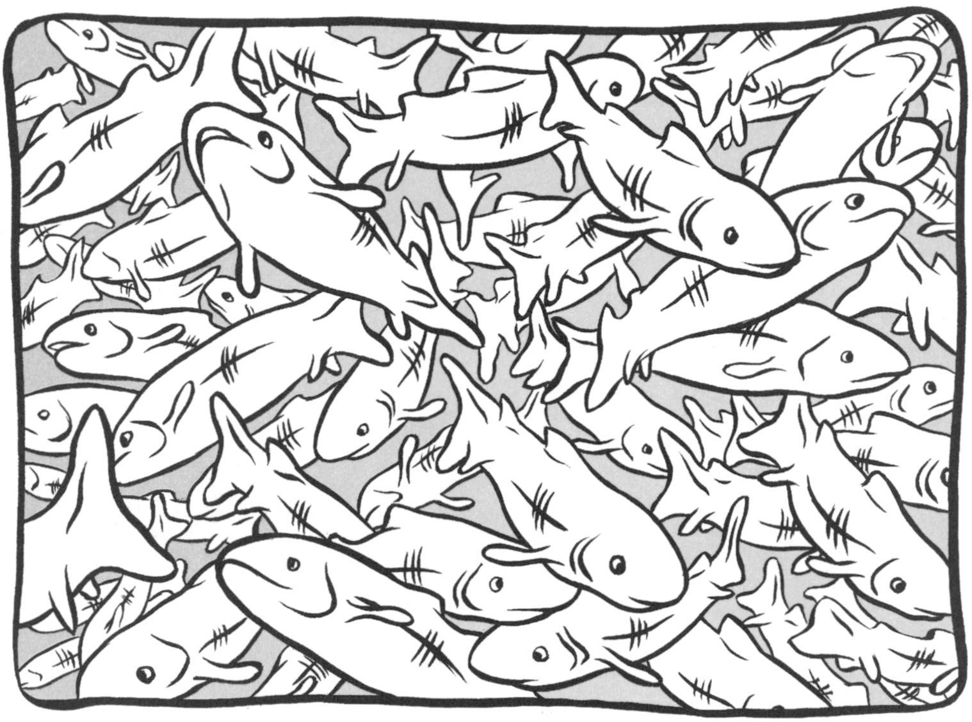

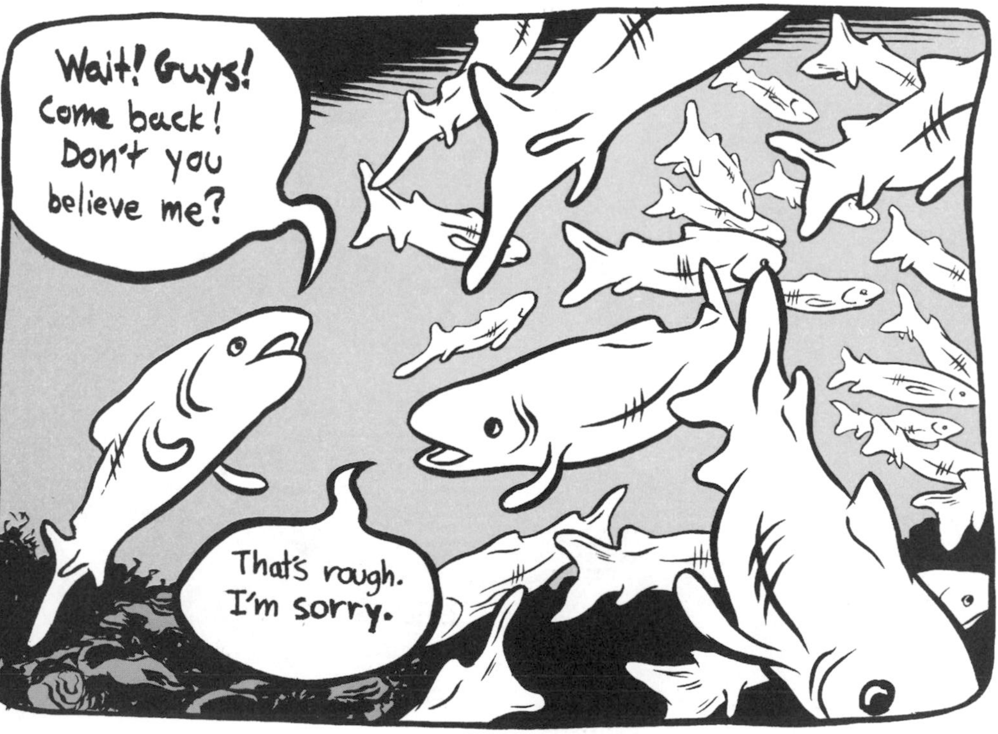
Wait! Guys! Come back! Don't you believe me?
That's rough. I'm sorry.

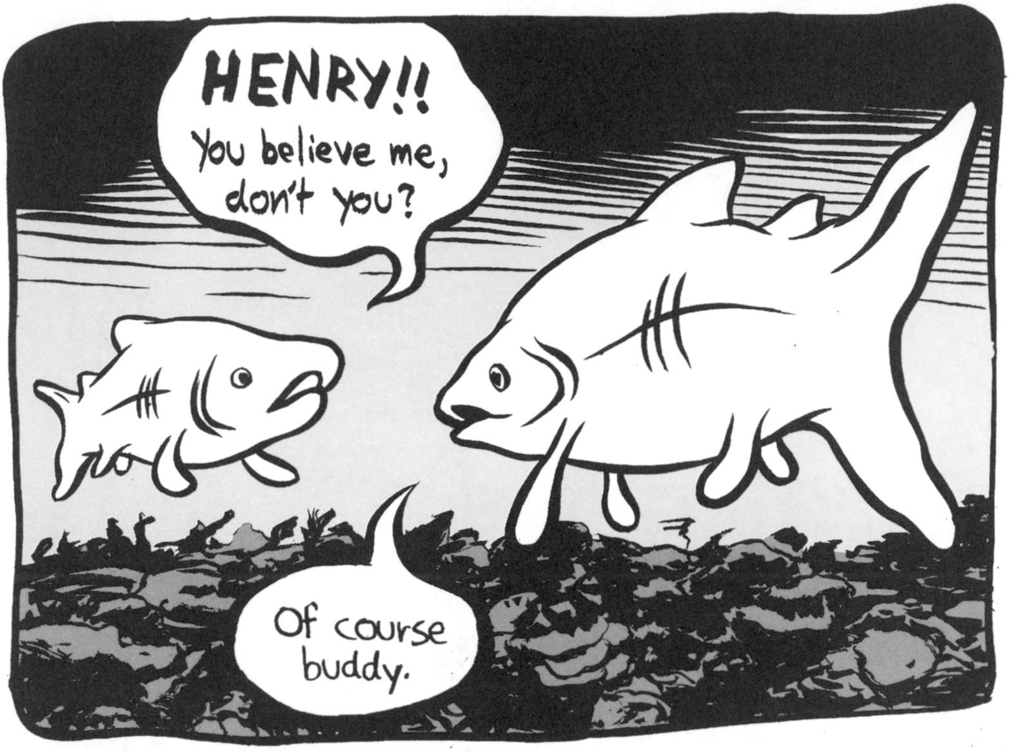
HENRY!! You believe me, don't you?
Of course buddy.

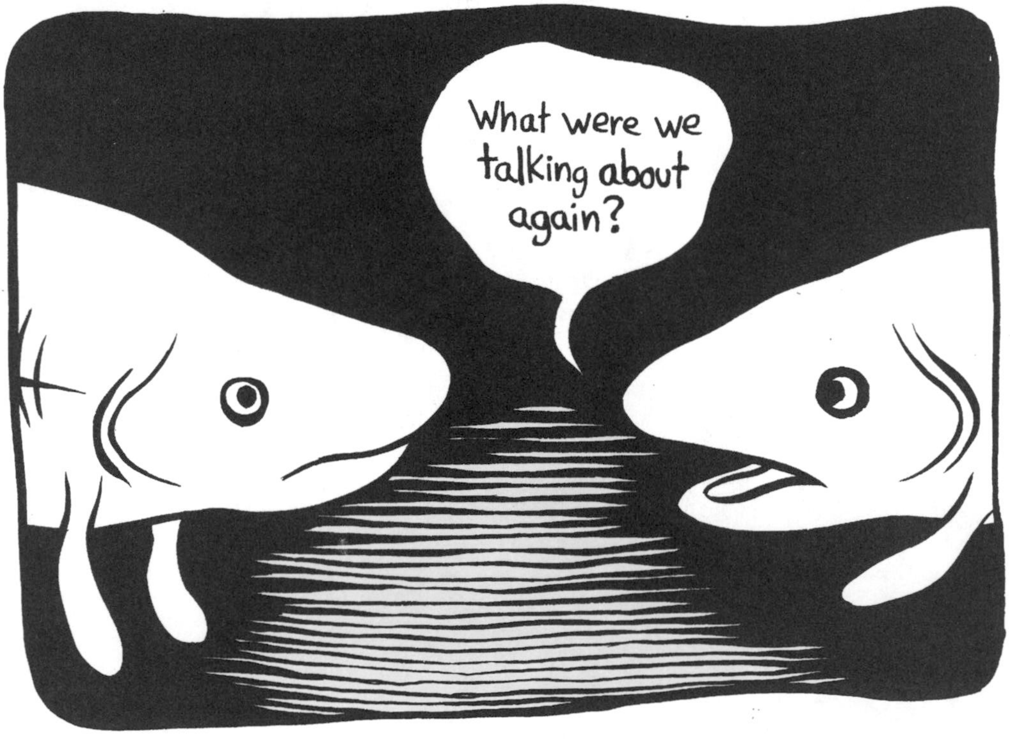
What were we talking about again?

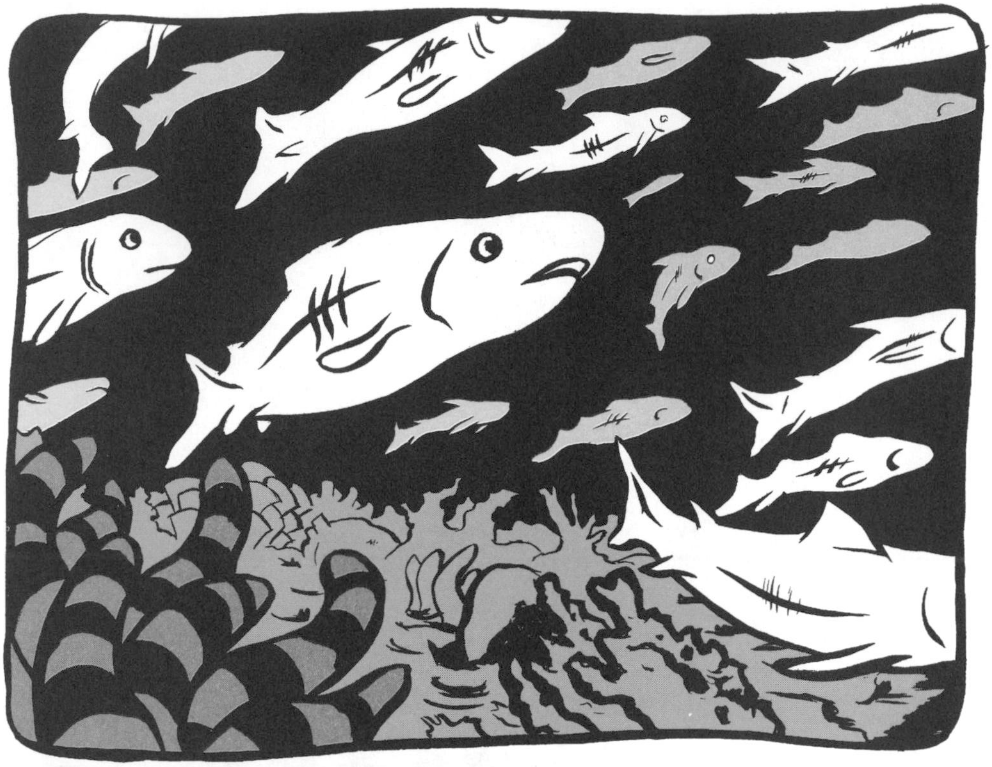

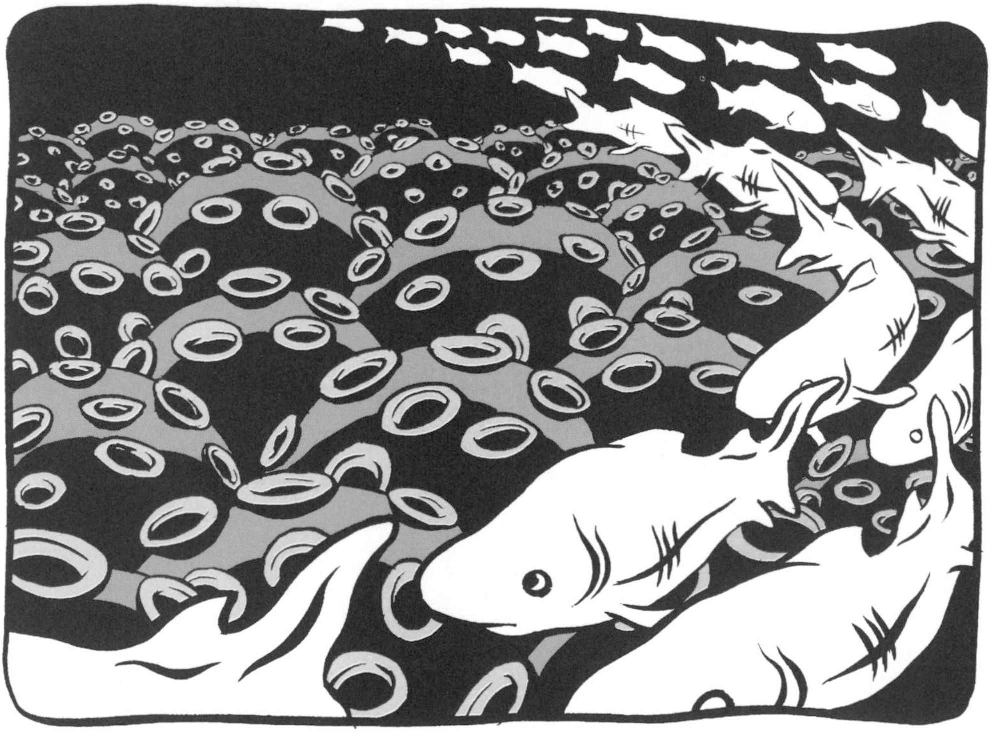

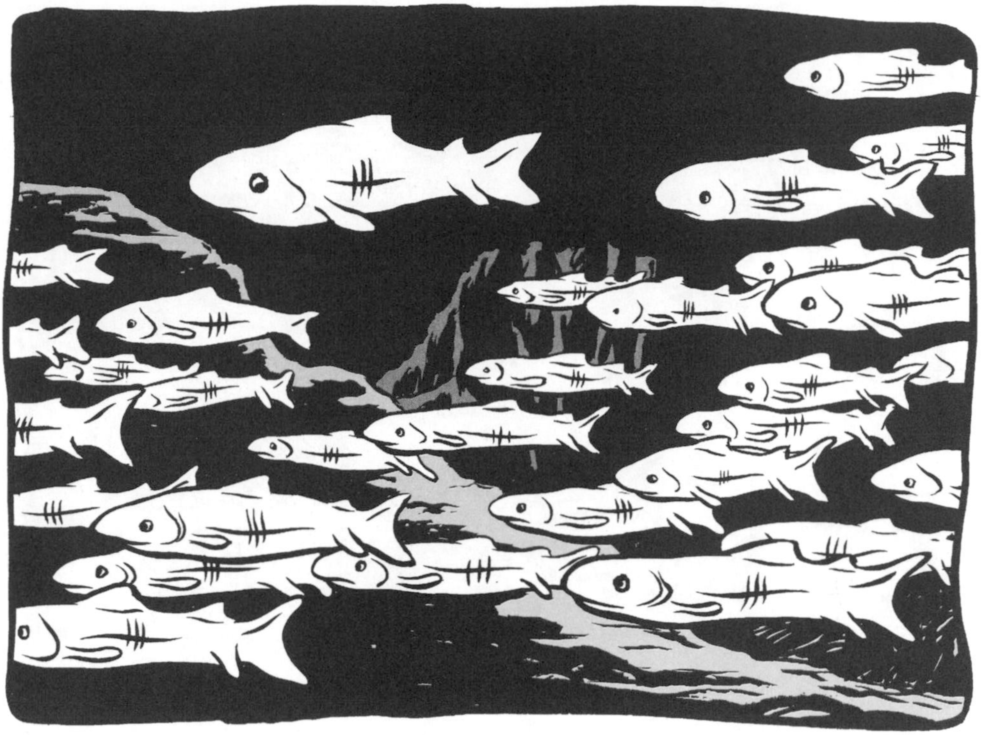

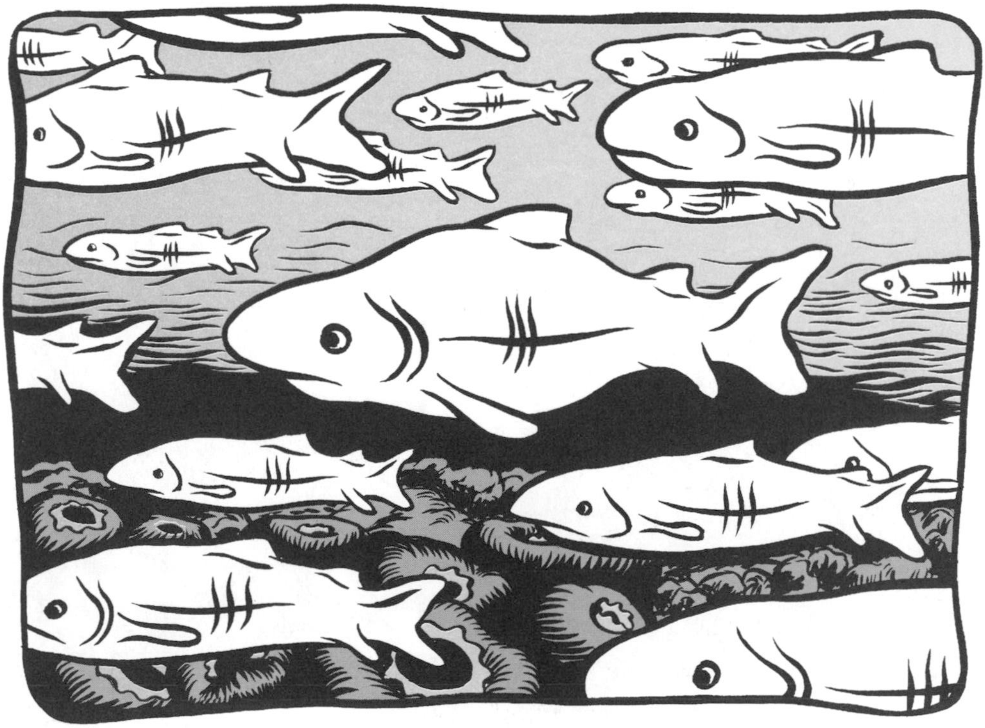

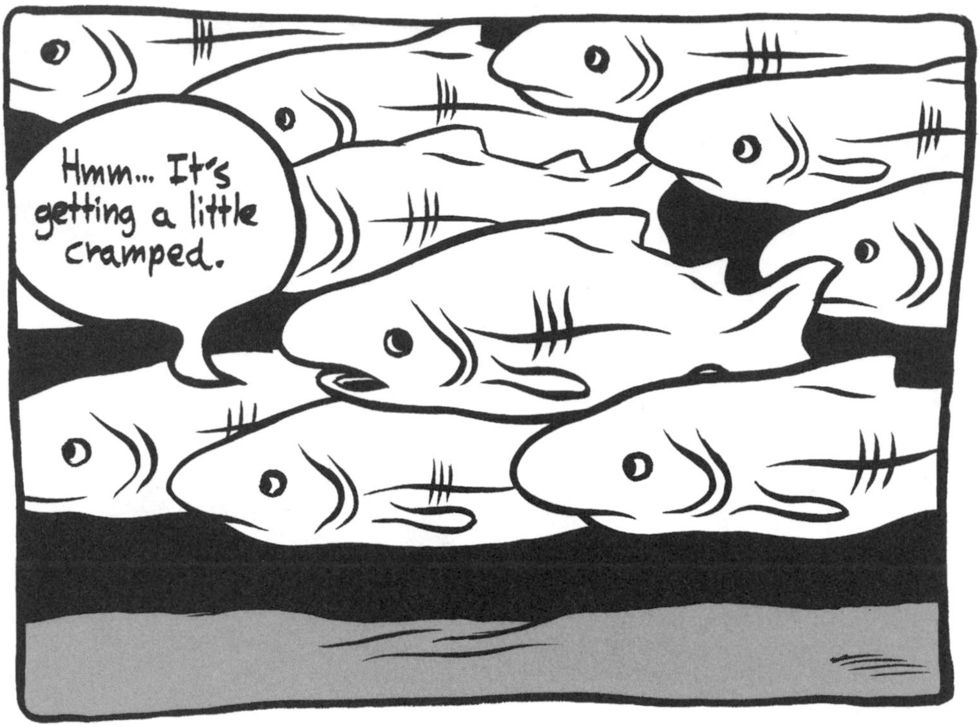
Hmm... It's getting a little cramped.

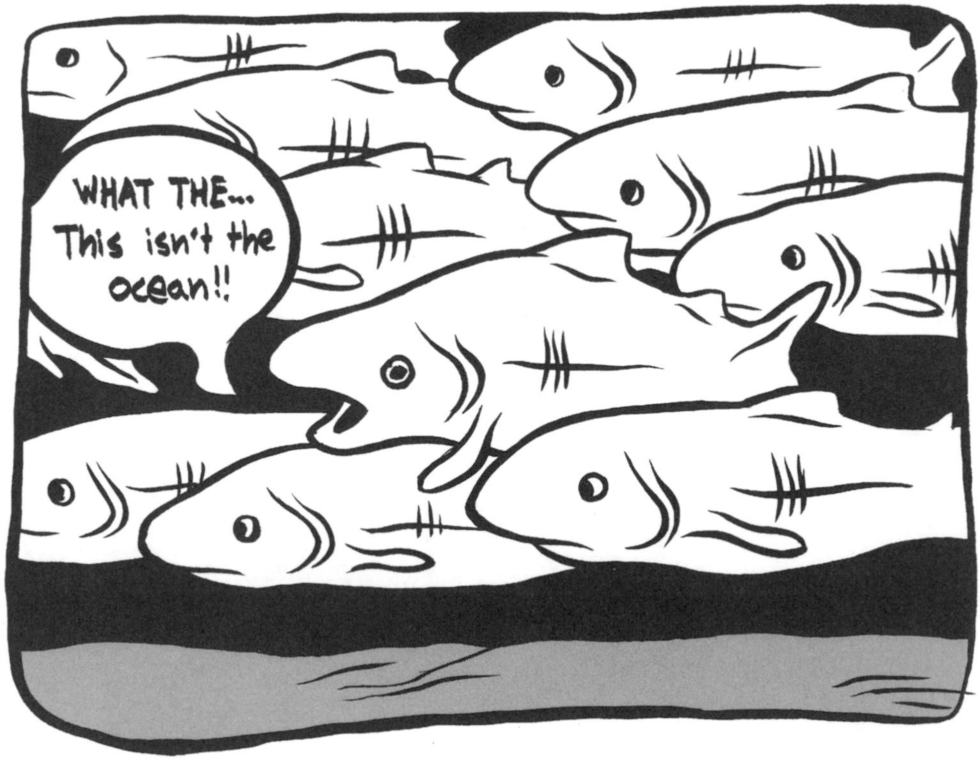
WHAT THE... This isn't the ocean!!

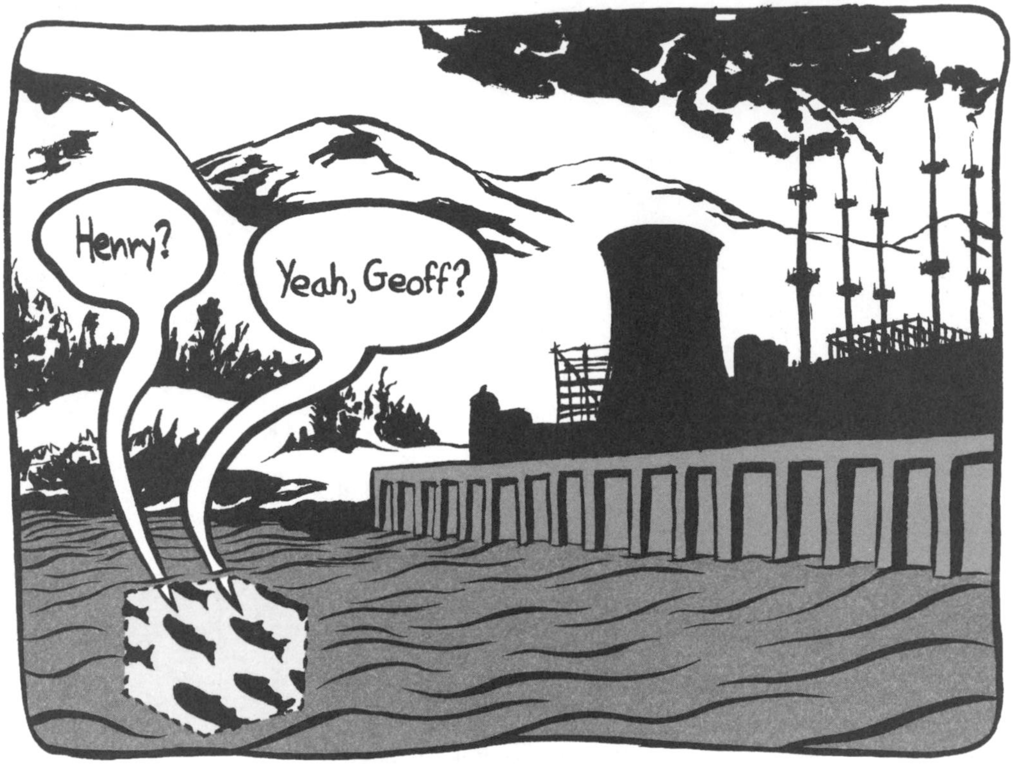
Henry?
Yeah, Geoff?

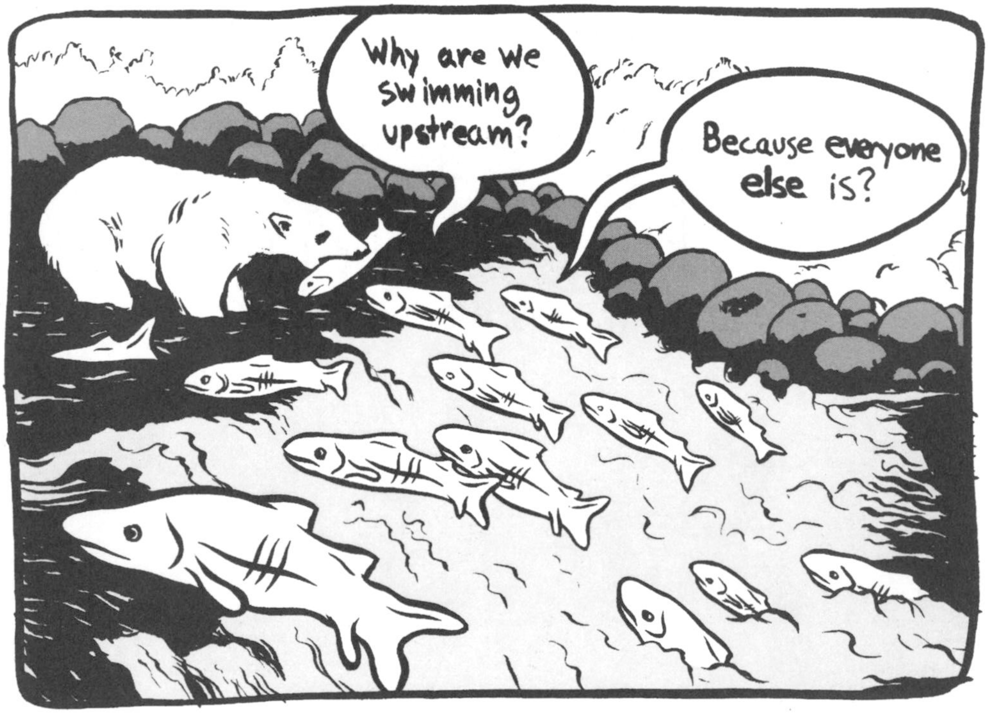
Why are we swimming upstream?
Because everyone else is?

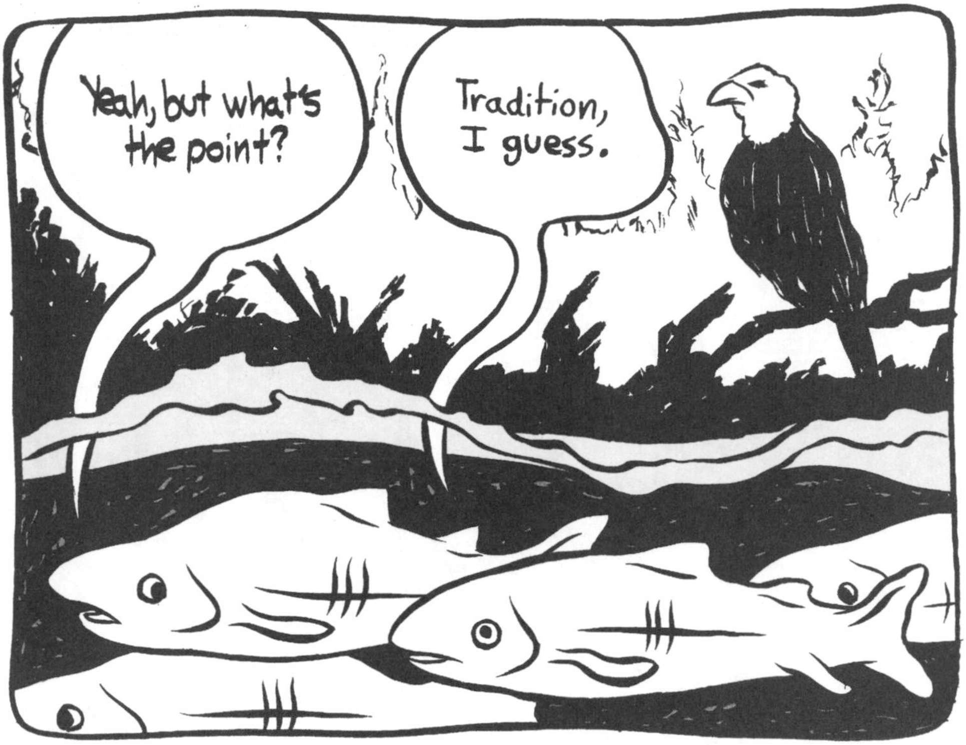
Yeah, but what's the point?
Tradition, I guess.

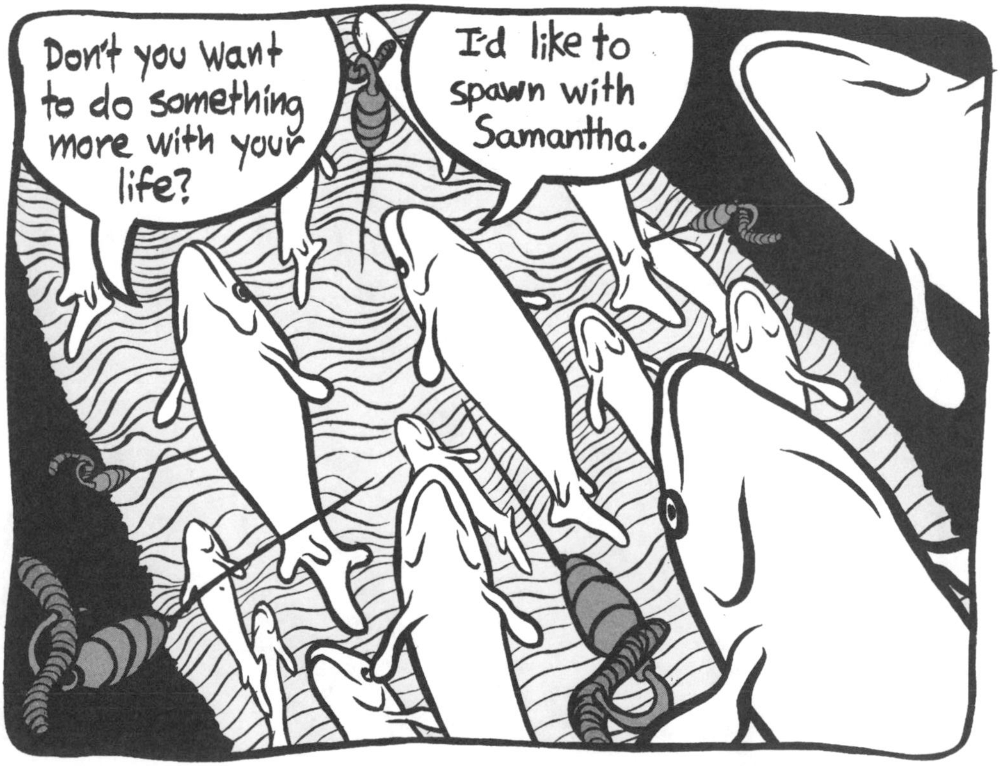
Don't you want to do something more with your life?
I'd like to spawn with Samantha.

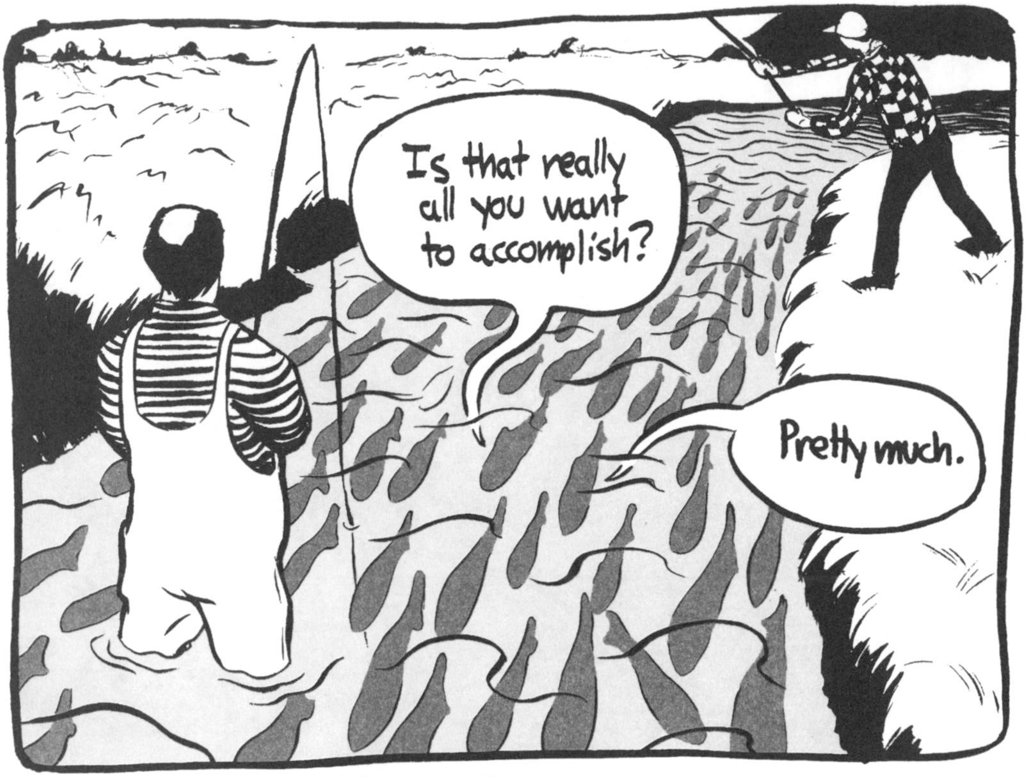
Is that really all you want to accomplish?
Pretty much.

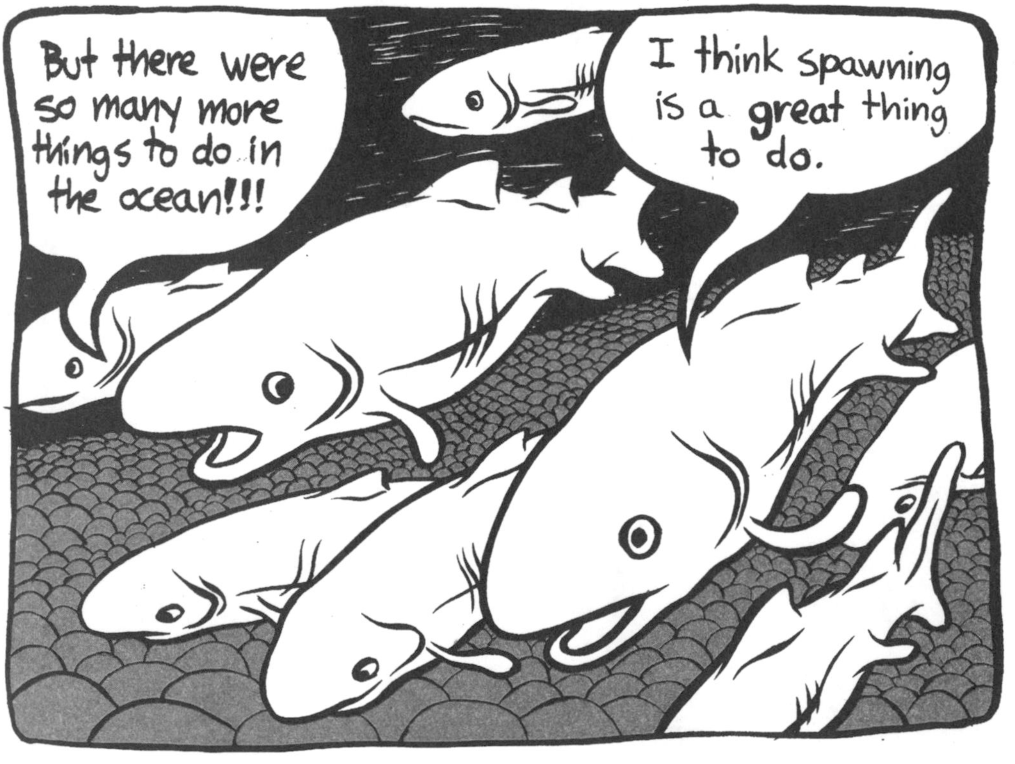
But there were so many more things to do in the ocean!!!
I think spawning is a great thing to do.

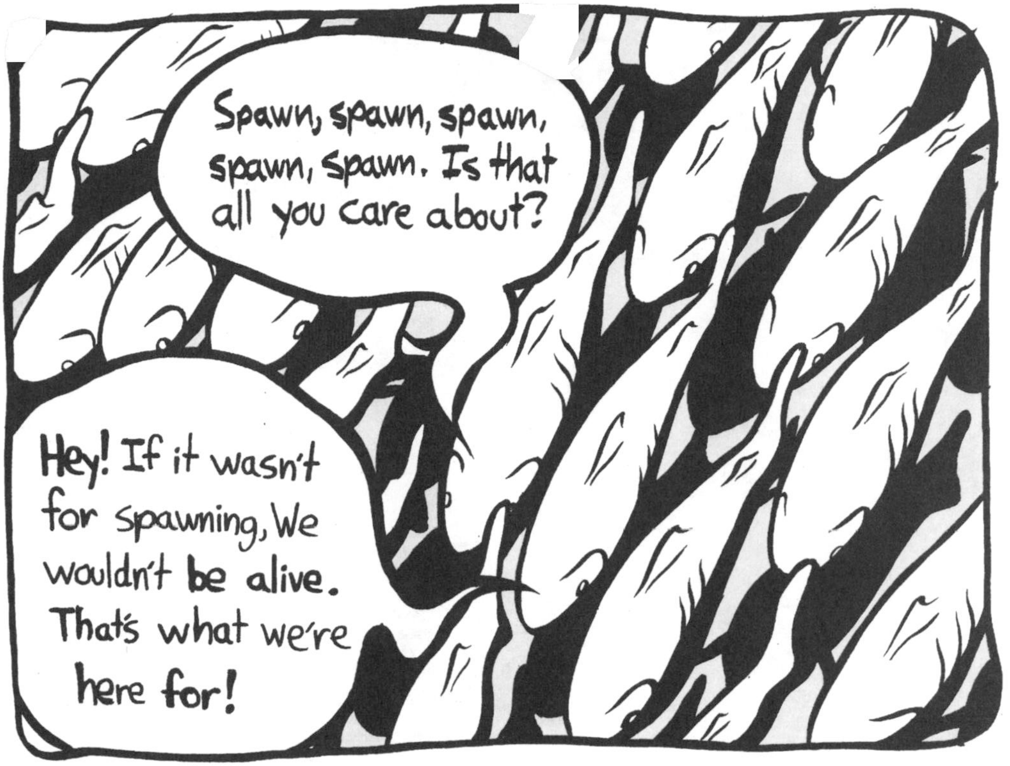
Spawn, spawn, spawn, spawn, spawn. Is that all you care about?
Hey! If it wasn't for spawning, We wouldn't be alive. That's what we're here for!

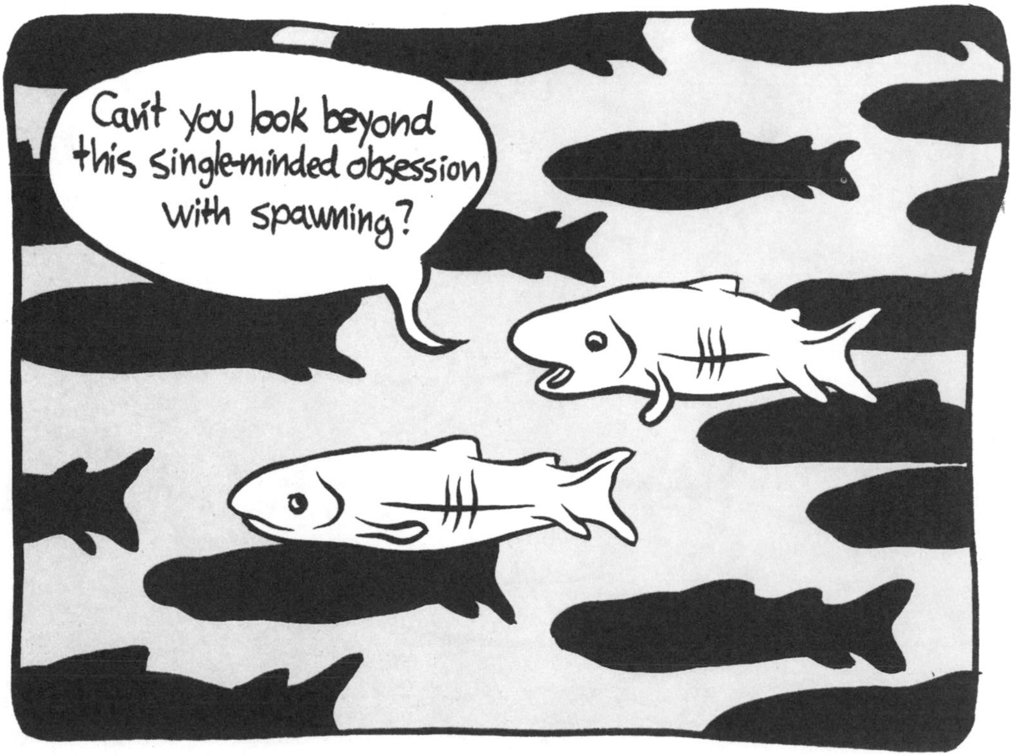
Can't you look beyond this single-minded obsession with spawning?

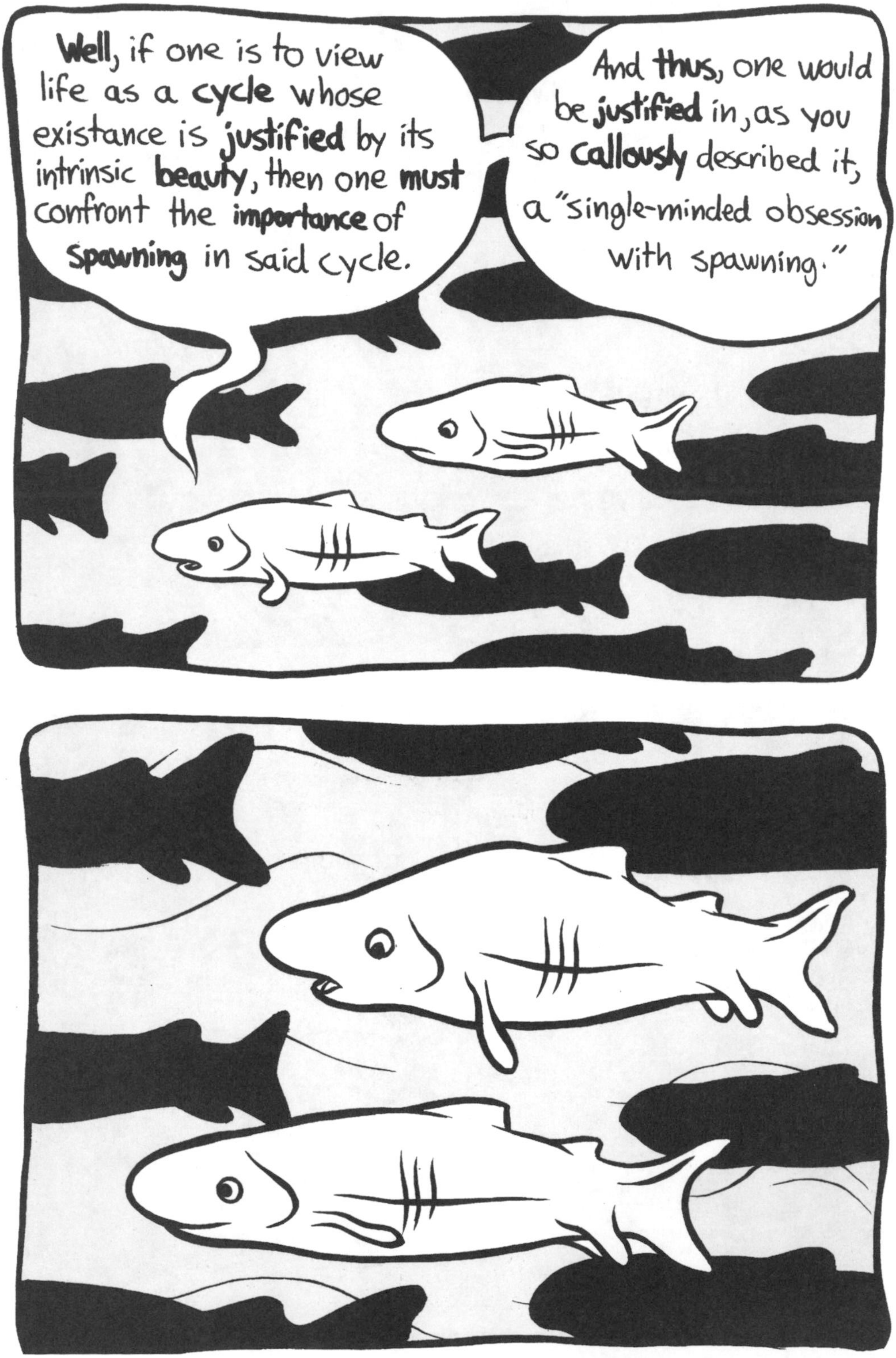
Well, if one is to view life as a cycle whose existance is justified by its intrinsic beauty, then one must confront the importance of spawning in said cycle.
And thus, one would be justified in, as you so callously described it, a "single-minded obsession with spawning."

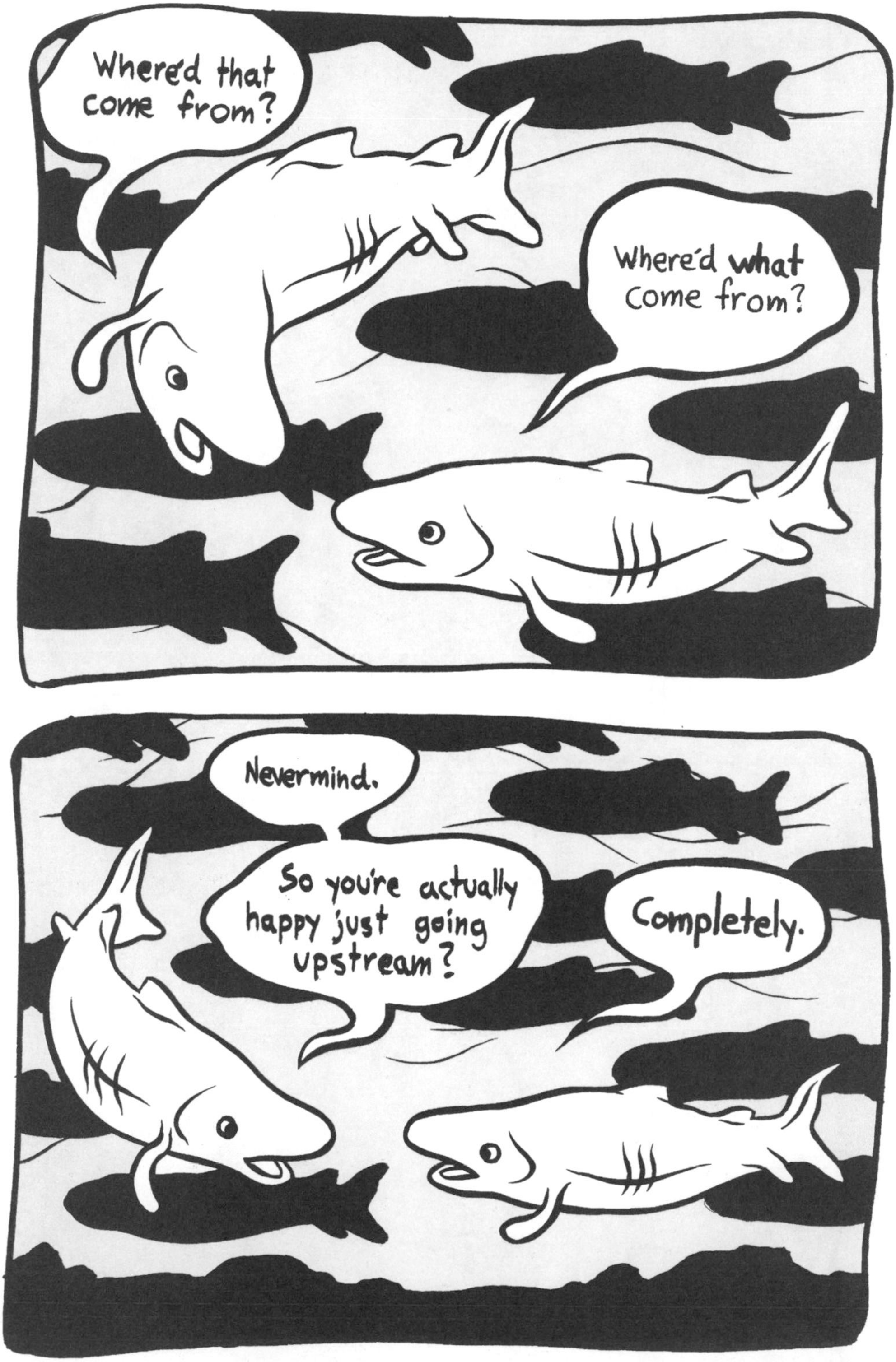
Where'd that come from?
Where'd what come from?
Nevermind.
So you're actually happy just going upstream?
Completely.

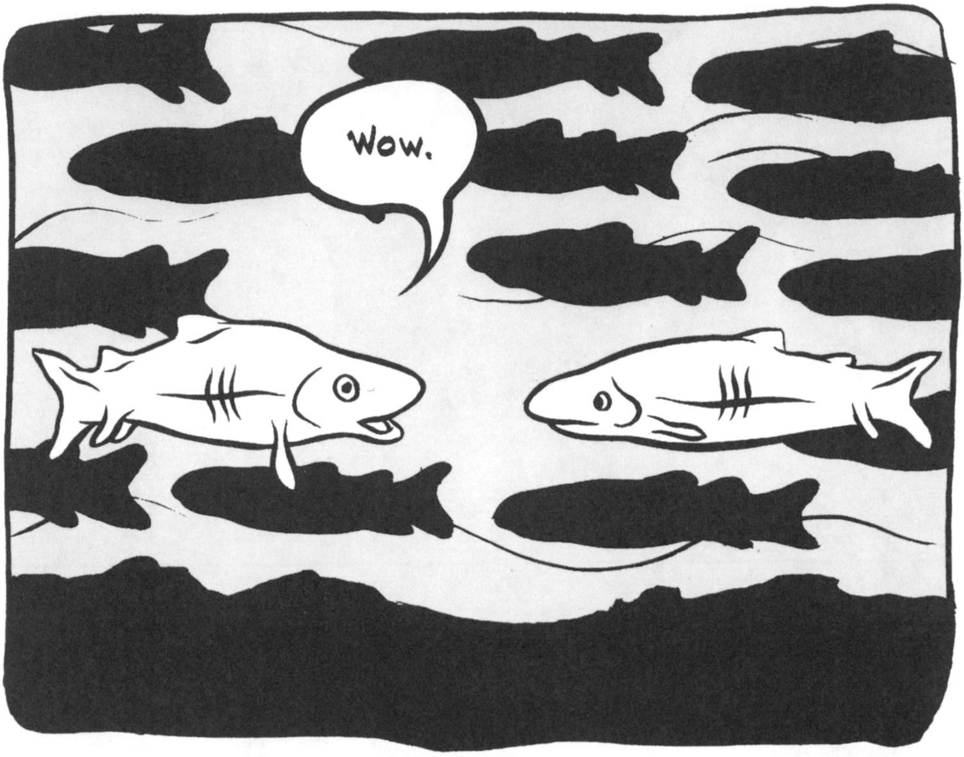
Wow.

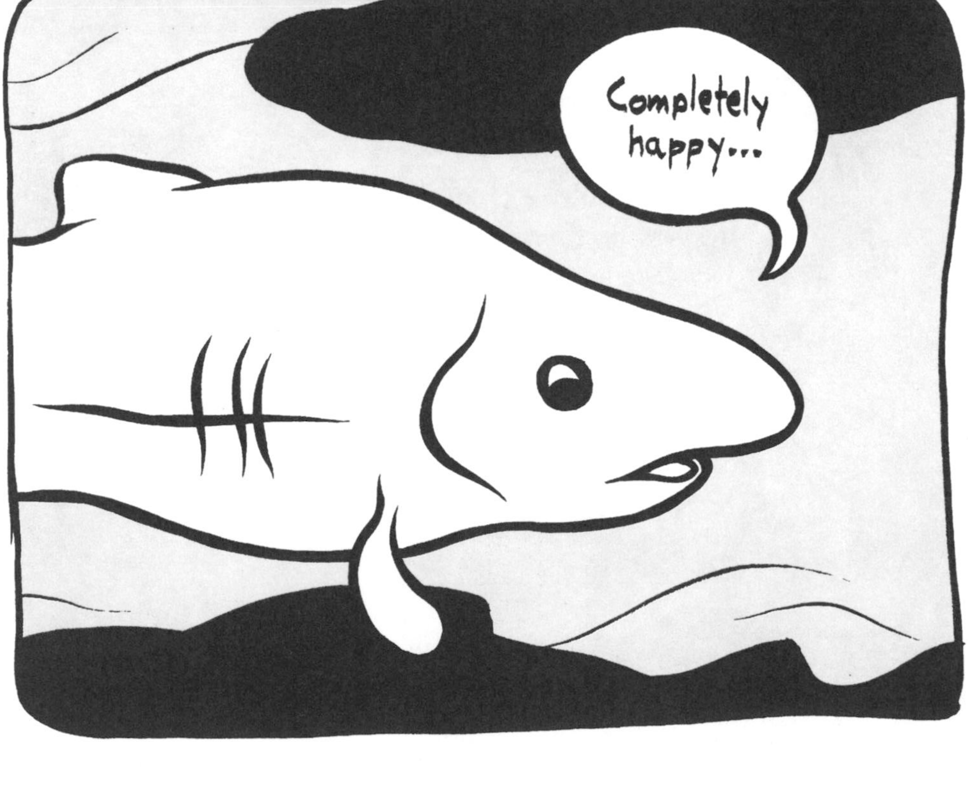
Completely happy...

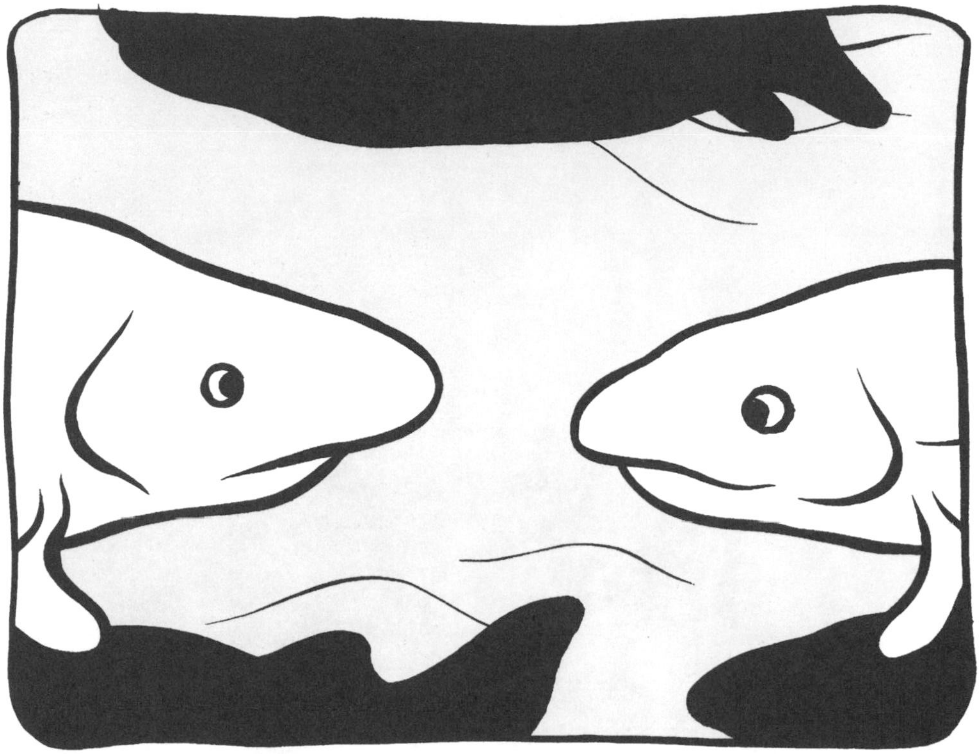

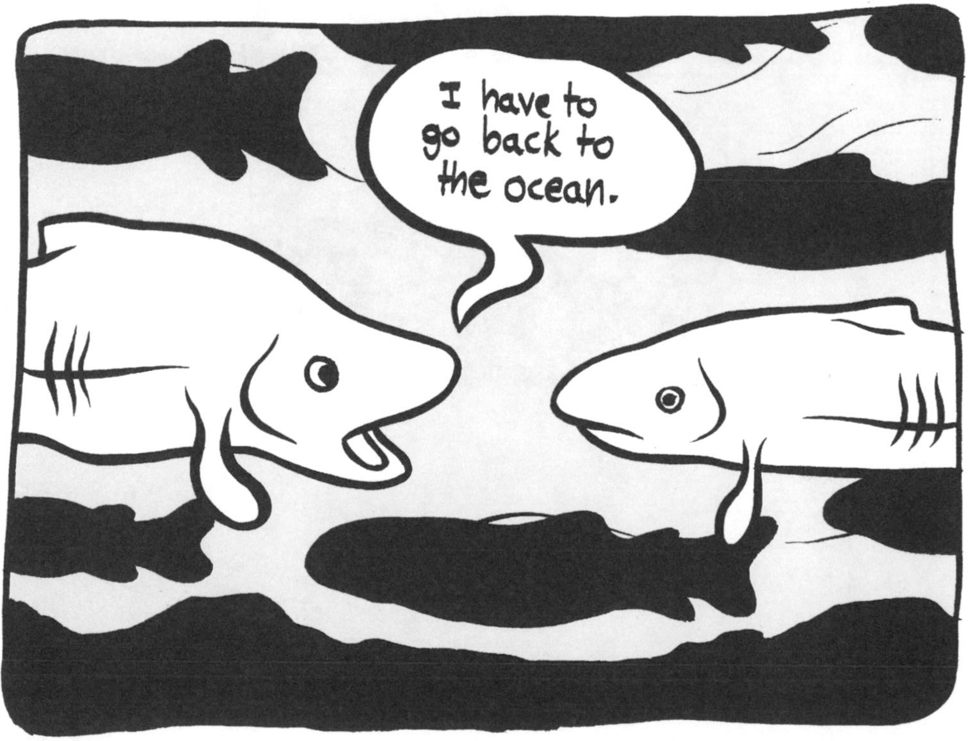
I have to go back to the ocean.

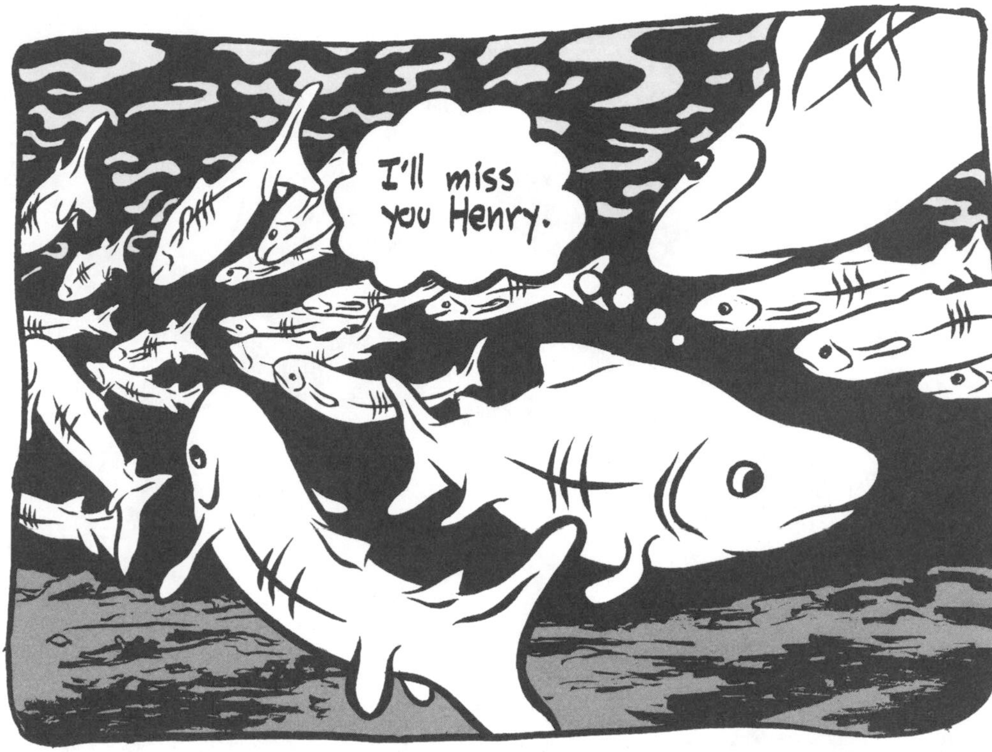
I'll miss you Henry.

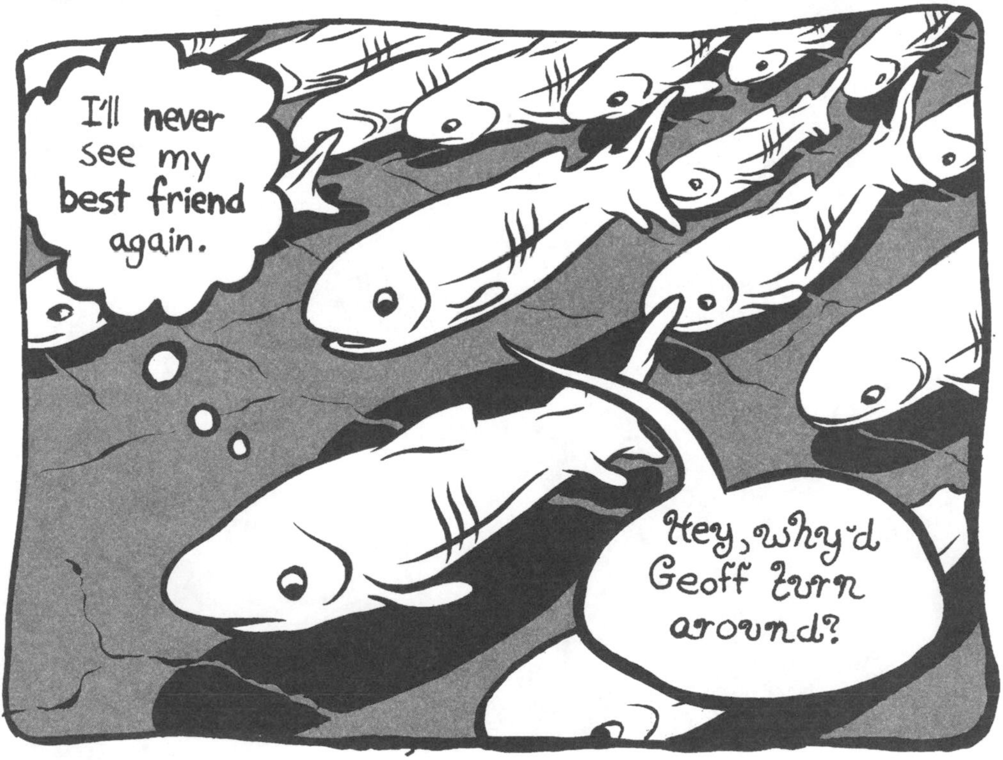
I'll never see my best friend again.
Hey, why'd Geoff turn around?

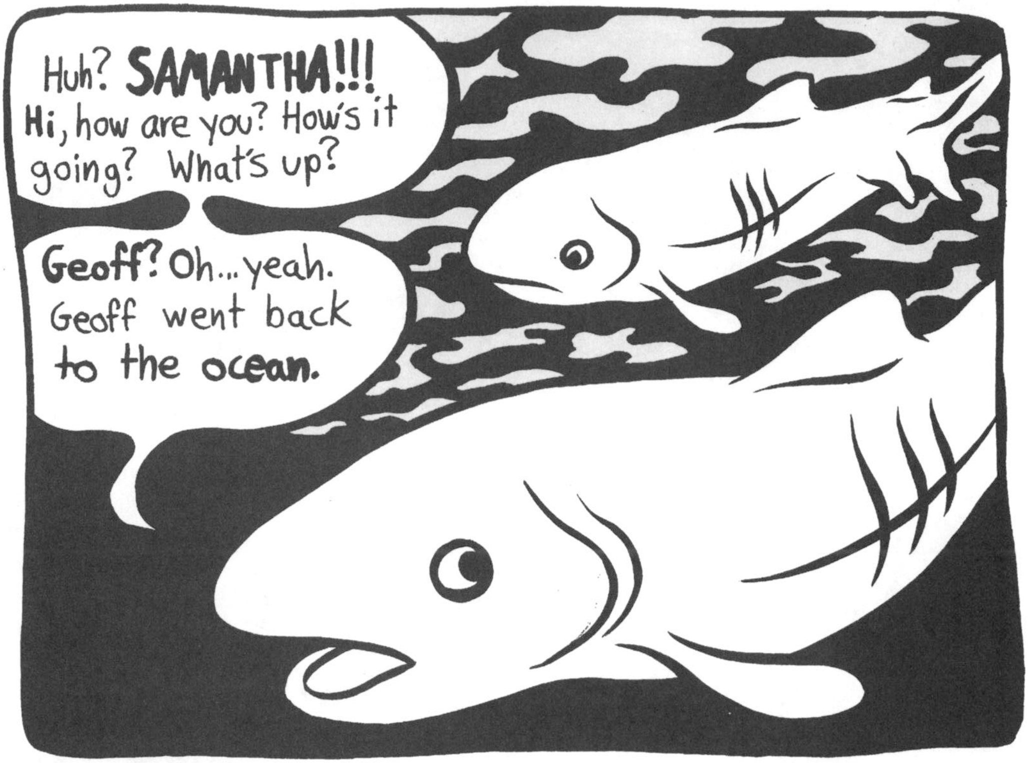
Huh? SAMANTHA!!! Hi, how are you? How's it going? What's up?
Geoff? Oh... yeah. Geoff went back to the ocean.

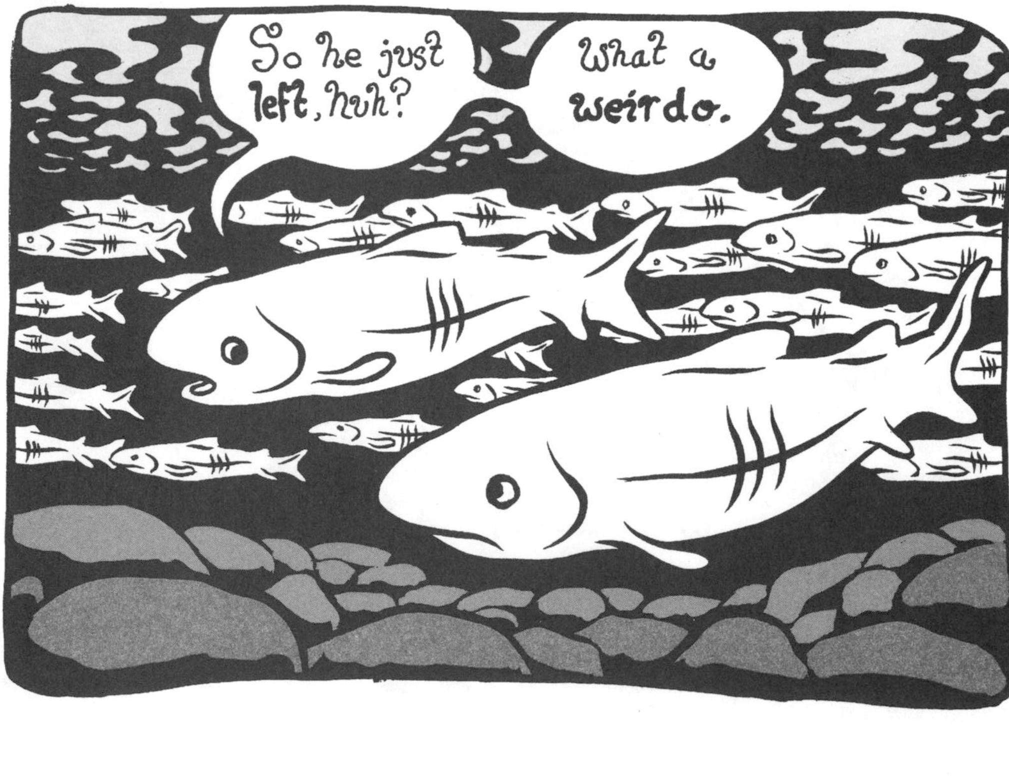
So he just left, huh?
What a weirdo.

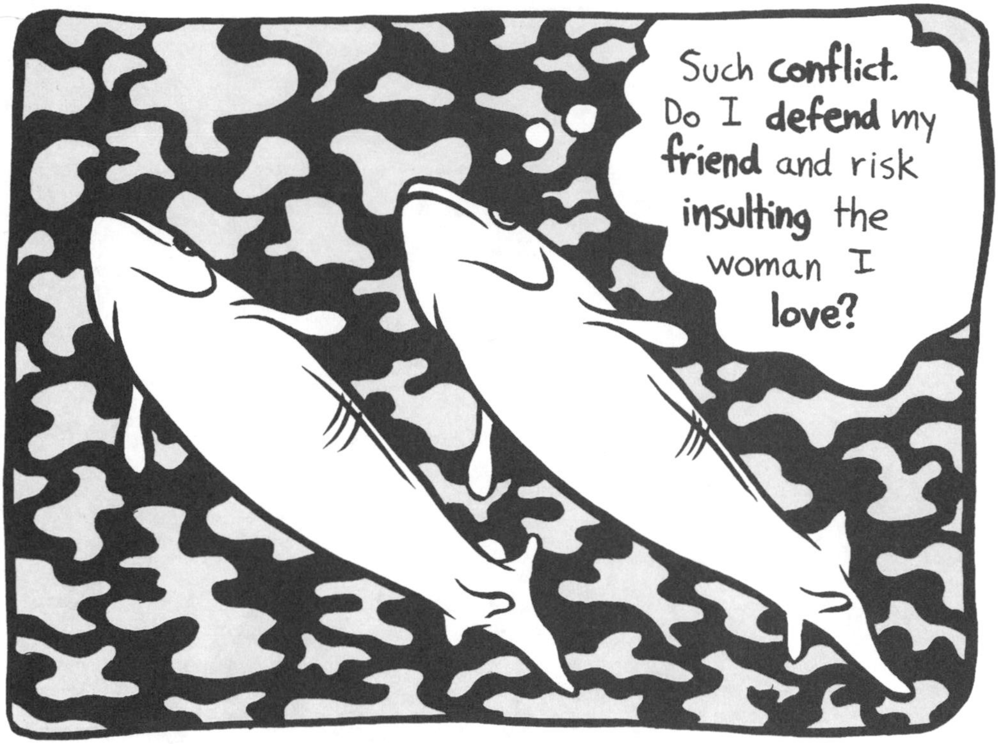
Such conflict. Do I defend my friend and risk insulting the woman I love?

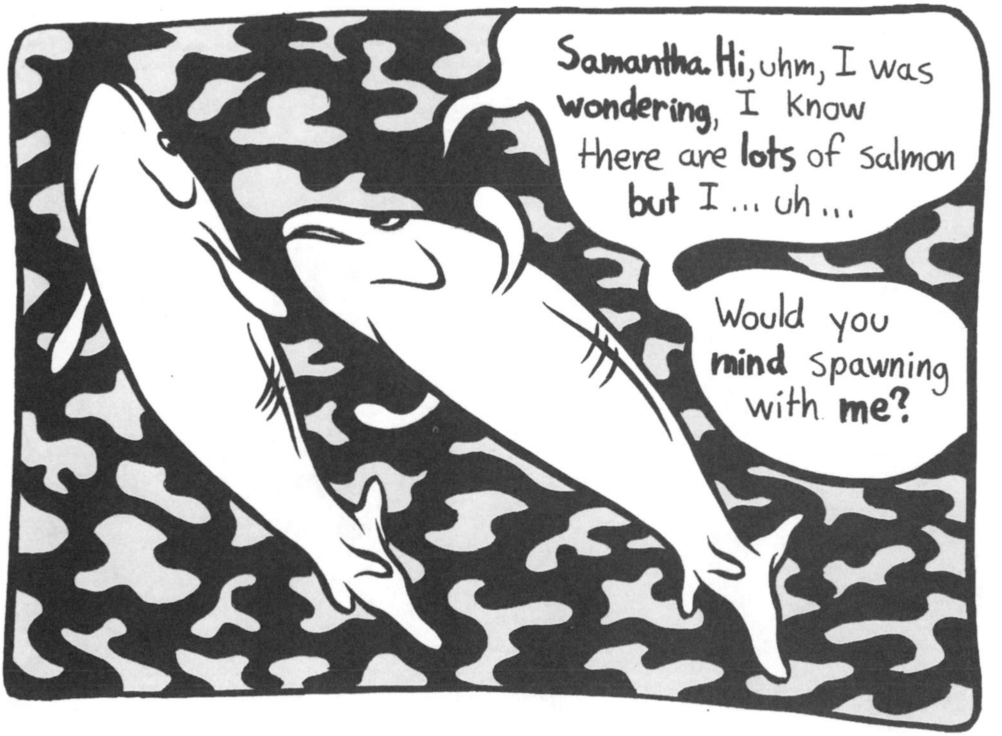
Samantha. Hi, uhm, I was wondering, I know there are lots of salmon but I ... uh ...
Would you mind spawning with me?

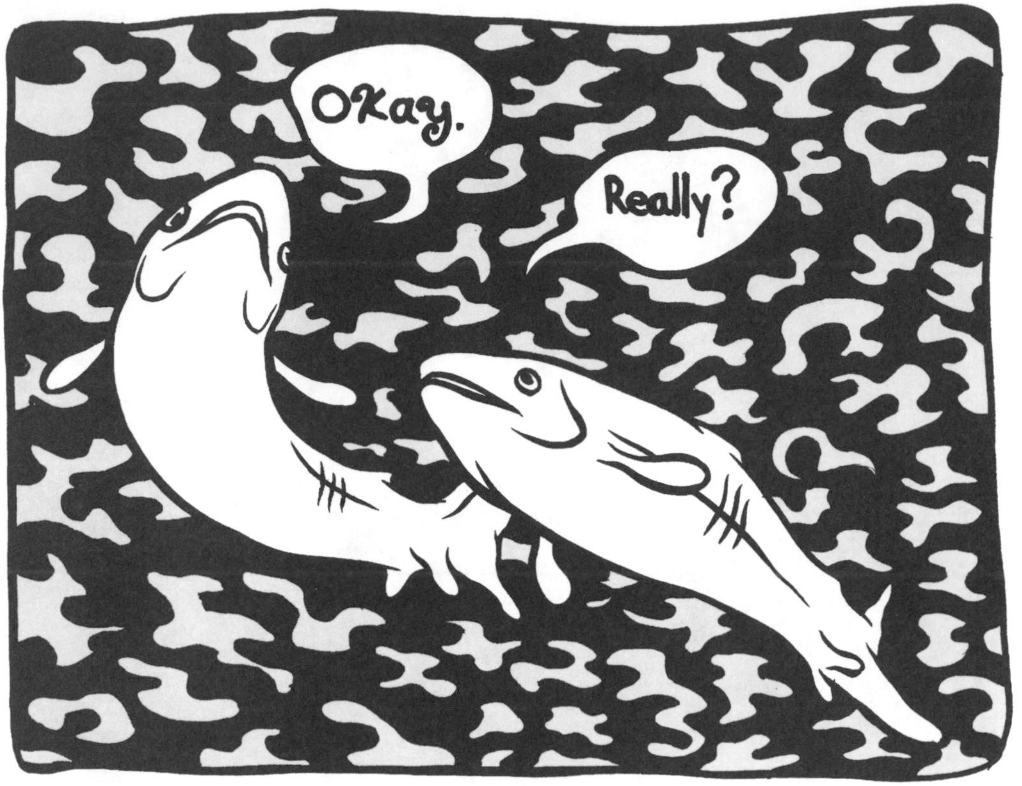
Okay.
Really?

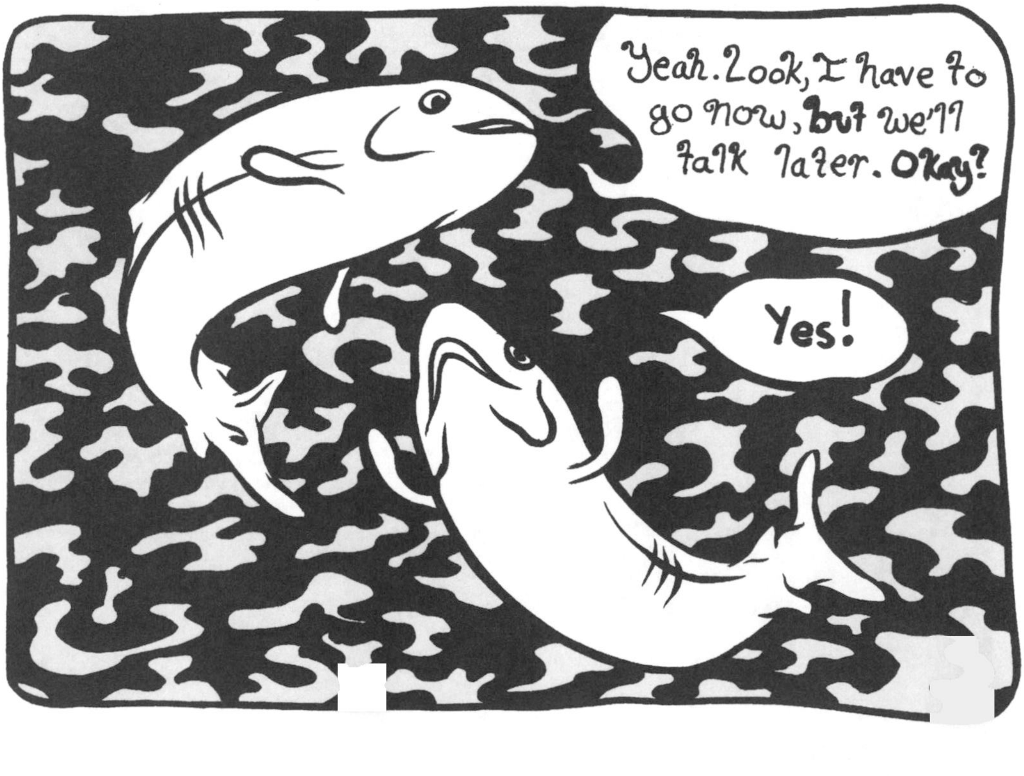
Yeah. Look, I have to go now, but we'll talk later. Okay?
Yes!

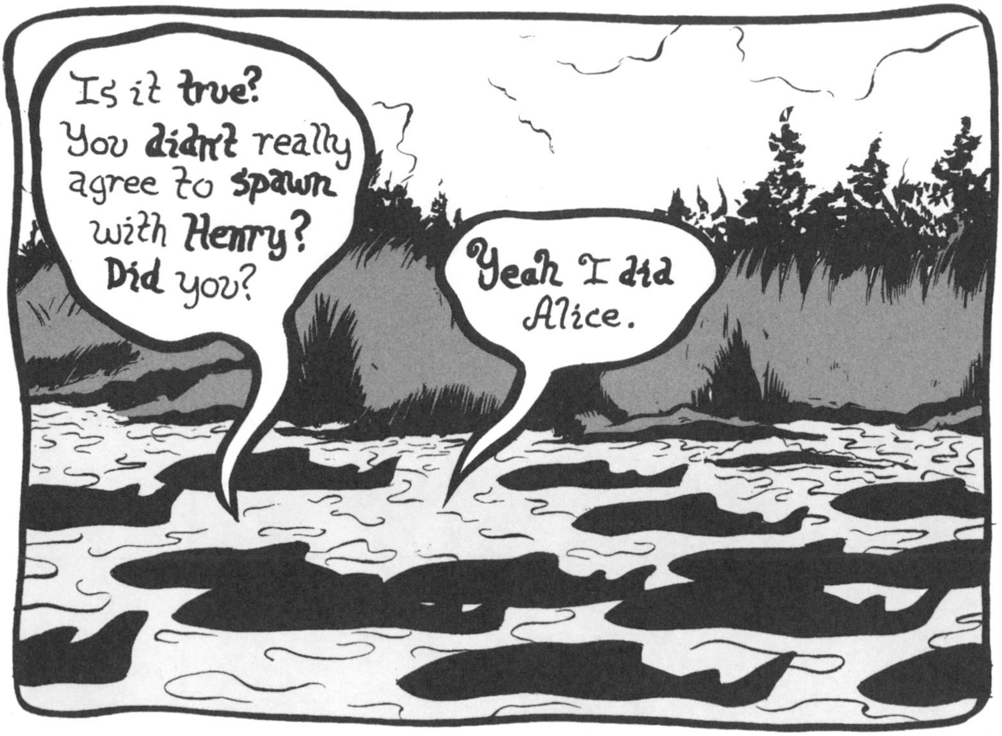
Is it true? You didn't really agree to spawn with Henry? Did you?
Yeah I did Alice.

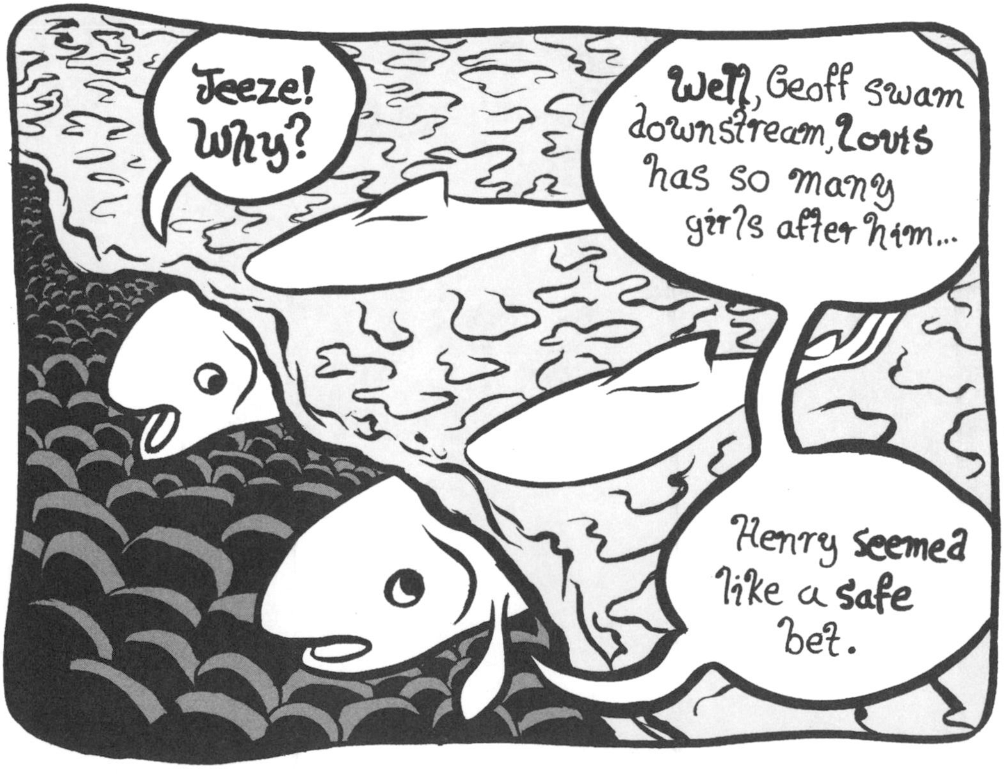
Jeeze! Why?
Well, Geoff swam downstream, Louis has so many girls after him...
Henry seemed like a safe bet.

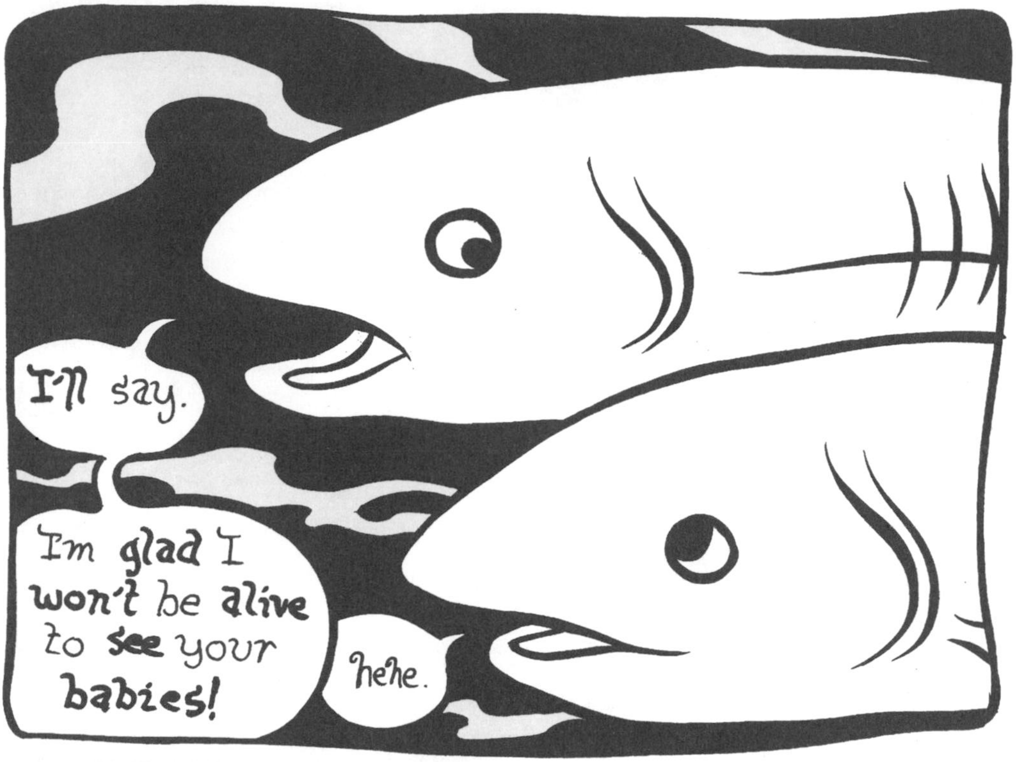
I'll say.
I'm glad I won't be alive to see your babies!
hehe.

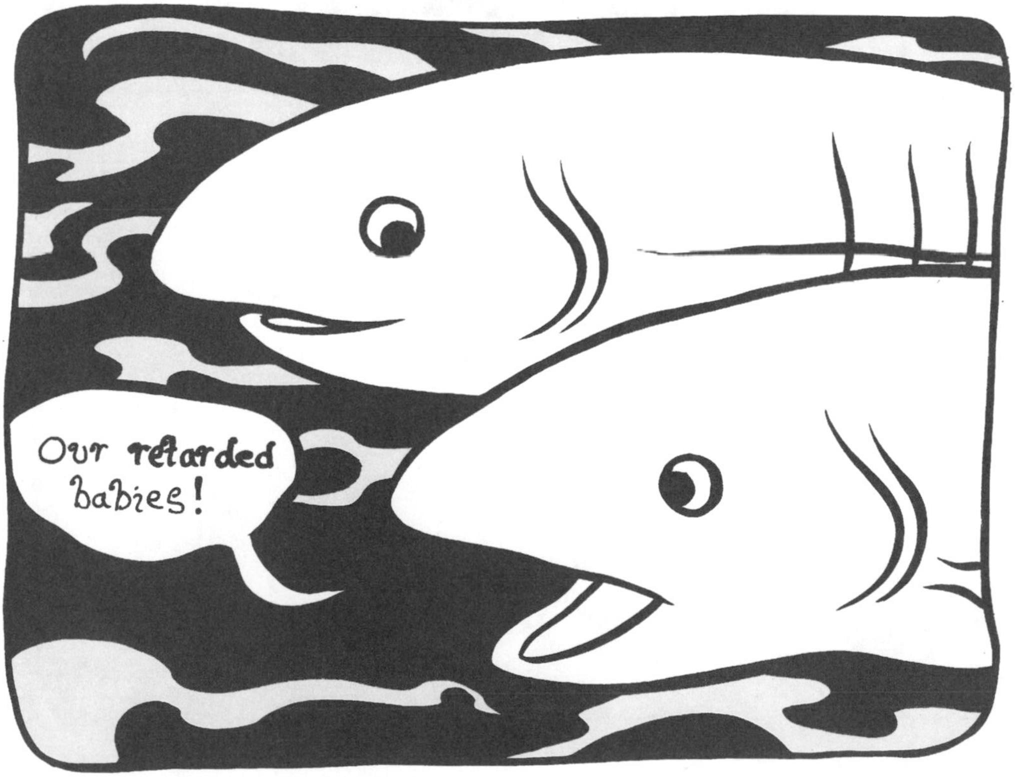
Our retarded babies!

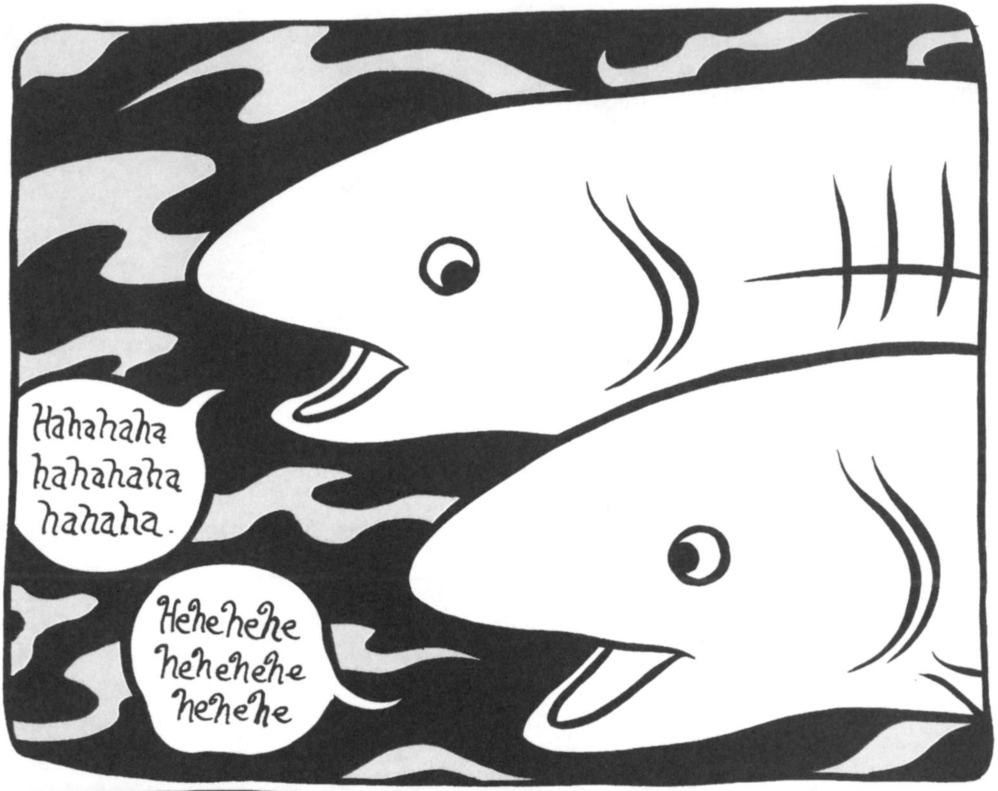
Hahahaha hahahaha hahaha.
Hehehehe hehehehe hehehe

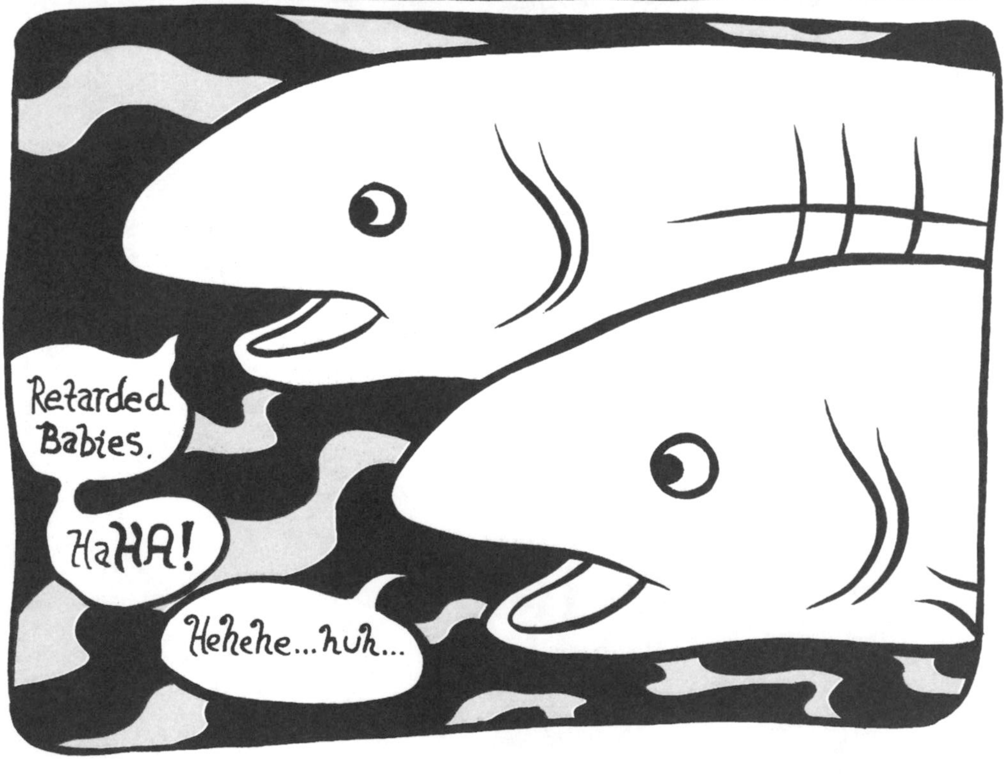
Retarded Babies.
HaHA!
Hehehe...huh...

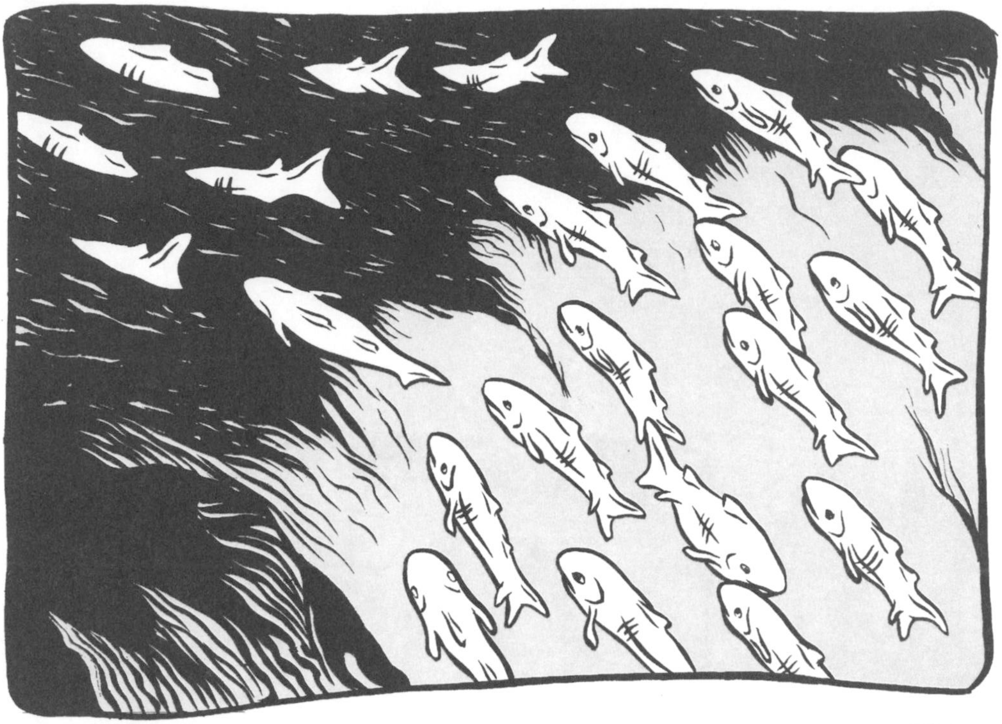

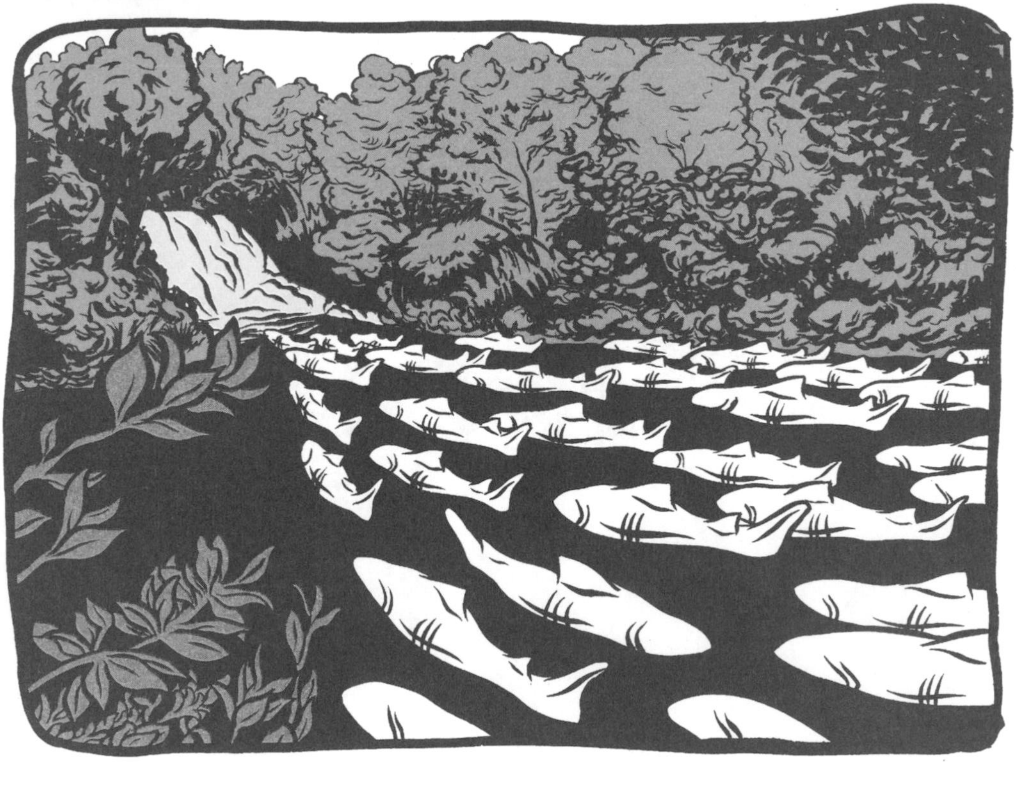

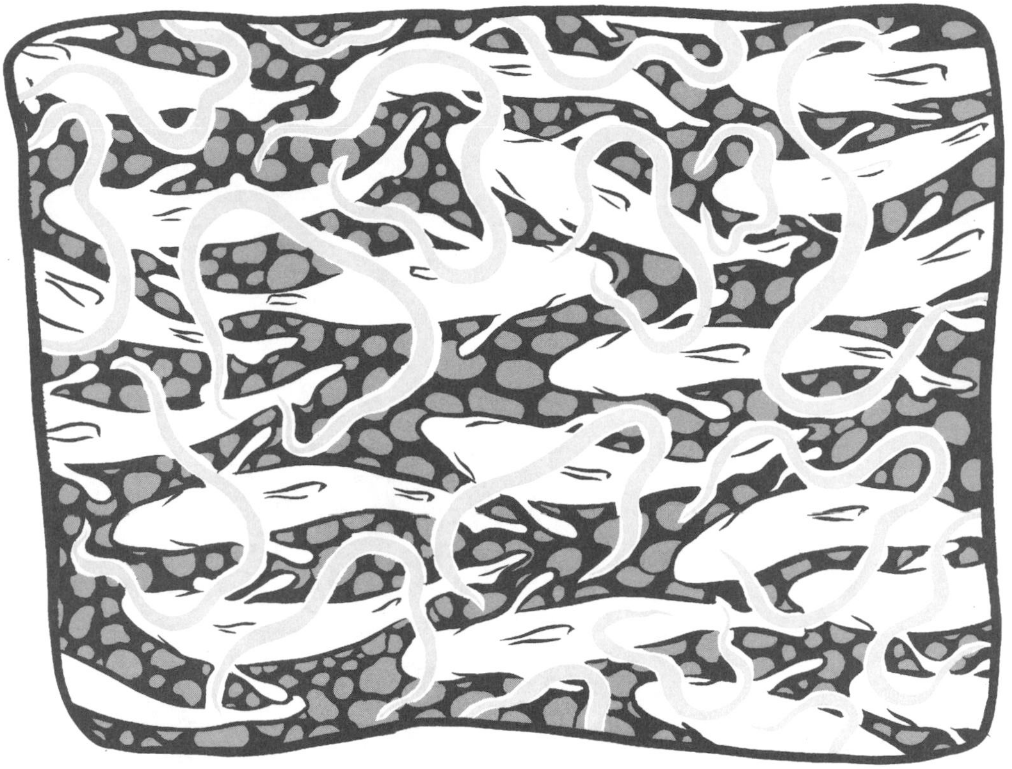
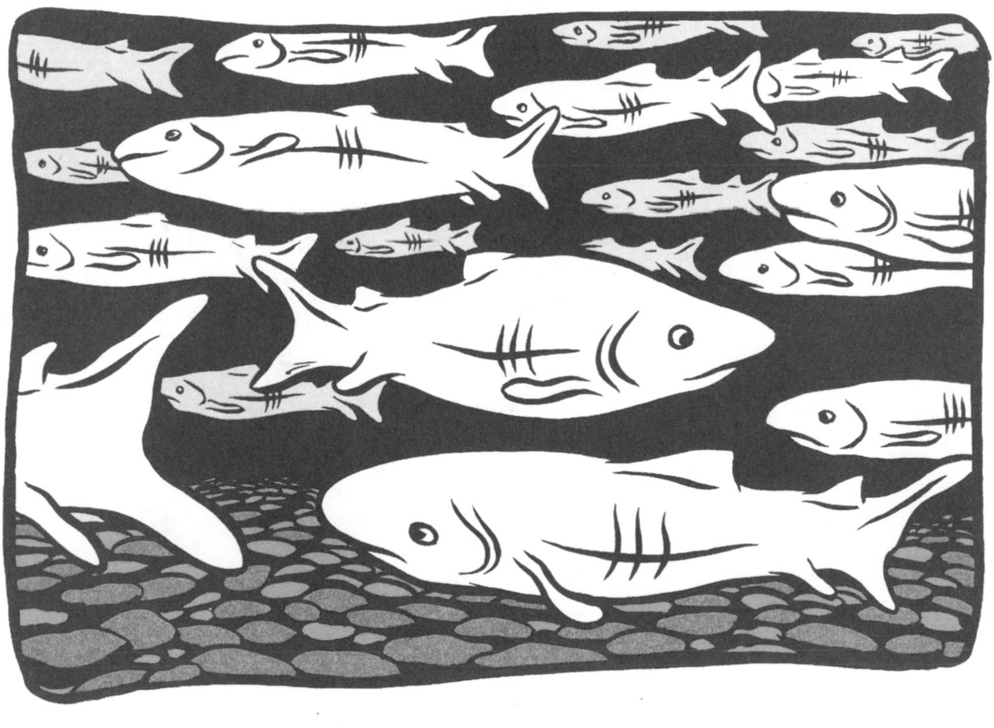

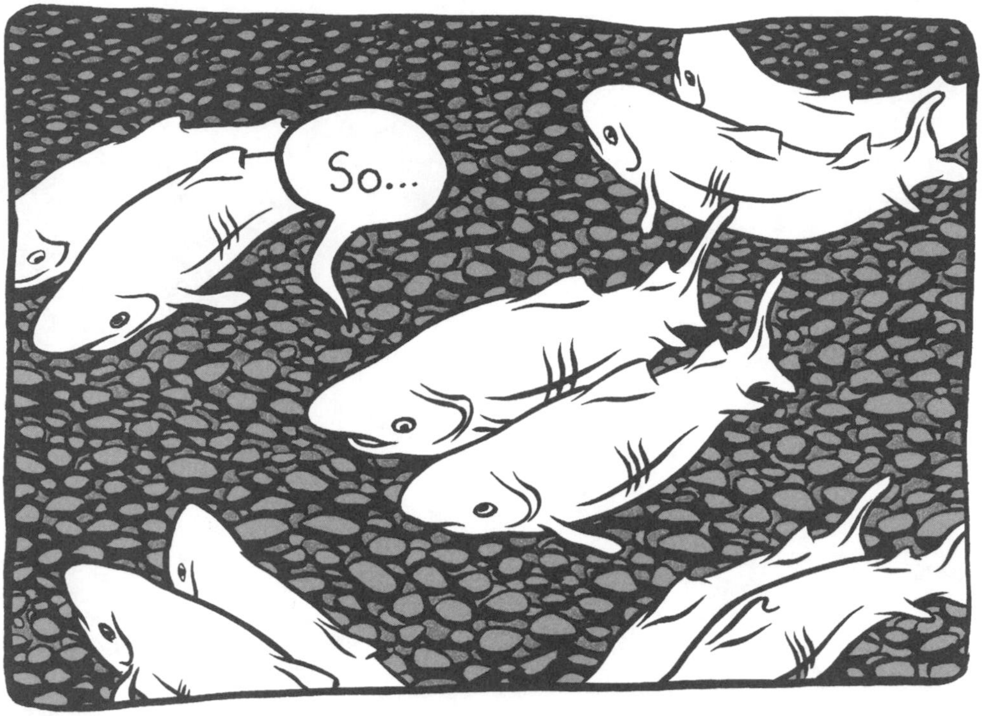
So...

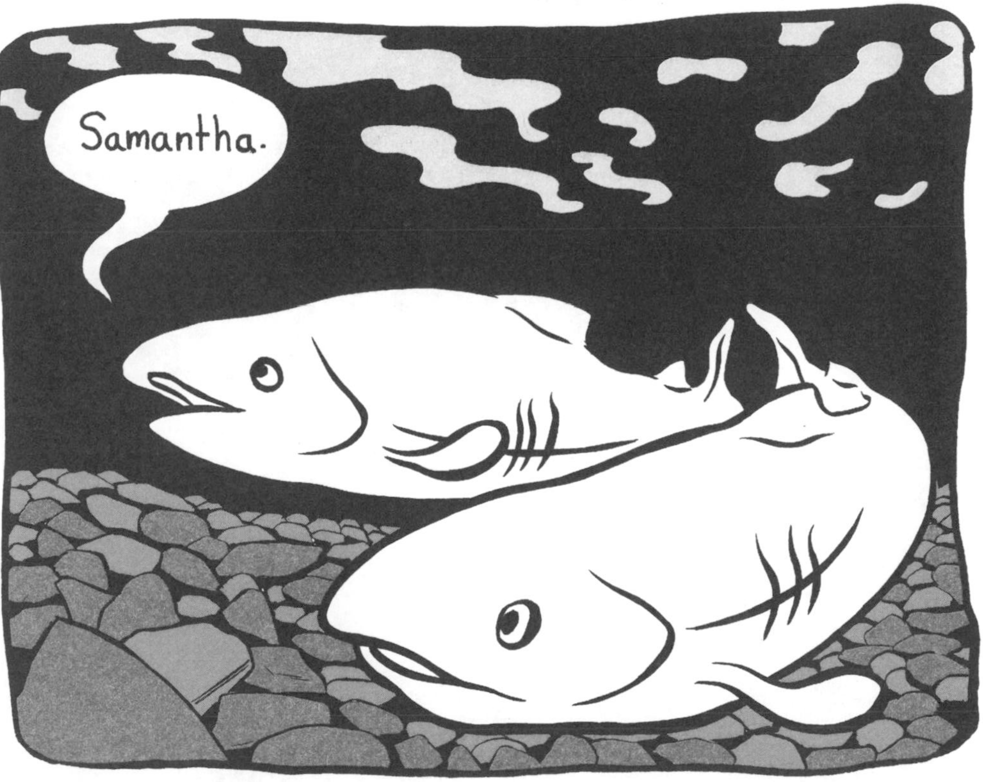
Samantha.

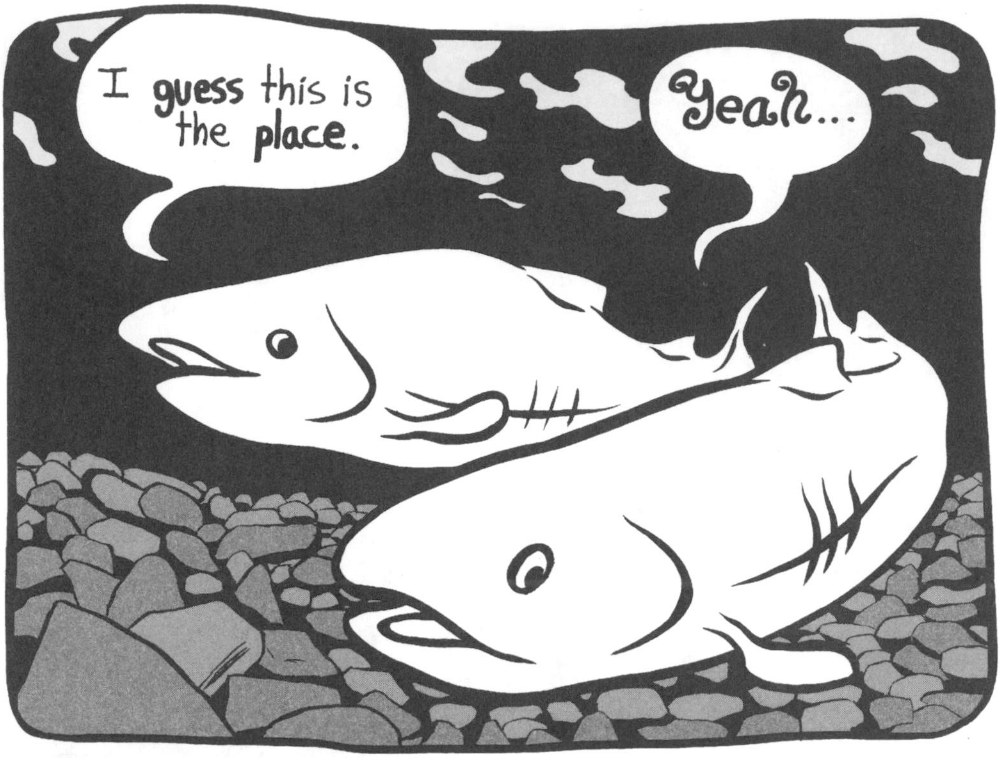
I guess this is the place.
Yeah...

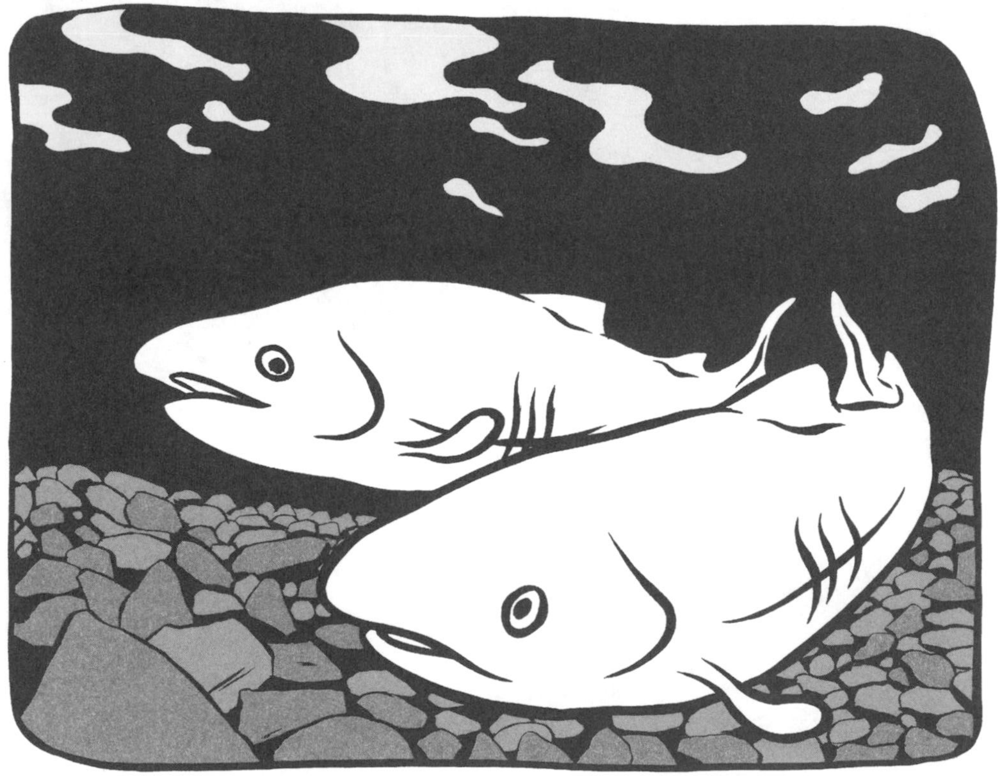

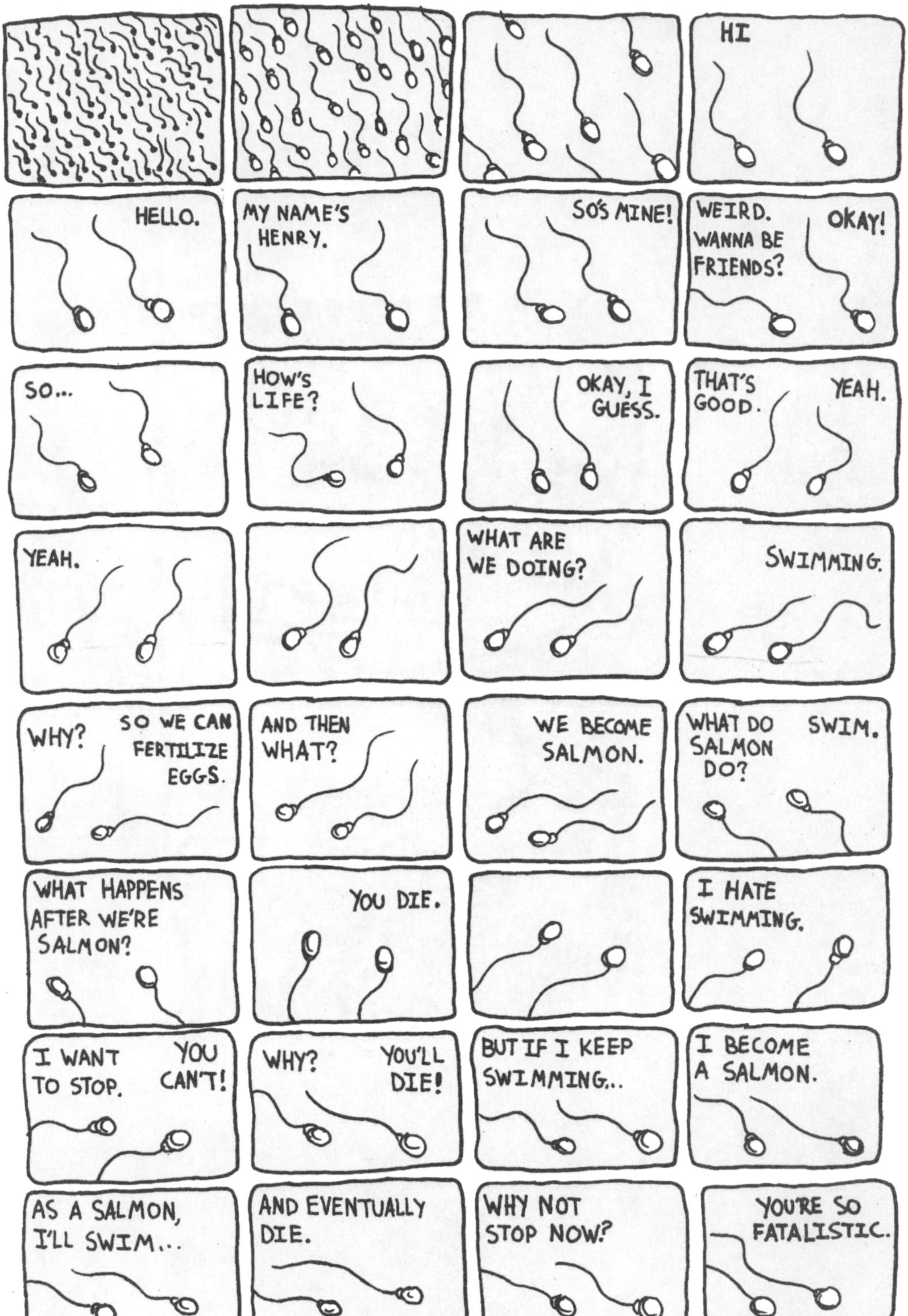
HI
HELLO.
MY NAME'S HENRY.
SO'S MINE!
WEIRD. WANNA BE FRIENDS?
OKAY!
SO...
HOW'S LIFE?
OKAY, I GUESS.
THAT'S GOOD.
YEAH.
YEAH.
WHAT ARE WE DOING?
SWIMMING.
WHY?
SO WE CAN FERTILIZE EGGS.
AND THEN WHAT?
WE BECOME SALMON.
WHAT DO SALMON DO?
SWIM.
WHAT HAPPENS AFTER WE'RE SALMON?
YOU DIE.
I HATE SWIMMING.
I WANT TO STOP.
YOU CAN'T!
WHY?
YOU'LL DIE!
BUT IF I KEEP SWIMMING...
I BECOME A SALMON.
AS A SALMON, I'LL SWIM...
AND EVENTUALLY DIE.
WHY NOT STOP NOW?
YOU'RE SO FATALISTIC.

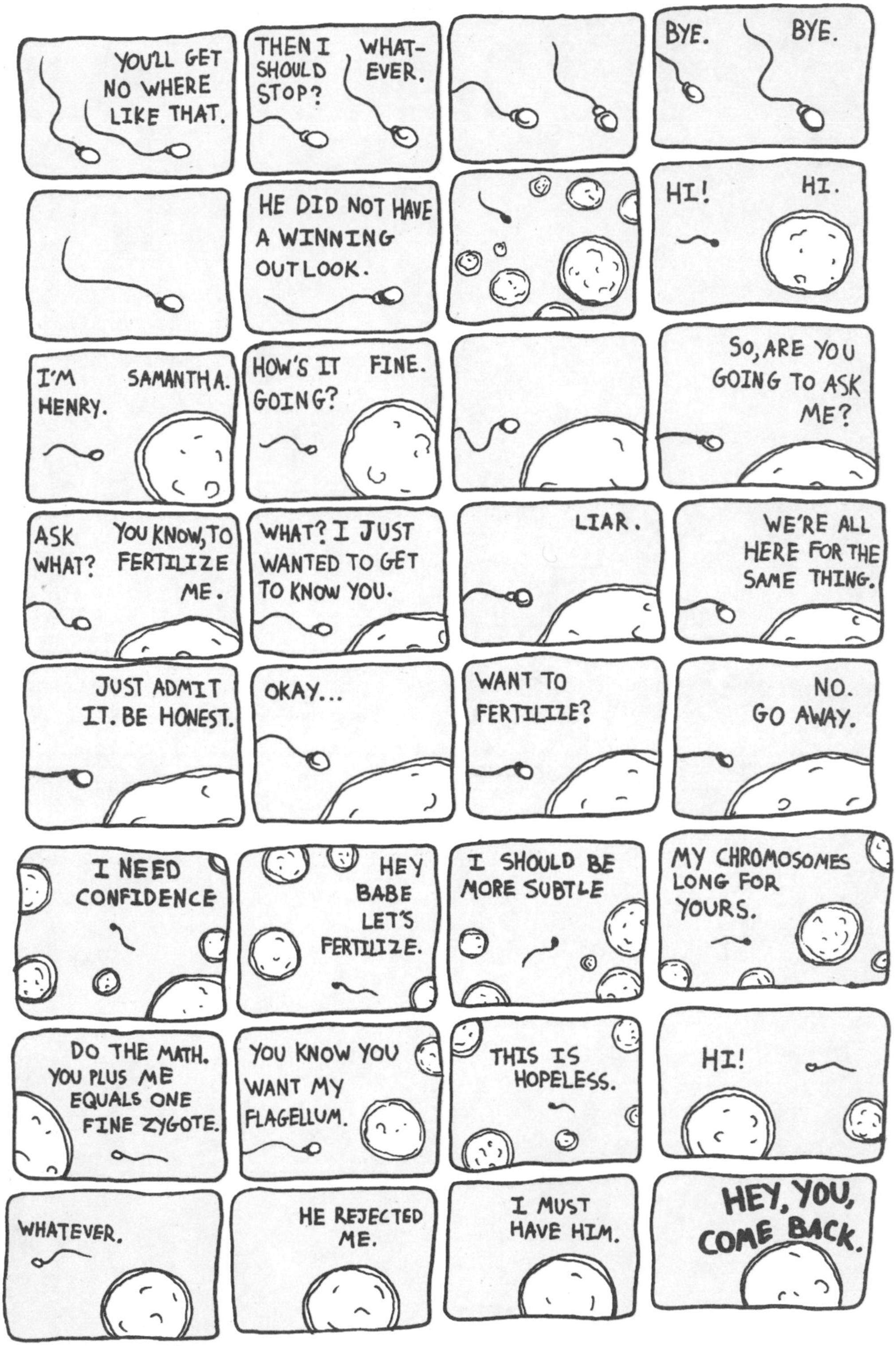
YOU'LL GET NO WHERE LIKE THAT.
THEN I SHOULD STOP?
WHAT-EVER.
BYE.
BYE.
HE DID NOT HAVE A WINNING OUTLOOK.
HI!
HI.
I'M HENRY.
SAMANTHA.
HOW'S IT GOING?
FINE.
SO, ARE YOU GOING TO ASK ME?
ASK WHAT?
YOU KNOW, TO FERTILIZE ME.
WHAT? I JUST WANTED TO GET TO KNOW YOU.
LIAR.
WE'RE ALL HERE FOR THE SAME THING.
JUST ADMIT IT. BE HONEST.
OKAY...
WANT TO FERTILIZE?
NO. GO AWAY.
I NEED CONFIDENCE
HEY BABE LET'S FERTILIZE.
I SHOULD BE MORE SUBTLE
MY CHROMOSOMES LONG FOR YOURS.
DO THE MATH. YOU PLUS ME EQUALS ONE FINE ZYGOTE.
YOU KNOW YOU WANT MY FLAGELLUM.
THIS IS HOPELESS.
HI!
WHATEVER.
HE REJECTED ME.
I MUST HAVE HIM.
HEY, YOU, COME BACK.

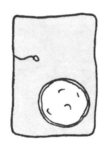

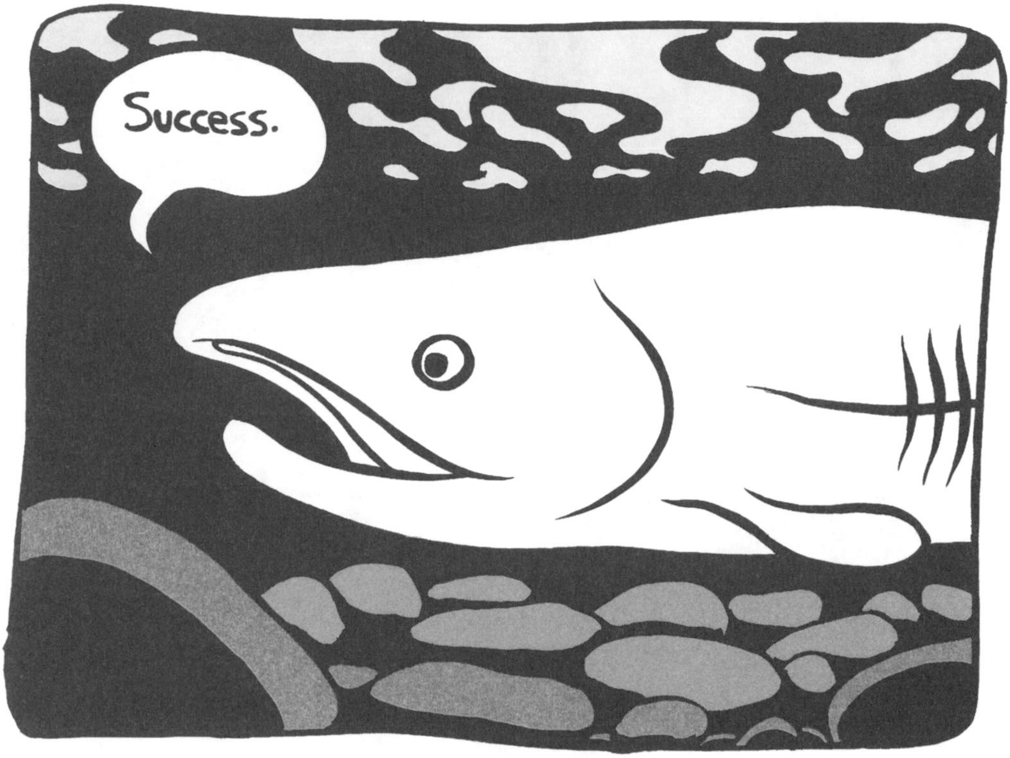
Success.

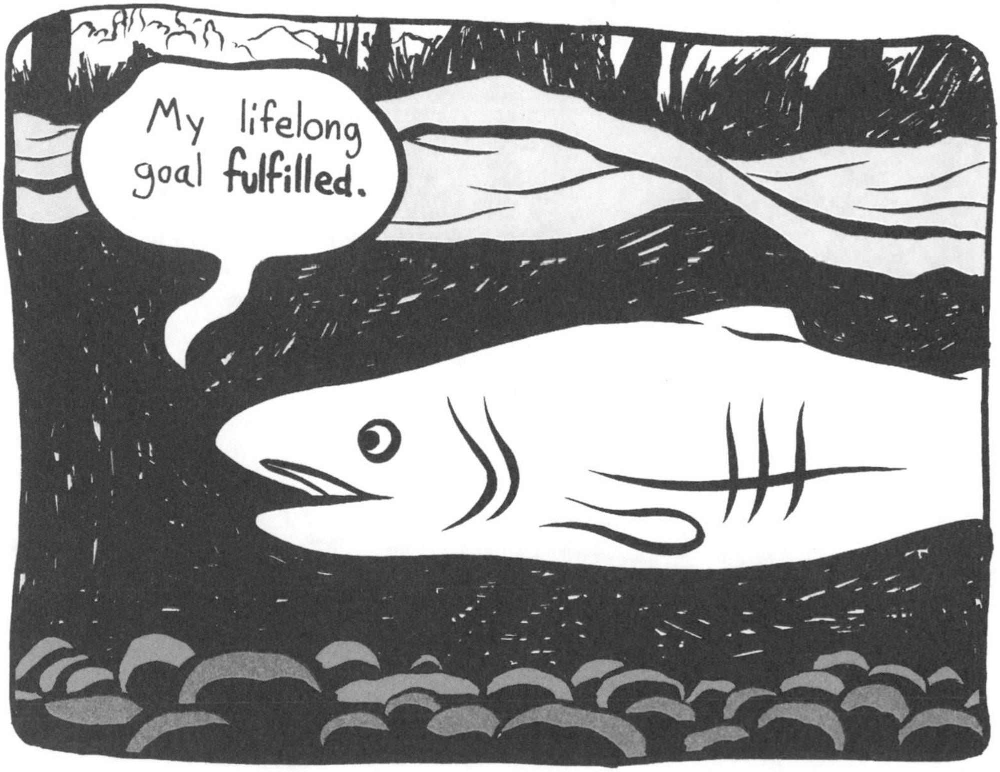
My lifelong goal fulfilled.

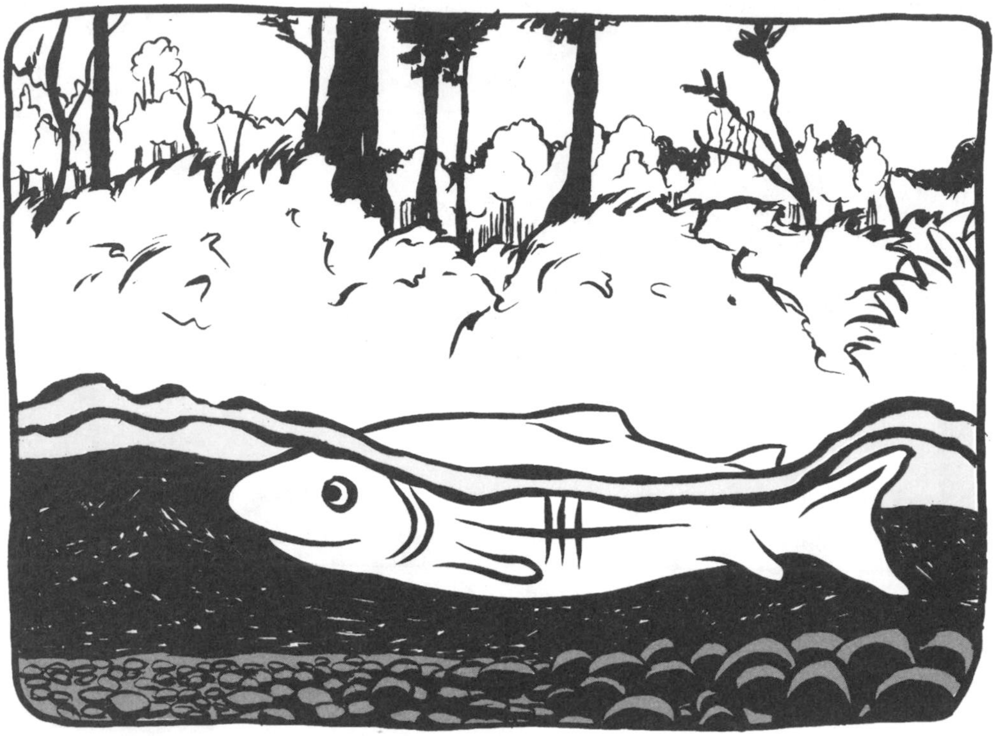

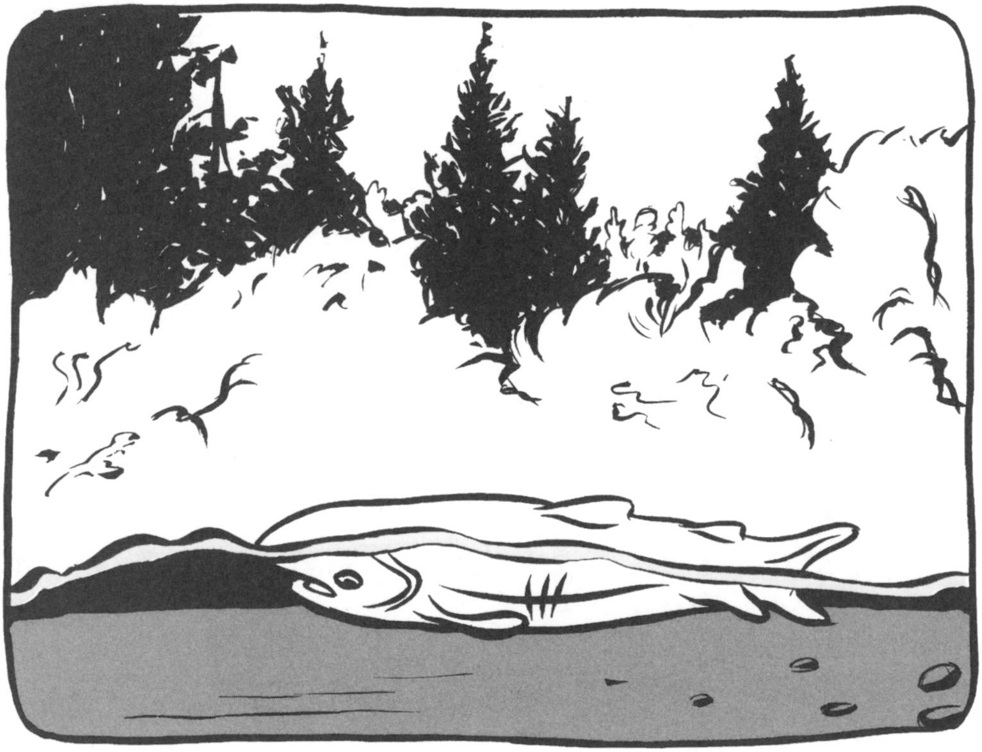

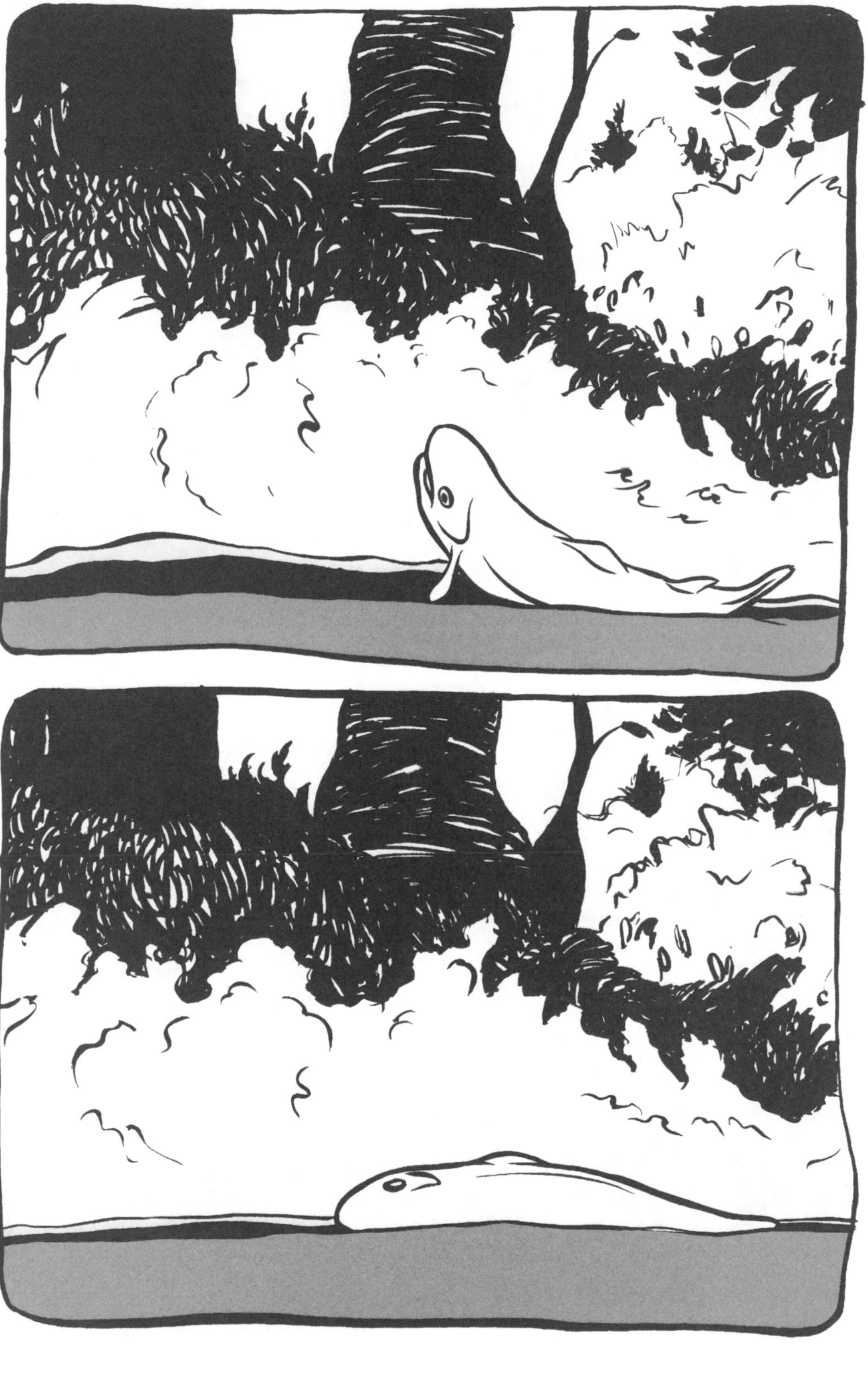

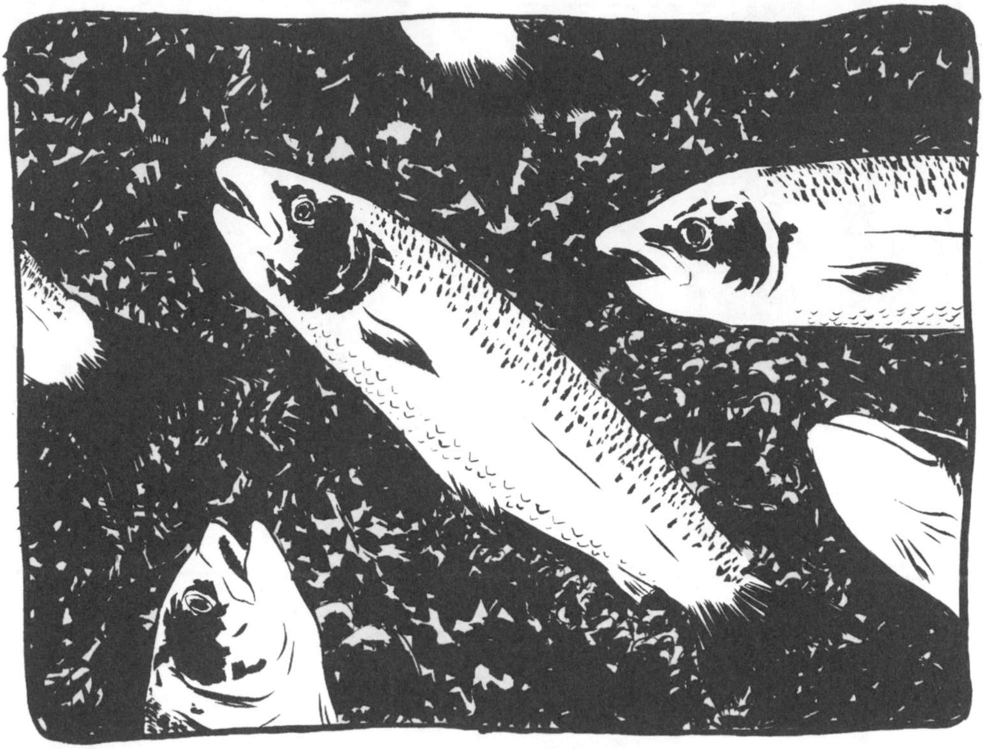

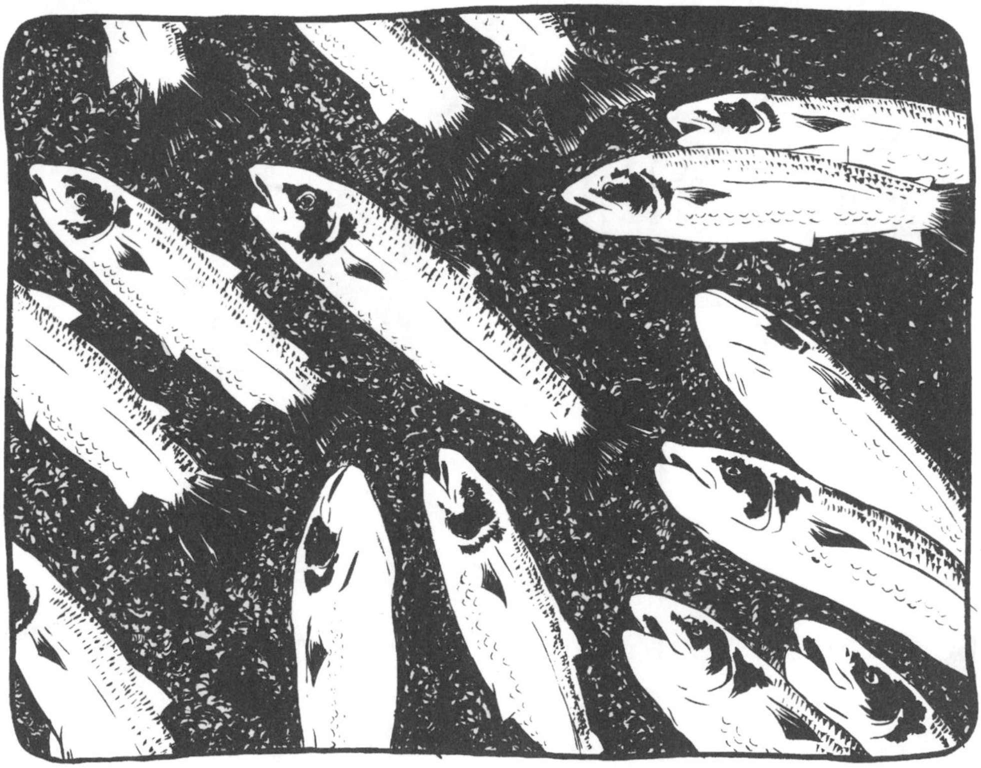

[redacted]

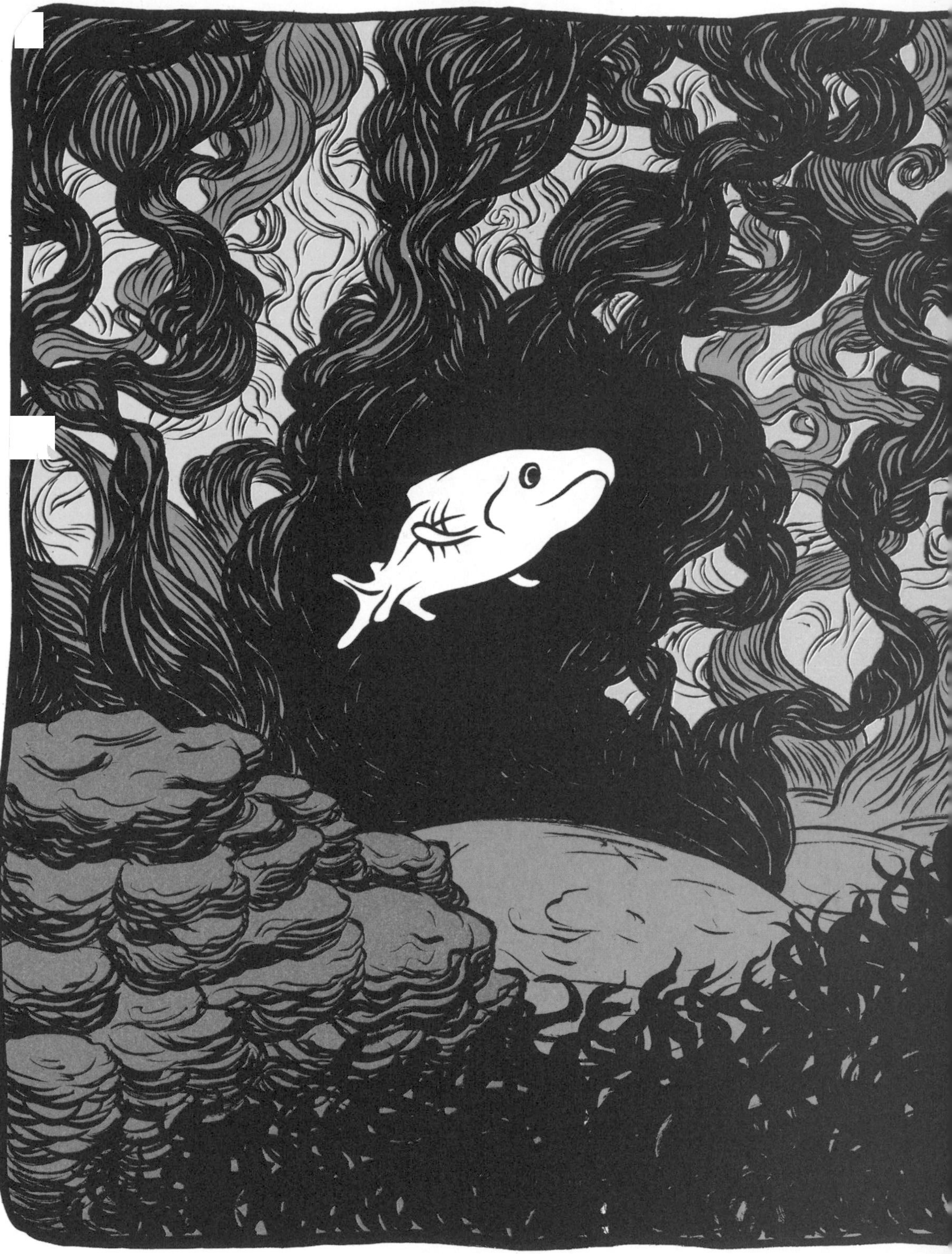

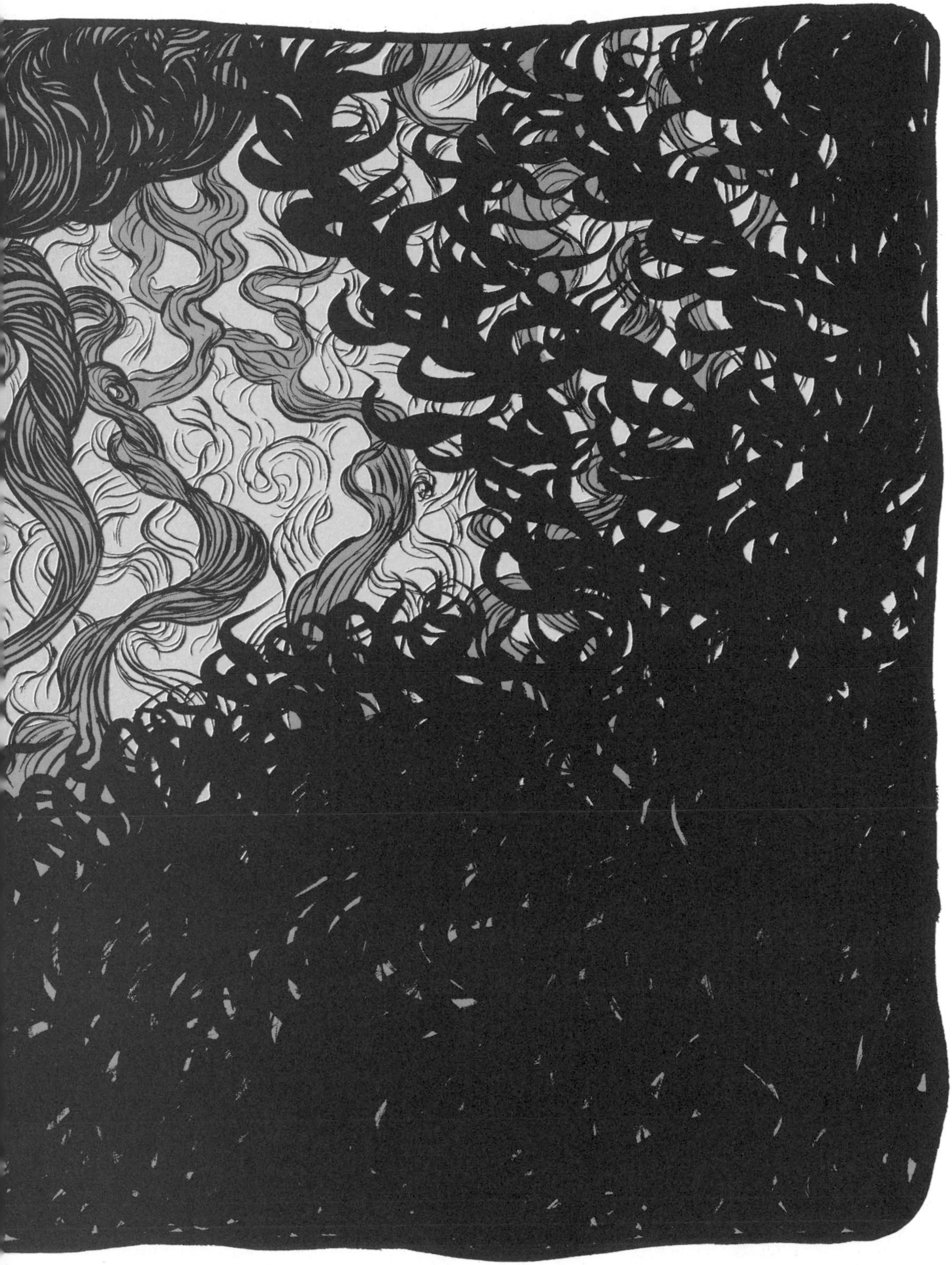

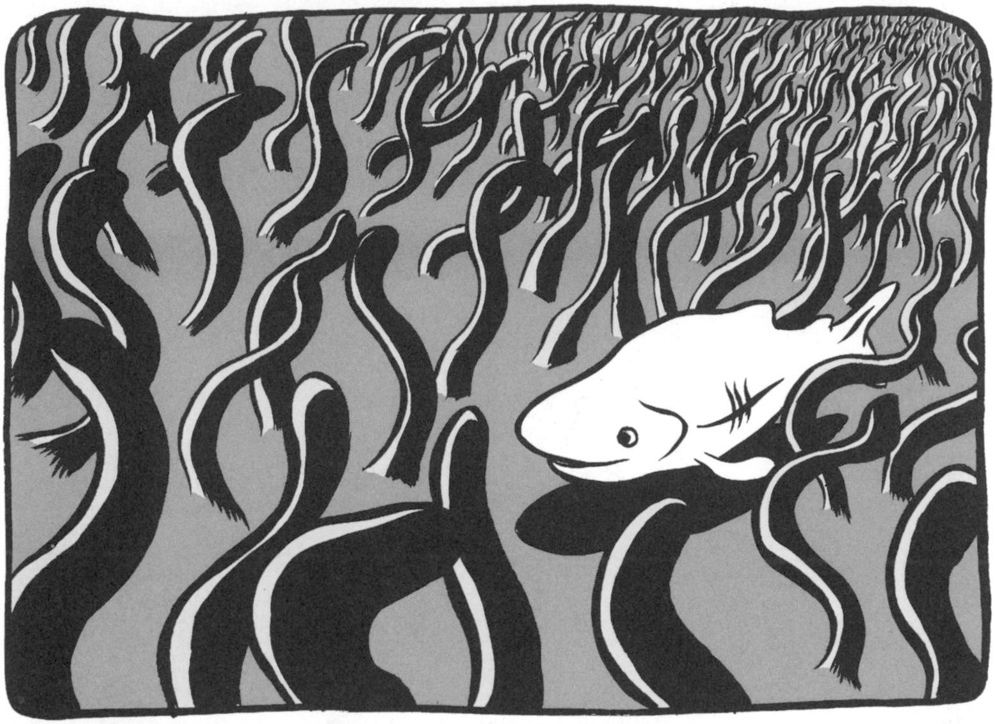

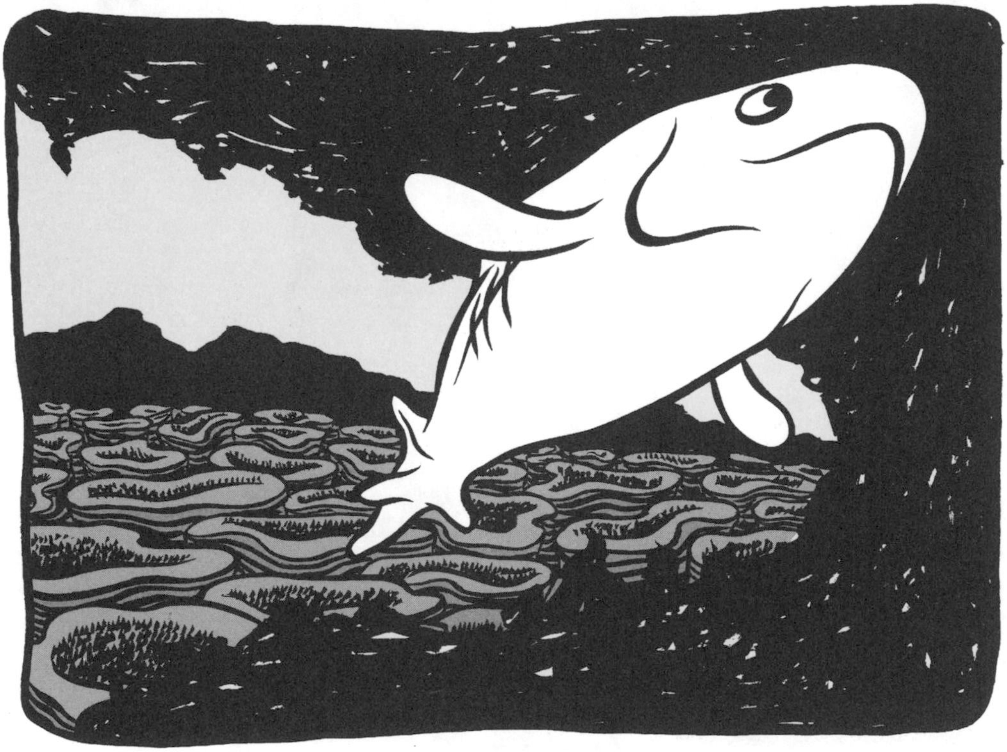

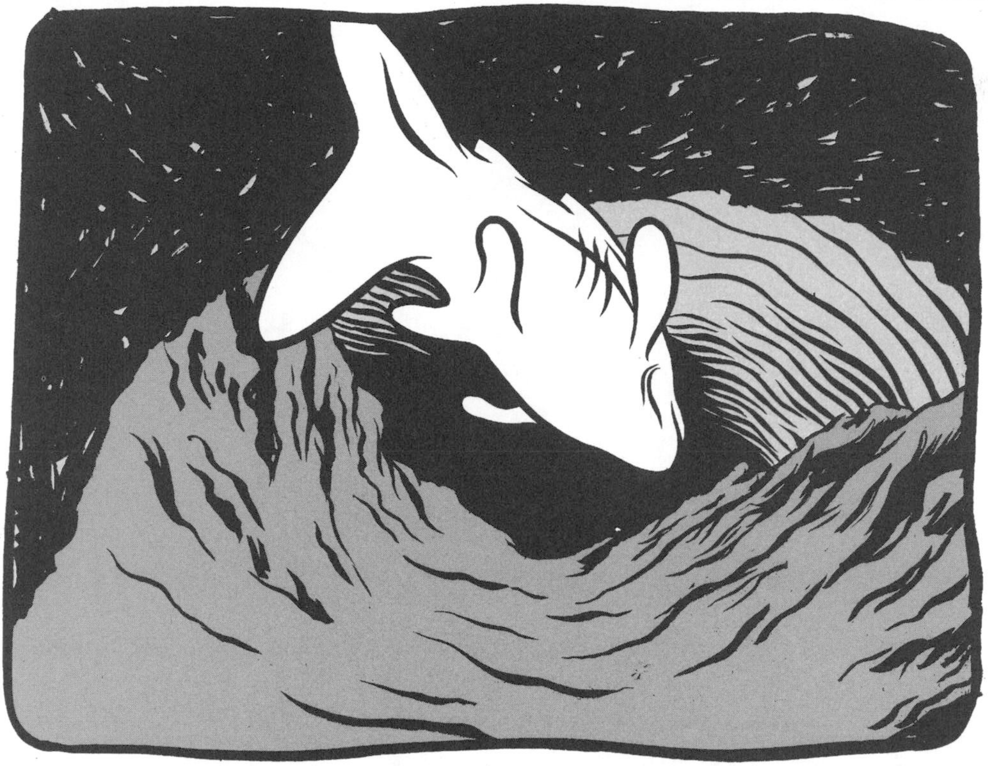

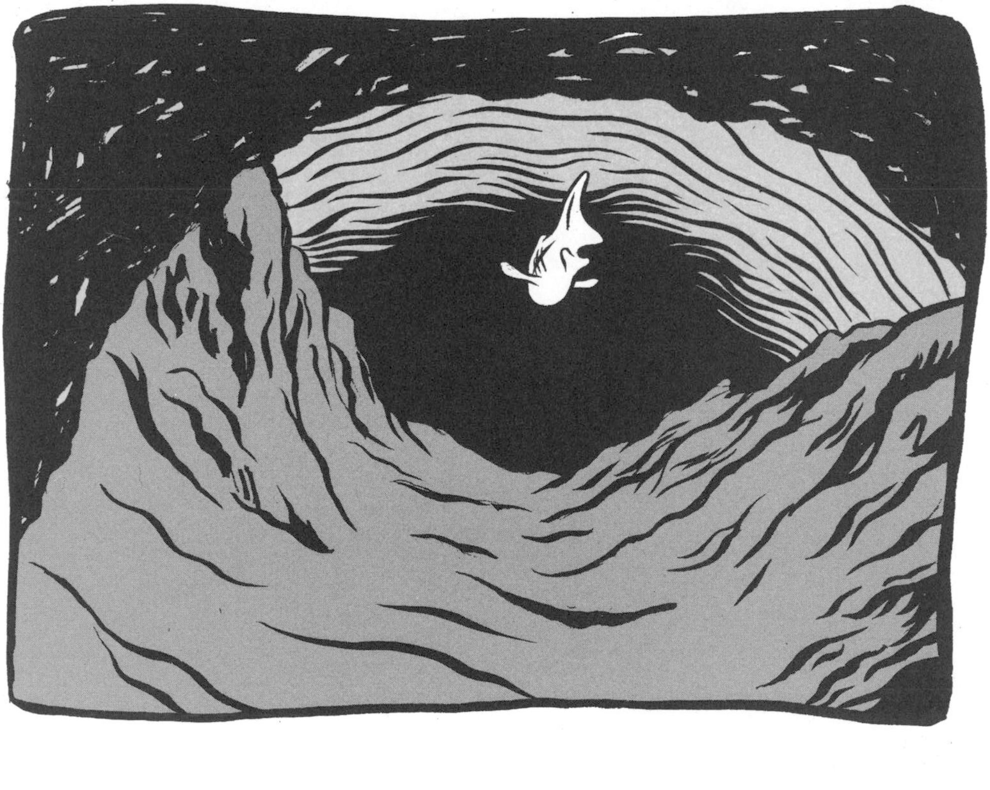